D1030911

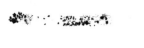

"The Labour Opposition Of Northern Ireland"

Complete Reprint of the first Labour newspaper in Northern Ireland, 1925-26

Introduced by
Joe Keenan

ATHOL BOOKS

10 Athol Street, Belfast, BT12 4GX

for the

South Belfast Constituency Labour Party

Other Works By Joe Keenan

The English Reformation, Chapter in Captain Francisco De Cuellar: "A Story Of The Spanish Armada.
An Argument On Behalf Of The Catholics Of Northern Ireland.
Scargill's Strike.

Other Publications Of South Belfast Constituency Labour Party:

Manifesto Of The South Belfast Labour Association.
Ireland by William McCullough (Reprints For The Future, No. 1).
Available from

South Belfast Constituency Labour Party,
Box 77,
Belfast, BT9 7BN

"The Labour Opposition
Of Northern Ireland"

Complete Reprint of the
first Labour newspaper in
Northern Ireland, 1925-6

Introduced by
Joe Keenan

ISBN 0 85034 054 3

is published for the
South Belfast Constituency Labour Party

by

Athol Books,
10 Athol Street,
Belfast,
BT12 4GX.
© **Athol Books 1992**

Contents

Illustrations appear throughout.

DEDICATION

To the memory of Patsy Keenan

(1925 - 1987)

"Bread *and* Roses"

Preface

The publication of reprints from Hugh Gemmell's **Labour Opposition** newspaper, 1925-26, could not be more timely. In the wake of the Labour Party's fourth successive General Election defeat, and even with Neil Kinnock's departure from the leadership, Labour's very survival as a serious contender for state power is in doubt. In the post-election reassessment, everything is up for grabs, including Labour's dubious "Northern Ireland policy".

Labour Party policy on Northern Ireland has been substantially similar to the Tory policy—to keep Northern Ireland at 'arm's length'. Don't, in Jim Callaghan's words, get sucked into the Irish bog, promote the nationalist interest if convenient, but at all costs, keep Northern Ireland at arm's length. This was made explicit when Tony Benn's Diaries were published and the details of the 1969 Labour Cabinet discussion on Northern Ireland's developing 'Troubles' was leaked. According to Tony Benn, the following exchange took place:

"Dennis [Healey] said he thought it was better to get Chichester-Clark [the Unionist Prime Minister] or another Ulsterman to carry the can... [Callaghan] said he thought Chichester-Clark was anxious to help because he was a very frightened man. Dennis stressed again: let's keep Chichester-Clark carrying the can. Jim agreed: 'Yes I too want to avoid responsibility...' Michael Stewart [Foreign Secretary] said... Britain could not entirely walk out of Ulster although we had considered it as an alternative. It was an interesting thing for him to have said because that would never have been admitted publicly. He thought that awful as it would be to take over responsibility, that would be less awful than walking out." (**Independent**, 14.2.1987.)

Sadly, the working class interest has rarely been paramount in the Labour Party's thinking on Northern Ireland. And, for the past generation, the Labour Party has actively tried to kill off Labour politics and Labour sentiment in Northern Ireland. But, despite the best efforts of Kevin McNamara, Peter Archer, Clive Soley, Roy Mason, Merlyn Rees and the rest, Labour sentiment has not been killed off—not, at least in the part of working class Belfast with which I am familiar. People often confide to me that, despite the Labour Party, despite everything, *"I'm Labour and so is my family, and always was"*. There is a strong sense of Trade Union solidarity in the Northern Irish working class and I know, in my bones, that there is a good Labour vote waiting to be got out.

*

Two things struck me on reading back copies of the Labour Opposition. Firstly its vigour! It was written by people who wanted to advance the working class interest, and believed in their cause with pride and conviction. Given what the Labour Party in Great Britain has become in the last 9 years—where bureaucratic manoeuvring, witchhunts and disciplinary 'strokes' mean everything and where public relations 'spin doctors', yuppie designer suits, opinion pollsters and rainbow coalition 'fads' are the primary political tools—it was a sheer joy to read a paper which stood four square for working people.

Secondly, however, the Labour Opposition failed to orientate itself to the new entity of Northern Ireland. This became the main failing, too, of the Northern Ireland Labour Party. The NILP polled close on 100,000 votes as recently as

1970, but collapsed in a heap as the civil conflict developed, for lack of a proper orientation towards Northern Ireland.

It is easy in hindsight, but perhaps less so at the time, to see that Northern Ireland was neither fish nor flesh. Northern Ireland is not, and never has been, a state. A part of the UK, but excluded from the Labour Vs Tory party system by which the UK was governed, it was subjected to a devolved government which no-one had asked for and which, since it required Protestants to govern Catholics, was bound sooner or later to aggravate sectarian tensions. This was the entity of Northern Ireland.

Labour, in the midst of this, took Northern Ireland to be a sort of state, took the Unionists to be the Tories (which they never were), and tried to act like a British Opposition. This left the foundations of provincial Labour being built on sand. In retrospect, it is easy to see that Labour's business is winning state power and governing in the interests of working people, or it is nothing.

The mirage of 'provincial' Labour is now over. *"Soda Farl Socialism"*, Paddy Devlin-style, is dead and gone. After the NILP, the United Labour Party, the Labour Party of Northern Ireland, and Labour '87, I do not believe there will again be a serious effort to establish a provincial Labour party which is not in the business of contesting for state power. But a serious effort had to be made to prove the point. The "Labour Opposition" was part of that serious effort.

The British Labour Party has consistently refused to organise in, or accept members from, Northern Ireland, despite the fact that it governs the area when it is in Office. However, the slow, painstaking work being undertaken to pressurize the Labour Party into organising in Northern Ireland on a basis that will represent working people from all sides, and repel neither community, is under way. The ballot of Autumn, 1991, in the Post Office Workers' Union, where over 70% of respondents favoured Labour organising, contesting elections and seeking a mandate in Northern Ireland, is indicative of a growing mood in the Trade Union movement in Northern Ireland. And it is essential that this generation has to hand literature and lessons from the past, like Labour Opposition. The orientation of those presently trying to get the Labour Party to set up in Northern Ireland is correct. If it gains half the head of steam and half the conviction of those behind the **Labour Opposition**, it will be hard to stop.

May, 1992,
Mark Langhammer,
East Antrim Labour Representation Group,
477 Shore Road,
Whiteabbey,
Co. Antrim.

Introduction

In 1892 the Belfast Trades Council which had been established ten years earlier involved itself in a strike of the Irish Linen Lappers Trade Union concerning wages, conditions and the right to organise. As part of its solidarity campaign it organised a Labour procession and demonstration (attended by some 1200 workers with about 30 or 40 bands) which was addressed by the Council President, Mr. Samuel Monro. According to a Belfast News Letter report of the occasion, Mr. Monro said that:

"That day, for the first time in the history of trades unionism, they had assembled in their thousands in Belfast at the calling of the United Trades Council. That day Orangemen and Nationalists had walked arm in arm (Cheers). Orange bands and Nationalist bands had vied with each other in discoursing pleasant airs..."

Another speaker ventured to hope that:

"...that day marked the emancipation of the working men of Belfast from the bigotry and prejudice which had hitherto separated them." (BNL 7/3/ 1892)

But the strike failed, and within a year, while Gladstone's second Home Rule Bill was making its way to the House of Lords, a fresh round of sectarian warfare broke out in Belfast and Catholic workers, for neither the first nor the last time, were expelled from the shipyards and elsewhere. Clearly trade union solidarity was not, of itself, enough to establish the degree of working class unity that would be proof against sectarian passions.

Exactly one hundred years on, though trade union solidarity has been demonstrated time and again in Belfast and throughout Northern Ireland, substantial working class unity remains an aspiration. Over the course of that hundred years it has occurred to many that the political organisation of labour is required to consolidate, build on and extend the basic solidarity of the workplace and dole queue. Over the last hundred years in Northern Ireland, Labour Parties have come and gone with depressing regularity: most recently the United Labour Party, the Labour and Trade Union Co-ordinating Group, Labour '87 and the Workers' Party have emerged, been briefly active, and gone, died or ossified; sectarianism and a divided working class remain. So far as the search for working class unity, the struggle against sectarianism, is concerned, the history of the last hundred years is a record of failure. But not unmitigated, and not always abject, failure.

The most substantial of the failed attempts at labour organisation was undoubtedly the Northern Ireland Labour Party. In respect of the extent of its organisation, the size of its membership, the degree of its support and the breadth of its activities and contacts, it stood head and shoulders above the rest. And, within the history of the NILP, there is a particular highlight, a phase of that party's development which throws into sharp relief the nature, the strengths and weaknesses, of the Labour Movement here. That is the period from March 1925 to June 1926 when the North Belfast Branch of the Independent Labour Party *published and controlled* the seventeen issues of **The Labour Opposition** Of Northern Ireland, edited by Hugh Gemmell.

The South Belfast Constituency Labour Party is here reproducing those seventeen issues of the first time since they were originally published. We are doing so in pursuit of the aim we announced while still a humble Labour Association: *"to familiarise the workers of South Belfast with the secret history of Labour politics in Northern Ireland."* Interest in that endeavour, and in the **Labour Opposition** material in particular, will, of course, extend far beyond South Belfast.

I hope in this introduction to present as succinctly as possible the context within which the **Labour Opposition** was produced and say something about the individuals and issues involved. Space does not permit, nor would the present state of our ongoing study justify, anything approaching a definitive history of the NILP, let alone of the Labour Movement in Northern Ireland.

It would be anachronistic to suggest that working class interest in independent labour organisation grew out of a desire to escape the social stranglehold of sectarian division. The roots of a specifically working class politics in Northern Ireland, as in the rest of the British Isles, lay in the requirements of the day to day economic struggle waged by the trade unions. As the Belfast Trades Council put the matter when it resolved in 1891 to contest municipal elections, its decision derived from a recognition that:

".....trade organisation, however perfect, cannot effect the reforms so essential to justice and good government while its efforts are confined to increasing wages and reducing hours of labour, as such efforts have to be made under laws formed and administered by trade union opponents, (who) would, if defeated in open conflict take away with their administrative hand the concessions wrested from their capitalist hand. It, therefore, proclaims its conviction that till labour is more fully represented in the council of the State justice cannot be secured to the labourer and as a first step in the direction of true reform recommends the adoption of one or more labour candidates to contest seats of the forthcoming municipal elections..." (BNL. 3/11/1891)

At the end of the nineteenth century such labour representation was as likely to be virtual representation, sponsored by the established bourgeois parties, as actual independent representation of workers by workers. Much of the political activity of the Belfast Trades Council in this period consisted of circularising candidates to discover their views on labour issues, advising its members how to vote and then monitoring the behaviour in office of the elected representatives.

Labour representation in Britain in this period operated under the tutelage of the Liberal Party (the Lib-Labs).

The idea of independent labour representation was pioneered in Belfast in 1885 by the then secretary of the Trades Council, Alexander Bowman, who contested the North Belfast Parliamentary seat, stating that labour:

"...wanted representatives who would be independent of any party in the State, who would not be dragged after any party for mere party purposes, but who would act in the interests of a class which had not received the recognition it deserved." (Northern Whig. 31/10/85)

Bowman's showing in the election was perfectly respectable; he polled 1,330 votes as against the successful Tory, William Ewart's 3,915. However, when, in 1886, he declared himself in favour of Home Rule the Trades Council was enraged and he was forced to resign.

Over the next seven years the Trades Council kept up its interest in the idea of independent labour representation without really getting anywhere. In 1891 it moved to establish an electoral committee to organise a Belfast Branch of the British-based (pro Home-Rule) Labour Electoral Association. March 1892 saw a decision to make election of the Belfast Electoral Committee an annual affair and establish a parliamentary fund.

An event of immensely greater interest and lasting significance occurred in 1893 when the Trades Union Congress (to which the Belfast Trades Council was then affiliated) met in Belfast. When the delegates dispersed, they left behind them a branch in North Belfast of the Independent Labour Party which had been formed some months previously at a conference in Bradford. (Associated with William Walker in founding the branch, which some 30 years later was to publish the **Labour Opposition** were Robert Getgood and Mrs. Ida Boyd who appear in its columns.

The point which must be stressed here is that the emerging Belfast Labour Movement in this period was developing unselfconsciously as part of the emerging British Labour Movement. It was the only area in Ireland to do so; a fact which was to have consequences. In 1893 the Belfast and District United Trades Council (to give it its full title for once) was affiliated to the Trades Union Congress. But in 1894 Trades Councils were debarred from membership. And in 1894 arrangements for special representation of Irish-based trade unions within the TUC were rescinded, which led to the formation in that year of the Irish Trades Union Congress. These facts also were to have consequences, for the Belfast Trades Council affiliated to the new Irish Trades Union Congress.

Essentially the position now was that, while continuing to evolve as an unselfconsciously organic part of the British Labour Movement, Belfast began to look south with a view to encouraging the development of independent labour representation in the whole of Ireland. Serious efforts in this direction began at the 1902 Congress in Cork. In the wake of the House of Lords' *"Taff Vale"* decision, Alexander Taylor of the Belfast Trades Council suggested that the money which unions were forced to spend on law suits could be better used for *"the advancement of direct labour representation in parliament"*. On the instruction of the Belfast Trades Council he proposed a motion calling *"on all elected representatives of Labour to observe the urgent necessity of abstaining from supporting the nominee of any political party unless he has been approved of by the local trades council, trade union, or other recognised Labour organisation"*.

Despite nationalist-inspired opposition from P. T. Daly, the motion was carried.

In 1903, the ILP and trade unions in Belfast formed a branch of the Labour Representation Committee. Three delegates from Belfast attended its third conference, after which Keir Hardie travelled to Belfast to open the ILP Hall in Langley Street (off Tennant Street on the Shankill Road). Hardie and Ramsay McDonald were then escorted to Newry to attend the 1903 Irish Trades Union Congress. Hardie addressed delegates on the advantages of independent labour representation, saying:

"...when the Labour members come from Ireland, as they would come, they would work together outside all the political differences that had weakened their ranks in the past, realising that they had one common interest, which was greater than national feeling, greater than religious difference, the principle of seeking to uplift the people to whom they belonged, and to make their life more worth living than it had been in the past."

When P. T. Daly again intervened, John Murphy of the Typographical Society (he was one of the first socialists on the Belfast Trades Council and a founder member, with Walker, Getgood and Ida Boyd, of the North Belfast ILP) proposed

"That this Congress of Irish Trade Unionists heartily recommends to the Trades Unions of this country an immediate affiliation to the Labour Representation Committee to promote the formation of independent labour representation in Ireland."

Again the motion was carried.

William Walker presided over the 11th Annual ITUC at Kilkenny in 1904 and used his presidential address to argue a clear, coherent, overwhelmingly practical case for what was becoming the *"usual"* Belfast resolution in favour of Irish unions affiliating to the Labour Representation Committee.

"The Trade Union movement is the most powerful working-class movement of today; its membership numbers almost two millions; its funds stand at almost four million pounds, and it has an electoral power that can make or unmake parties. The membership has hitherto been divided, one section voting with one party, and the other section with another, thus each section neutralising each other's power; its funds have been spent on strike after strike which has arisen not always because of the desire of the employers not to concede terms, but often against economic conditions which can only be changed by Parliamentary action. If then we can establish a movement which can not merely unite these 2m. voters but which will also have the support of the huge army of workers not organised but receiving the benefits which trades combinations confer upon the working classes, then we shall be directing a power and instituting a movement that shall eliminate all iniquities and substitute co-operation in lieu of the competitive waste now prevailing. To do this, of course, means money. But surely Trades' Union funds can be devoted to nothing better than improving the social conditions of the members. Surely it is a saner and wiser policy to spend £1,000 in the return of a member to the House of Commons than it is to spend ten times that amount in a strike which is often not successful, and even if successful entails upon the members participating in such strike great privations."

Cutting a long and repetitive story short, every year between 1903 and 1911 motions supporting affiliation to the LRC (from 1908, with the Labour Party) were carried at the Irish Trades Union Congress, by steadily decreasing majorities. And nothing happened. The Dublin Trades Council and the Irish-based unions quite simply, very consistently, refused to affiliate or send delegates to the Labour Party. And that was that.

It is clear that the representatives of the Belfast movement were simply flummoxed by the behaviour of Southern Labour. They took it for granted that, having won the arguments and having won the votes, they would have their way. But it didn't happen like that. They thought that they were dealing with something very much like themselves. But it wasn't and they weren't.

The Southern Labour Movement took its attitude to political organisation in the first instance from the "father of the land league", Michael Davitt. While doing fifteen months in Portland Prison, Davitt prepared his **Leaves From A Prison Diary** in which he argued that workers in Britain should strive for independent political organisation. To that end he advocated making election expenses a charge on the rates, and payment of MPs. Leaves From A Prison Diary was published in 1885. In practice, however, Davitt's close connection, on nationalist grounds, with the Liberal Party made him lukewarm about the reality of independent labour representation as it worked itself out around Keir Hardie, the ILP and the LRC. And all along, in respect of Ireland, he was utterly opposed to workers engaging in politics on their own behalf. There he insisted that the Irish Parliamentary Party was the vanguard, the engine, and the only possible vehicle of social reform, within which the Irish working class would have to organise itself. When a Dublin conference of trade unionists in 1891 called for the election of labour representatives, Davitt saw to it that the IPP agreed to select a number of *"Labour Nationalist"* candidates. Two of these were elected to Parliament in 1892 and the agitation in Dublin for independent representation ceased.

J. P. Nannetti MP, Lord Mayor of Dublin, was invited to address the ITUC in Athlone in 1906 and argued that:

"...they in Ireland were in the happy position that they had a Labour Party already in England. The Irish Parliamentary Party were the Labour Party, and he asked them to take advantage of that party... They were purely labour as well as Nationalist.... not a single constituency in Ireland would return a man on the labour question purely."

Nannetti here differs from Davitt only in the forthrightness which was entirely foreign to Davitt on this subject. But then Nannetti did not have to look over his shoulder at a British Labour constituency which he was simultaneously trying to persuade of his progressive credentials. Nannetti could afford to be forthright.

In 1911, acquiescence in virtual representation through the IPP, and opposition to the Labour Party's advocacy of *"godless education"*, led to the narrowest vote yet on Belfast's usual resolution. It was carried, but by only 32 votes to 29.

(The debates at which nationalist opposition to Labour Party organisation concentrated on its policy regarding secular education boded ill for the future of socialist values in an Ireland under Home Rule. In 1903, a resolution to the 10th Irish Congress in favour of secular education was rejected despite its movers disclaiming any *"desire to ostracise Catholics from their religion"*.

It is interesting to note that Catholic Church control of its schools was long an issue dividing the working class in Liverpool. David Logan, a Labour MP and founder of a Chapter of the Knights of St. Columba in the city, refused to vote with the party on the 1931 Education Act. In 1933, when Sydney Silverman contested the Exchange constituency for Labour, his Conservative opponent played the Catholic card, distributing a leaflet outside the Churches on Sunday, which stated:

"1. As Catholics you cannot accept the extreme socialist policy of Mr. Silverman, it is not sound, it is not good for the working class

2. You cannot expect Mr. Silverman to further the just claims of our Catholic Schools."

After his defeat Mr. Silverman commented:

"...this was a triumph of religious prejudice over political conditions. My opponent throughout fought the campaign purely on a religious basis and managed to persuade enough hungry, ill-clad, badly housed people to vote for him on the basis of the similarity of their religions."

The politics of Liverpool are no longer dominated by sectarian issues and stratagems, precisely because of the organisation and growth of the Labour Party. They continue to dominate the social and political life of Northern Ireland precisely because of the British Labour Party's refusal nationally to consolidate and build on the spirit and vigour of our local **Labour Opposition**.)

In 1912, Connolly and Larkin joined the Redmondite IPP'ers to vindicate the principle of national labour organisation. Connolly's motion:

> "That the independent representation of Labour on all boards be, and hereby is, included amongst the objects of this congress"

was carried by 49 votes to 18. The Irish Labour Party was formally launched in 1914.

In short, the strategy which Davitt had pioneered, of misrepresenting the Nationalist Party as the vanguard of social reform, while simultaneously manoeuvring against any possibility of independent labour organisation, had the result in the end of leaving the Southern Labour Movement with the worst of both worlds. The Irish Labour Party was responsible for its own activity, it was no longer virtually represented, in the sense of obliging a stronger interest to patronise it; effectively, it had ceased to count as a distinct interest within the nation. At the same time it had deliberately rejected association with the burgeoning social and political power of British Labour, choosing instead to organise itself on the narrow ground of its own weakness. It had nowhere to run to, nowhere to hide, it was doomed, some four years before De Valera stated the obvious, to wait.

The Belfast Labour Movement meanwhile was being itself, an energetic region of British Labour, active in its branches of the Independent Labour Party and the Labour Representation Committee. In 1906 the LRC nationally decided to change its name to the Labour Party. Its first annual conference under that title was held in Belfast in 1907 (something which it now affects to have forgotten).

In 1905 William Walker, with Ramsay McDonald as his election agent, fought North Belfast, where Bowman had stood twenty years before, in a bye-election. The contest was close-fought, with Walker losing by some 500 votes in a poll of over 8,000. At the general election held a few months later he reduced the majority of his opponent, Sir Daniel Dixon, to some 300. Though he fought the seat again in 1907, his hour had passed and North Belfast was left to be taken for Labour (in a Stormont rather than a Westminster election) by Sam Kyle of the **Labour Opposition** in 1925.

In 1910 Walker, who had several times been a member of its National Executive Committee (and in 1911 was to be its vice-Chairman), fought the Scottish seat of Leith Burghs for the Labour Party. After engaging in a momentous dispute with James Connolly in the pages of the Glasgow ILP paper, **Forward,** Walker retired from politics to help administer Lloyd George's new National Insurance scheme to which he was deeply committed. He died in 1918. (The Connolly/Walker controversy is too significant in itself to attempt to deal with it in outline here. It will form the core of a future SBCLP reprint.)

The margin of the Belfast Labour Movement was full of a life that can only be sketched here very briefly. In 1897, Alice Milligan and her brother Ernest helped form a Belfast Socialist Party which was associated with Connolly's Irish Socialist Republican Party. Eight years later the Belfast Socialist Party and the Trades Council founded the short-lived Belfast Labour Party.

A Belfast Branch of the Workers' Educational Association was founded around 1910 by, among others, Sam Kyle and William McMullen who, like Kyle, was later to be associated with the **Labour Opposition** (and the Stormont Parliament, and the ITGWU, and much else, see next paragraph).

William McMullen was the first chairman, in 1912, of the Belfast Branch of another of Connolly's attempts to nationalise Irish labour organisation, the Independent Labour Party (Ireland). The ILP(I) achieved nothing and is of little significance in itself. That it was set up at a conference which was attended by, along with the BSP and the SPI that one would expect at such an event, four of the five Belfast Branches of the ILP (North was the stop-out) indicates the extent to which, by 1912, the mainstream of the Belfast Labour Movement was becoming reconciled to what was increasingly felt to be the inevitability of Home Rule.

One element of the strategy which Davitt appears to have pioneered required the Irish Parliamentary Party to present itself in Britain as THE party of social reform in Ireland. In Britain, the Party's nationalist rhetoric was, of necessity, subsumed within a carefully constructed presentation of Home Rule as the essential precondition of good government, effective government, above all, socially progressive government in Ireland. The Liberal Party, which towards the end of the nineteenth century was entering on the terminal stages of the illness that led to a notably strange death, bought that bill of goods, literally sight unseen. The Labour Party, which in every major particular developed its instincts and prejudices under Liberal tutelage, carried that dogmatic commitment to Home Rule with it in its baggage when it set up on its own. Both the Liberal and the Labour Parties were blind to the naked reality that the land reform of the Tory, Balfour, which ended landlordism and established peasant proprietorship, had completely answered the social reformist case for Home Rule.

Balfour's Land Acts of 1903 were literally the last reform that the former tenant-farmers, now farm owners, felt they needed or desired. What they now felt they needed and most definitely desired, and supported Home Rule in order to ensure, was an end to reform. The Irish Parliamentary Party in consequence led the opposition to extension of Lloyd George's 1911 National Insurance Bill (the essential legislative and administrative basis of Beveridge's much more comprehensive plan) to Ireland. The Liberal and the Labour Parties took Redmondite opposition on board in the transparently sincere belief that it would be wrong to shackle the more advanced reformers of Ireland with the inferior, relatively primitive, social arrangements appropriate to Britain (and if the workhouse wraiths of Free State days could have laughed they might have stopped weeping).

The British Labour Party at the beginning of this century had no intimate connection with and no practical knowledge of the peasant proprietors of Southern Ireland, the new ruling class which was beginning to flex its muscles preparatory to remoulding its social environment in the image of Rome and Rome's canon law. British Labour believed about them what the Irish Party and Connolly told it it should believe. That is fair enough. What is tragic is that the Labour Party conveyed its illusions to the representatives of Belfast Labour when it met them, as it naturally did when they naturally appeared at Trades Union Congresses, ILP Conferences, meetings of the National Executive Committee of the Labour Party and so on. Even worse, in fact utterly unforgivably, it insisted on conducting its relations with these Belfast people, with whom it had intimate connection and of whom it had practical knowledge, on the basis of those illusions about an entirely different set of people.

The political priorities of the individuals comprising the Belfast Labour Movement in this period are not difficult to discover; they had not changed by 1925 and can be read month by month in the **Labour Opposition**. Essentially, they were concerned above all to cherish and nurture the limited degree of cross-community working class unity which existed (these are the people who had sweated blood to achieve it): the individuals concerned were predominantly Protestant and, I strongly suspect, did not know enough Catholics well enough to realise that we are by no means as sensitive as Protestants tend to assume we are. In any event, that very natural, praiseworthy, concern, led them to refuse to discuss sensitive political matters in any trade union forum whatsoever, from Trade Union Branches to meetings of the Trades Council itself. The issue of Home Rule was, of course, discussed in the ILP but no decision, for or against, was ever officially arrived at.

What was arrived at was arrived at in accordance with the second of Belfast's political priorities; its heart-felt concern to continue to develop politically in step with the British Party. Belfast Labour had no more notion than had British Labour of the actual social nature of Irish separatism. Its instinct was to suspect it, but that instinct was suppressed in the interest of shop-floor unity. British Labour had no instinct which applied to the situation but believed it had knowledge of it. That knowledge was conveyed energetically to its Belfast region. When commitment to Home Rule became Labour Party policy the Belfast people, who had no functional grounds of opposition and no tradition of passive acceptance, decided to look on the bright side of the measure.

Of course there were a few individuals who had decided views for and against Home Rule (William Walker immediately springs to mind as one of those who was very much against; Jack Beattie, the beginnings of whose turbulent parliamentary career are charted in the **Labour Opposition**, would have been its most prominent supporter) but, of the majority, I do not think more can be said than that they resolved to look on the bright side.

Certainly, the unofficial but generally accepted, view of Home Rule which prevailed in the Belfast Labour Movement from about 1912 on was a triumph of its determined optimism over its experience, from 1903 to 1911, of the Southern Labour Movement. It allowed itself to be persuaded that Home Rule was an administrative measure which would facilitate the good government and encourage rapid development of Ireland. Allied with the Southern Labour Movement in the Irish Parliament, it would work to provide independent representation for a united working class. That class's representatives at Westminster would work with the British Labour Party to build Socialism in a yet more United Kingdom. In short, it accepted the inevitability of Home Rule, informally adopted Labour Party policy on the matter, and resolved, in characteristically ebullient spirit, to make the best of whatever occurred. And in the meantime it got on, insofar as it was allowed, with being itself, an energetic region of the British Labour Movement.

In 1917 the Trades Council convened a conference in Belfast of the Independent Labour Party branches and the trade unions at which the Belfast Labour Party was reconstituted. This put forward four candidates at the *"coupon"* election of 1918. Sam Kyle stood in North Belfast. None of the four was elected, but they all managed a respectable poll.

The Belfast Labour Party was then forced to face up to a *"worst-case"* scenario which had hitherto been dismissed as unimaginable. 1920 and 1921 were not good years for Labour in Belfast. The Government of Ireland Act partitioned the country and set up an administration in the North which was entirely novel, a constitutional experiment the implications of which were revolutionary in the most disturbing sense of that often misused word. No criteria existed by which to gauge the survival prospects of the new arrangements but they did not, to put it mildly, seem good. And, in 1920, the ILP Hall in Langley Street was burned down by a loyalist mob.

Having thus been marginalised by circumstances over which it had absolutely no control, the Belfast Labour Movement was thrown brutally back upon its most basic instincts; the political priorities which had guided its activity since 1885. Consequently it refused to adopt any formal position with regard to partition, simply expressing its general support for the policies of the British Labour Party.

Though the Belfast Labour Party decided not to contest the 1921 elections, some individual socialists stood, describing themselves variously as Labour, Independent or Labour-Socialist. Among these was Harry Midgley in East Belfast and the Rev. J. Bruce Wallace in North. Midgley's career was just beginning, Wallace's was coming to an end, and this may be a good point at which to refer to his activity, the influence of which pervades many of the seventeen issues of the **Labour Opposition**.

A formative work in the development of British Socialist thinking in the late 19th century was Henry George's **Progress And Poverty**, published in 1879, which advocated land nationalisation. George was brought to Belfast in January 1885 by the Irish Land Restoration Association and addressed a meeting in the Ulster Hall. The secretary of the Association was Alexander Bowman of the Belfast Trades Council. Its Chairman was the Rev. J. Bruce Wallace. A month after the public meeting, Wallace debated the issues raised with the notorious *"Roaring"* Hanna. In the course of that debate, which is quoted forty years later in the **Labour Opposition**, Wallace expounded the labour theory of value. Forty years on, *Sowseed*'s prescription for Northern Ireland agriculture owes a very great deal to Henry George, by way of Wallace.

The independent candidates in 1921 were comprehensively defeated; their negligible vote simply proved Labour's irrelevance in an election concerned solely to test the new state's determination and ability to survive. Labour, official and independent, kept out of the 1922 Westminster elections.

1923 was a different matter. When Joe Devlin declared at the end of October that he would not be standing, Harry Midgley, who was fast becoming the driving force behind labour in Belfast, was pressed to contest the West Belfast seat in the Westminster elections of that year. Though he entered the election with only a fortnight to go to polling day, Midgley fought a classic campaign against the Unionist, Sir Robert Lynn, editor of the Northern Whig. The final result was Lynn, 24,975 votes, Midgley, 22,255.

Midgley lost in West Belfast, but the result nationally was the return of a minority Labour Government at Westminster. That conjunction and Midgley's organisational drive energised the movement. At a meeting in Ye Olde Castle Restaurant in Belfast on the 8th. March 1924, the Belfast Labour Party was reconstituted as the Labour Party (Northern Ireland). Sam Kyle was elected President, with Robert Dorman as vice-President and Harry Midgley as Secretary. The question of a full and complete constitution was left to a further conference in September.

The September conference approved a constitution based on that of the British Labour Party. On organisational matters it stated:

"The Central Labour Party shall consist of affiliated Trade Union Branches, Co-operative Societies, Socialist Societies, The Trades Council and Trades Federations, and the Local Labour Parties in the area".

As the Irish Labour Party was established on a purely trade-union basis, the new LP(NI) could not consider affiliation with it (its ILP branches would have been excluded). Its relationship with the British Labour Party, being a live issue which had to work itself out, was more complex.

Since 1893, the major vehicle within which Belfast labour had forged its development as part of the broad British movement was the Independent Labour Party. This was an entirely normal state of affairs at the time.

Until 1918, when the British Labour Party adopted a new constitution, the only way to join it was through an affiliated organisation: a trade union; or socialist society. In practice, the path by which socialists entered the Labour Party was through the ILP, in Belfast as in Bradford, as in Birkenhead.

In 1918, the Labour Party became a "national" party, acquiring the form of constituency organisation and the staff to service it. The recently reconstituted Belfast Labour Party applied to affiliate to the British Labour Party two Divisional parties, which it had organised apart from the ILP. The Labour Party refused affiliation on the grounds that local party organisation in Belfast was a matter for the Irish Labour Party. The reasoning behind this was that Home Rule for Ireland was expected to take place, a policy which British Labour supported. Northern Ireland Labour was thus in a catch-22 situation. It could not affiliate to the Irish Labour Party without isolating some of its strongest elements; and it was not permitted to affiliate to British Labour, on the grounds of that Party's position on the Irish Question.

It therefore remained the case in Northern Ireland after 1918 that membership of the British Labour Party was only possible by way of membership of an affiliated socialist society, the ILP. It was in fact the case that, bureaucratic anomalies aside, Belfast labour was still a functioning part of the new "national" Labour Party.

The mutual connections which had been developing since 1893 were not rationalised out of existence in 1918. Far from it! It is evident from the pages of the **Labour Opposition** that Belfast remained very much on the ILP/Labour Party itinerary. Visits to Belfast by G.D.H. Cole, A. A. Purcell (vice-Chairman of the TUC), James Maxton MP (Chairman of the ILP), David Kirkwood MP and Ellen Wilkinson MP are vividly recounted there. Charles Philips Trevelyan, who was in charge of education in the 1924 Labour Government, spoke in the Ulster Hall on May Day 1926.

(The anomaly thus remained, allowing Northern Ireland Labour an organic connection with the British Labour Movement, until 1932, when the ILP nationally disaffiliated itself from the Labour Party. At that point, the loyalty of its Belfast members being first and foremost to the Labour Party, the ILP organisation in Northern Ireland dissolved itself.)

The new constitution of the Labour Party (Northern Ireland) became operative from 1st February, 1926.

The second local Northern Ireland election (the last to be held under Proportional Representation) was held on 25th April, 1925. Three candidates were put forward; Jack Beattie in East Belfast, Sam Kyle in North and William McMullen in West. Beattie topped the poll in East Belfast, Kyle was elected on the second count and McMullen got in as the fourth member for West Belfast after five counts.

In these circumstances, with this history, the **Labour Opposition** Of Northern Ireland set out to do battle with the Unionist administration of a unique constitutional arrangement called, for lack of any but a geographical precedent, Northern Ireland. No one knew what to expect. Though the Unionist Government was widely suspected of being capable of any perfidy, its real character was not as yet known. Its capacity to sustain itself was still, at this early stage, a matter of speculation. The situation was ripe for propaganda and Hugh Gemmell (whose biography, with many others, will be found in the following pages) was just the man to supply it.

Such then are the origins of the **Labour Opposition** Of Northern Ireland. It should now begin to speak for itself. It is well capable of speaking for itself. And what it says, it says with a kick!

Joe Keenan

NOTE:

What follows is the complete text of the 17 issues of the **Labour Opposition** Of Northern Ireland. Technical problems in transposing a newspaper into a book have made it difficult for us to give the full flavour of the newspaper in the form in which it originally appeared on the streets. Each issue of the **Labour Opposition** was illustrated with photos of labour figures prominent at the time. These have proveddifficult to reproduce. We have included some, despite their poor quality, in order to give an idea of the person portrayed; others we have had to discard.

Most particularly, we would ask readers to bear in mind that the few trade union and labour notices and advertisements which are scattered through this edition are no more than a representative sample. In the original, each issue carried a full page of advertisements, in addition to others which appeared in the body of the paper. The Trade Union and Labour Movement in Belfast endorsed the **Opposition**, used the paper to further their objectives, and supported it financially by means of these advertisements.

❧ THE LABOUR ❧
OPPOSITION
OF NORTHERN IRELAND.

VOL. 1—No. 1.   MARCH, 1925.   ONE PENNY

Scandalous Housing Conditions near Belfast

BY SAM KYLE.

ACCORDING to evidence submitted at the Home Office Inquiry into the £40,000 scheme for the Belfast Rural Council, for the erection of 118 labourers' cottages, the housing conditions of the people in Hyde park, Glengormley and District are anything but pleasant, or conducive to that healthy and prosperous state of affairs we hear so much about from the Unionist orators. If the same orators would pay more attention to remedying the scandalous state of the housing of their " loyal " supporters and less to the caterwauling of the clergy, who apparently are only concerned about compelling teachers to do their work for them, they might perform something worth while.

One witness at the inquiry stated, and he was an ex-soldier, that before he left that morning " we had to bale the water out of the kitchen. I have no house, I have only one room 12 feet square. We have to go very night to get into bed and out of it." Which reminds me of Jack Jones' story of the man who had to put his feet and legs out of the window to get his trousers on in the morning.

No, while people are compelled to live in stables, barns and tumble down houses, the Parliament of Northern Ireland should be more concerned with remedying this scandal than prating about Flags and Empire and Borders, and the necessity of Religious Instruction by Amateurs. The facts of the matter are that it is much easier to talk about non-essentials than it is to do practical every day things.

Compare the condition of the ex-service man that has served his country in France and Flanders, with the case of the Duke of Abercorn for whose house the taxpayer is being mulcted to the tune of over £80,000 despite the fact that the Duke is not really in need of a house as he has more than one already, or again let any of our readers go up to Stormont and look at the elaborate preparations for another house for the Speaker of the House. We think everybody will agree that the present Speaker of the House has no need for another one. The sum of £80,000 would provide 160 houses at £500 each, for the people who are in such dire need of house. The conditions revealed at the inquiry on evidence given by the people of the district, discloses a terrible state of affairs, and even the employers have joined in demanding the erection of labourers' cottages for the homeless people in and around Belfast. Take the millions that are being spent at the Parliament House and Buildings, a thing which in another generation will probably be called England's Folly or the Unionist Party's Disgrace, how many thousands of ordinary working men's houses might be erected with this money which so far as the ordinary man in the street is concerned is so much money thrown away.

The Labour Opposition Of Northern Ireland

Vol. 1.—No.1   March 1925.   One Penny

Scandalous Housing Conditions near Belfast.

BY SAM KYLE

According to evidence submitted at the Home Office Inquiry into the £40,000 scheme for the Belfast Rural Council, for the erection of 118 labourers' cottages, the housing conditions of the people in Hydepark, Glengormley and District are anything but pleasant, or conducive to that healthy and prosperous state of affairs we hear so much about from the Unionist orators. If the same orators would pay more attention to remedying the scandalous state of the housing of their "loyal" supporters and less to the caterwauling of the clergy, who apparently are only concerned about compelling teachers to do their work for them, they might perform something worthwhile.

One witness at the inquiry stated, and he was an ex-soldier, that before he left that morning "we had to bale the water out of the kitchen. I have no house, I have only one room 12 feet square. We have to flit every night to get into bed and out of it". Which reminds me of Jack Jones' story of the man who had to put his feet and legs out of the window to get his trousers on in the morning.

No, while people are compelled to live in stables, barns and tumble down houses, the Parliament of Northern Ireland should be more concerned with remedying this scandal than prating about Flags and Empires and Borders, and the necessity of Religious Instruction by Amateurs. The facts of the matter are that it is much easier to talk about non-essentials than it is to do practical every day things.

Compare the condition of the ex-service man that has served his country in France and Flanders, with the case of the Duke of Abercorn for whose house the taxpayer is being mulcted to the tune of over £80,000, despite the fact that the duke is not really in need of a house as he has more than one already, or again let any of our readers go up to Stormont and look at the elaborate preparations for another house for the Speaker of the House. We think everybody will agree that the present Speaker of the House has no need for another one. The sum of £80,000 would provide 160 houses at £500 each, for the people who are in such dire need of houses. The conditions revealed at the inquiry on evidence given by the people of the district, discloses a terrible state of affairs, and even the employers have joined in demanding the erection of labourers' cottages for the homeless people in and around Belfast. Take the millions that are being spent at the Parliament House and Buildings, on a thing which in another generation will probably be called England's Folly or the Unionist Party's Disgrace. How many thousands of ordinary working men's houses might be erected with this money which so far as the ordinary man in the street is concerned is so much money thrown away.

Hits and Misses.

By MARKSMAN.

A well known business man was boasting in a hotel bar the other evening that he was born in Co. Derry, 42 years ago without a penny in his pocket. His companion, who evidently had a sense of humour replied. "Well, of course, we can't all be born with silver spoons in our mouth."

      *   *

In a hotel bar one can hear things said which are never overheard in the ice cream saloon. For instance, I heard that six "old-town-hallites" are to be appointed by the local Education Committee as inspectors.

      *   *

I also heard of a highly placed Government Official who cloaked the discrepancies of his junior and when the facts leaked out, threatened to dismiss some person or persons, for circulating a *false* report.

      *   *

I am a teetotaller as a rule, but as Jack London says, its wonderful what you can get to know over a social glass.

      *   *

There are bad times in store for the working class unemployed. Of course, the "superior" class of unemployed will continue to live pretty well by drawing "Rent Interest and Profit." And the rich unemployed do not have to line up in queues, nor have they to face the "court" in order to prove that they are "genuinely seeking work", or that they are "normally in insurable employment".

      *   *

I do not know what instructions have been issued to Branch Exchange Managers of the Ministry of Labour, Northern Ireland, but I find that the "Coort" is usually composed of one representative of the workers, and three representatives of the employers, with the result that two out of every three applicants are being denied their benefits. I am speaking now of the Rural and Urban Districts. The remedy for this state of affairs is in the hands of the working class themselves. Let them organise in their Trade Unions, and vote Labour at election times. Wake up! Henry Dubb, Wake up!

      *   *

Yes, Henry, the "Coorts" are being packed against you, because one Branch Manager admits having notified only one labour representative to each "Coort" and notifying three employers. The regulations are clear that there should be equal representation.

      *   *

I say, Henry Dubb, do you remember when the British Empire Union and the National Citizens Union took action against the Belfast Corporation to prevent them paying 1/2 per hour to Builders' Labourers?

We heard so much about the British Empire Union's concern for the pockets of the ratepayers, and oh! the lofty ideals they preached. It was "Down with the Russian Gold", and "down with the Socialist Sunday Schools".

      *   *

But Oh, what a change! We now find these lofty souled British Empire Union's and National Citizens Union's engaging Messrs. Wolkowski and Nadia, and the Russian Cabaret Company to perform in the Ulster Hall, Belfast for five successive nights.

      *   *

However, the morals of the working class are not to be corrupted by witnessing a wicked Russian Cabaret. Oh no; the British Empire Union have seen to that, Henry.

      *   *

In order to enjoy this Cabaret with its sit down supper, and a running buffet, you have got to pay two guineas per night for you and your wife, or if you take some other fellow's wife, well, no questions are asked. And of course there is a taxi to pay for and the tips. So you will understand, Henry, if your employer pays you a living wage, well how can he go to the Russian Cabaret in the Ulster Hall? It simply cannot be done.

      *   *

Seriously, however, I hope that the "Sunday-go-to-meeting-people" who subscribe to the funds of the British Empire Union, will take note, and might I point out that if these well meaning people really want a new Heaven and a new Earth, they should send their subscriptions to the Independent Labour Party.

      *   *

At the last monthly meeting of the Belfast Corporation, I was sitting in the public gallery, and heard the debate on British *v* French Cement. I noted that some of our Labour Representatives voted "for" and some "against". I realise that there is a good deal to be said on both sides. For instance if you vote for French Cement, it proves you are an internationalist, and it also proves that you are out to smash the British Cement Trust, and the fact that eight British firms tendered and all quoted the same price proves there is a trust, ring, or combine to keep up prices.

      *   *

On the other hand if you vote for British Cement, it proves that you are anxious to give employment to our own people, and it is said that the conditions of labour are better here than in France.

* *

Incidentally I heard something else which was not mentioned in the debate, and that is that British Cement was quoted at 52/6 per ton, as against the French tender of 48/- per ton, I was told that the French Company cannot tender here, unless they can secure a big order, and had there been no French tender, the British combine would have charged 60/- per ton, as they *are* charging at present where the French Company are not in a position to compete.

* *

Might I appeal to the Labour men to come together and hold a meeting previous to each meeting of the Corporation, in order that they might decide their policy on certain questions, such as Cement Contracts.

* *

Some Councillor named "Texas Jack" took a prominent part in the Cement debate,

and it seems to me that he is a "poor Prod" for his historical references were not quite correct. For instance, he raved about Derry, Aughrim and Magheramorne! Well, any Belfast man knows this is wrong. What he should have said was Derry, Aughrim, and the Boyne. Of course, we are all liable to make mistakes. For instance, we have all seen the Orange Banners with pictures of King William crossing the Boyne, and King William landing at Torbay. Torbay as you know, is in the South of England.

* *

A prominent Orangeman (who was a member of a public board in Belfast), was at Torbay last year, and was told that the Prince of Orange landed there. He pitied the poor Englishman, who told him that story, and informed him that Carrickfergus was the place where the Prince of Orange landed. However, to his amazement he learned that the Prince landed at Torbay before ever he landed in Ireland, so you see we are all liable to make mistakes as well as "Texas Jack."

Labour Men of the North.
WILLIAM WALKER.
BY BOB M'CLUNG.

The subject of our sketch was born in 1871, and died in 1918.

A joiner to trade, he was appointed, when only twenty years of age, as Delegate to Belfast Trades Council, and in turn held all the important offices of that body. A staunch and energetic member of the Independent Labour Party from its inception in 1893, and the founder of the North Independent Labour Party, his energy and enthusiasm was mainly responsible for the building of the only Independent Labour Party Hall in Ireland, which was burned down in 1920. Walker was early singled out for hatred and abuse. Whilst hatred and abuse may be the lot of early pioneers of new principles, Willie Walker by his fearless courage and determination was successful in winning the regard of his fellowmen and to-day lives in the hearts of hundreds of his old comrades who remember him with deep affection and

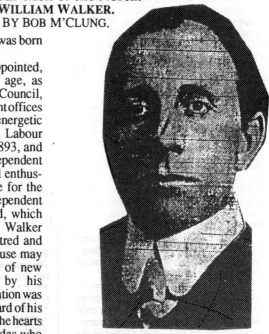

William Walker

regard.

In 1894 and 1895 Walker had to be almost continuously under police protection, because of his advocacy of the principles of Socialism. In 1899 he was elected a member of Belfast Poor-Law Board, and in 1903, was elected as Councillor for Duncairn Ward. In the same year he was elected as organising delegate of the Carpenters' and Joiners' Trade Union, which has since become the Woodworkers' Trade Union.

He was defeated in four parliamentary contests, but as Comrade Walker used to say:

"There's many a victory surely, decisive and complete,
Has meant a sight less fighting than a hardly fought defeat;
And if people do their duty, every man in his degree,
Why defeat may be more glorious than a victory needs to be."

Gilford And The Prince Of Wales
BY X.C.

If the Arts of man joined to the Powers of Hell, conspired to inflict their greatest evils on any town or village in the land, they could hardly produce more painful results than the demon of unemployment, ably supported by the callous indifference of National and Local Governing Boards, has inflicted upon the unfortunate Textile Workers of Gilford, Co. Down.

With a population of about 1,000 there is scarcely a home in the whole village that is not suffering from the effects of 4 years of under-employment.

As I write there are about 350 out of work, and of that number over 100 have not received any Unemployment Benefit since the 1st. January, 1925, and most of those who **are** working are on short time.

After the Ministry of Labour had done its worst, the question of granting relief from the Public Funds through the Banbridge Board of Guardians was discussed at two of their meetings, but the Home Office, though asked over a month ago to give specific guidance on the point as to whether the Guardians have the power to give relief in cases of this kind, have up to the present ignored the definite request of the Board.

We are a proud people here in Gilford and many, I have no doubt, would willingly undergo the tortures of the damned rather than accept relief in this form.

For all such I have the utmost respect, but I must also remind them of this other undeniable fact, that they are not the only people who are in receipt of maintenance out of the Public Purse, for it is out of the same Pocket that the Prince of Wales draws his dole of £220,000 per year and for which he need never sign the register!

Nor is this all our story, for even here in our peaceful village there may be heard the prancing of the Horsemen of the Apocalypse, even here has been experienced many of the curses of a capitalist system of society, where consumption has taken its dreadful toll and even the Asylum has had its quota. The latest victim in this connection was a girl who, having had her unemployment benefit stopped and no prospect of finding work, and an ailing sister dependent upon her, her mind gave way under the dreadful strain and in her more coherent moments she could be heard asking for "her bureau".

Besides this we have had many migrations and emigrations during the past 4 years, yet we have often heard it stated that Socialism would destroy the home, but after our experience here in Gilford where many happy homes have been shattered through unemployment, I have no hesitation in asserting that it is the lack of Socialism which is responsible for our present plight.

It is the knowledge of this fact that has driven so many thoughtful people to the conclusion that our only salvation can be found along the lines of Public Ownership, and Production for use instead of for profit, where all shall give according to their ability and receive according to their needs.

Application Form.

If you wish to join the North Belfast Branch of the Independent Labour Party, and you agree with the principles of the Party, then sign your name and address underneath and post the form, together with P.O. for 1/- to the Secretary, North Belfast Branch, I.L.P., 48 York Street, Belfast. It will be attended to at once!

Name,..................................
Address,...............................

The Labour Opposition

OF NORTHERN IRELAND.

Published and Controlled by the
North Branch I.L.P.
Advertising Rates, Two Shillings
per single column inch.
Subscription Rates, 1/3 per year, Post
Free.
Address all communications to
The Editor, 48 York Street, Belfast.

Fighting To Win.

We had originally intended to publish The Opposition once a month, and this issue should not have been on sale until the beginning of April. However, the uneasy haste with which Sir James Craig plunged into the turmoil of a General Election, makes it imperative that we should alter our plans and meet the arrogant challenge of a Tory Monopoly, by issuing a special number of The Labour Opposition.

Thus No.2 will be out at the end of the month, and we hope its opportune birth will be an augury of its future success. It has come to stay. **The Opposition is not an experiment. It is an institution.** And high sales, low sales, we do not care, we will hold on and fight and fight until the Labour Opposition grows into a Government in our Northern Land, and we have ousted the Tories from their political Gibraltar. As we write, great names that are gone rise up before us and inspire us with their steadfast courage and noble manhood. Had it not been for the pioneers who blazed the trail in the dark days of Ulster Labour, we could not have launched this venture now. We live for Socialism and all that that sacred word implies, and from month to month in our columns, we will expound some aspect of that world embracing philosophy. In our next issue, the Labour Candidates will develop the practical programme of Labour in Ulster, and in our columns lay the foundation of a vigorous and alert Opposition.

That we can win representation we know, but how many men we can send depends entirely upon you. We need workers, agents, money, and if these are forthcoming, we can return such a Labour Party to Parliament that will make the Tories hesitate before they again insult us with a Criminal Lunatic Asylum, instead of houses for the people. If this be error and upon us proved, then we never wrote and no man ever loved. It has been a long march and a bitter struggle, and if in the past we have marched from defeat to defeat, let us now consolidate our forces for a triumphant victory. Perhaps you are weary of political strife and lack of victory, and have determined to seek rest and solace in less exciting spheres. Don't do it! Be a man; be a woman, and help us in our noble cause. The world is astir and Labour is marching-on. Sometimes when we look around we grow sad at our slow progress in Ulster, and say we will never win. Don't be deluded! We are on the eve of victory. Do not think for one moment that you are an isolated band fighting a forlorn hope. Far from it! Remember that from Fairhead to the Cove of Cork, the torch of liberty is aflame throughout the land, and the army of the Working Class marches on to battle. And we will fight, and fight to win!

OUR FIGHTING FUND.

We appeal to all friends, sympathisers and well-wishers who desire to see a strong, alert and effective **OPPOSITION** in the Northern Parliament to send a subscription to our I.L.P. Fighting Fund. Any sum, much or little, will be welcomed, and will be acknowledged with thanks in these columns. Send your "sub." c/o. this Office at 48 York Street, Belfast.

SAM KYLE,
HUGH GEMMELL.

Workers' Union, No. 1 Branch	..	£15	0 0
Joint Committee I.L.P.	..	3	3 6
William Moneypenny	..	1	0 0
H. B.	..	0	10 0

Health *versus* Wealth
BY MARY KYLE.

As Socialists we are all agreed that we want, and must have, an efficient health service run by the community, and for the community. Women should be particularly alive on this question, for it is on them that the nursing of the sick and infirm generally falls, and they see the tragedies that often happen through sheer neglect. Granted that with higher wages and better conditions, we should have gained the most important item on our health programme, yet even then there are various provisions for health that we shall require, and we must fight for them now, just as we fight for higher wages. On both fields it is a case of opposing the cheeseparing policy of the economy mongers who always put the accumulation of wealth (in their own pockets) before everything else.

One very urgent matter that is *practical politics at the present moment* is the feeding of school children. Under the Education Act, provision is made for the feeding of necessitous school children, but now there is wrangling and delay owing to the stingy policy of some of the thoroughly comfortable.

The Belfast Education Committee wants to provide meals for 4,000 children, but the Government think they cannot possibly afford meals for more than 3,000. What meanness, what false economy, and what a

SCANDALOUS ATTACK ON THE CHILDREN.

No limit should be fixed except that meals should be provided for all those children who need them.

So too, there is the question of medical inspection and treatment of school children. Provision is also made for this under the Act, and a beginning has been made, but the whole thing needs speeding up. For instance, it is useless for reports to be put into the Press showing what a large percentage of Belfast children have bad eyesight. Nor is it any use blaming cross-word puzzles or cinemas. We must have adequate provision made for the physical well-being of the children, and the money must not be grudged. There are many such practical details that need the attention of Labour men and women, both inside and outside the Council, for *public opinion* can make itself felt, as witness the stir that is being caused at present in Government circles by the opposition to certain parts of their Education Act. If *we* could raise as much uproar to see that some of the provisions of that Act were immediately put into effect, what might we not get! But to turn to the general question of Health, we suggest that the proposal recently made in evidence given before the local Government Commission that a Ministry of Health for Northern Ireland should be set up is a good one, and

---

Pointers From Labour's Programme

1. To provide an Opposition in the Northern Parliament.
2. To resolutely oppose the spending of public money, without getting adequate safeguards that the money so spent will be recouped by the people.
3. Old Age Pensions on the same terms as in Britain.
4. Pensions for widowed mothers.
5. The establishment of a Ministry of Health.
6. The provision of work or maintenance for the unemployed.
7. The abolition of the Poor Law Guardians, and the substitution of direct control by a Committee of the Local Bodies, and thus abolishing the most iniquitous and wasteful scheme ever foisted on the Public.
8. Adequate provision of homes for the people.
9. Nationalisation of Railways.

---

should receive our active support. Not that we have everything when we get a Ministry. Far from it!! But it is a beginning, and we might reasonably hope that then more attention would be paid to some of the shocking housing conditions that were brought to light in connection with a recent

HOME OFFICE ENQUIRY;

that more attention might be paid to the care of mothers and infants; which in Belfast is very far behind that of many large towns in England; that more attention might be paid to the physical well-being of school children and to the general health of the whole population. The scheme for a Ministry of Health was clearly outlined in the evidence given, and while not agreeing with every detail it should have our general support, and we should insist on having representation of working men and women on the various Councils and Committees proposed. The argument that we cannot afford these things—that rates and taxes will go up —will of course be used. But we must insist that we cannot afford to neglect the public health. The workers grind their lives away in the factory, not to put large profits into the pockets of a few, but to secure the well-being of their own families, and the families of their fellow-workers. **We demand our rights when we demand that more money shall be spent on better provision for health.**

MAXTON And KIRKWOOD are great pals, and it was Maxton, as executive member of the Labour Party, who instructed Davy in the matter of the Prince's Tour. Everybody knew it would create a great sensation, and a man of such penetrating political vision, and possessing such forensic acumen, must be worth listening to. Apart from that, Maxton has a deep pitched, sonorous voice that could be heard in every corner of the Albert Hall in London, and he has a genius for dramatic gesture that sets him in the forefront of our orators. Applications for tickets

ARE COMING

in fast, and when the tickets are sold that's everything finished. This is not an effort to stampede you into buying a ticket too soon. It is an earnest warning that you will hold on to your shilling until it is of no use. You know perfectly well what Election Time is like in Belfast. Well, Maxton speaks in the Ulster Hall, on Monday, the 30th March, three days before the Poll! No ticket, no admission— and no money taken at the doors . Buy one now, and give Maxton a rousing welcome

TO BELFAST

Hugh Gemmell.

The Invisible Government of Northern Ireland.
BY HUGH GEMMELL.

THE POPULATION OF THE SIX COUNTIES IS 1,284,000.

No Government of modern times has been so hostile to the Working Class as the Government of Northern Ireland, and no Government on the surface of the globe has legislated with such unprincipled class bias. After dragooning the Democracy of Ulster into giving them an absolute monopoly, the Tory Government immediately thrust its hand into the public purse, and enriched a multitude of Departmental Officials with the spoils. From the first day they took office, Ulster sank from a prosperous community with only a small margin of unemployed to the position it occupies now, a community with 48,000 totally unable to obtain work, and thousands more only partially employed.

Gaunt famine sweeps our borders from end to end, and in our industrial cities disease born of starvation takes its nightly toll. In Belfast, the Capital of the Imperial Province, close on 40,000 workers vainly seek an honest outlet for their energies, and instead of bread are afforded the spectacle of the state opening of Parliament. The kept press of Belfast, already discredited in the minds of honourable men, and in one instance actually suspended from publication by order of the Government of Britain, seeks to stave off the pangs of hunger with promises of orders for our ship-building yards, and orders for our linen mills, but despite the persistent clamour of the Press, no work has matured, and our army of unemployed has steadily grown throughout the entire ministry of Sir James Craig.

BANKRUPT

Commercial stagnation holds Belfast in its grip, and our business men are appalled at the bankruptcies listed each week in the Gazette. How could it be otherwise, when the Government itself was compelled to effect a financial arrangement with its largest creditor, and where the Treaty provided that Ulster should pay £7,920,000 per annum, to the Imperial Treasury, we are only able to pay three and a half million pounds. Is it any wonder that our legislators have destroyed Ulster's credit on the Stock Exchange, and made us a hissing and a by-word among the nations of the world. Yet only last week, in the Northern Parliament, during the mummery that passes for legislation with the political neurotics who govern our destinies, a Mr. Leslie, speaking of the Loans Guarantee Act, said: "I do not think the measure should leave the House without public attention being drawn to the highly satisfactory state of public credit in Northern Ireland". Let us test it!

During August, 1924, shortly after the death of Lord Pirrie, Messrs. Harland & Wolf, decided to go to the London Stock Exchange in order to raise a capital of £4,000,000 with which to rehabilitate the shabby condition of the largest shipyard in the World. Every publicity was afforded by the Press to the venture, and every astute device to conceal defects and exalt slender virtues was resorted to by the promoters, yet when the books were closed, instead of a subscription of four million pounds, only one and a half was received. **The Credit of the Loyal and Imperial Province lay shattered in the dust.**

The hectic finance of our Government had frightened the Money Lords, and the biggest shipbuilding yard in the world was allowed to lie idle.

Credit at that vital moment would have saved our people, but our futile Government has brought our industries into unsavoury repute in the financial centre of the universe.

Two months later, the imperialists

who refused to invest in Ulster's Industries subscribed £120,000,000 in *two hours for Germany,* where only £30,000,000 was asked for by that clever industrial competitor of Britain.

But what a difference when it comes to voting money for their own class, because when the big farmers pleaded poverty of production to the Ulster Government, they immediately granted them £180,000 in relief of agricultural rates and calmly paid it out of the public treasury without a blush. No wonder the Duke of Abercorn when proroguing Parliament last November could tell the public that "the weather, which has proved so unfortunate to agriculture—*our greatest industry*—and the continued slackness in our shipyards, have prejudicially affected conditions in Northern Ireland, but prices for agricultural produce are showing an upward tendency, which will mitigate the losses sustained by the farmers".

What brazen insolence!! The Government actually rejoices that the people have to pay more for their food! Surely that is

CLASS LEGISLATION

with a very pronounced class bias. Look where you like, and examine any Act you like, the story is the same. The Government of Northern Ireland legislates against the people.

Is it old age pensions?

Why, everybody knows that they took advantage of our feeble and infirm old people, and robbed them of the advantages conferred upon them by the Labour Administration of Mr. Ramsay MacDonald.

Is it unemployment benefit?

Why, everyone knows that the increases so humanely conferred, upon the people by the people's own Labour Government, was discounted by the Northern Government, and conditions imposed that left the increase at the will and discretion of the Minister of Labour.

Too well we know the result of that

astute and subtle political device, for sickness and death have reaped their harvest of the class bias of Ulster's Government.

But look again how open handed they are when it is a question of securing their own safety, and making the six counties safe for *autocracy.* On the same occasion of the proroguing of Parliament, the Duke of Abercorn concluded his address from the Throne with the following significant warning to Democracy. "This sum £400,000 will be utilised in connection with a Training College, and Hostel for School Teachers, a Depot for the Royal Ulster Constabulary, a Convict Prison, a Borstal Institution and Criminal Lunatic Asylum, and Institutions for Agricultural Instruction and Research."

In plain words, £400,000 for Bombs, Bayonets, Bullets and Benzine, but not a halfpenny for the Working Class. I suppose we deserve it. We voted for it and we got what we voted for. When we vote Tory, we undoubtedly vote for a lunatic asylum, and when we vote Labour we vote for taking people out of the lunatic asylum, as Mr. Ramsay MacDonald did with the ex-service men, whom a Tory administration in Britain had condemned to a living death.

The time has come in Ulster to give our Class Government its quietus. They have been on the run ever since they were born, meeting now in the City Hall of Belfast, now in College Green, now in Stormont Castle, and anon on the banks of the Thames. Always invisible and like all invisible things working potently for evil against the people, let us now run them to earth and replace them with sane legislators of the people themselves. Let us be honest and admit our errors of the past, and profiting by our bitter lesson, vote Labour, Labour, Labour all the time.

Look out for our special Election Number. It will be ready at the end of the month, and will give the Tories a fright. It will be full of ginger.

Stop Thief!

Why are the poor, poor?
BECAUSE
They are robbed by the rich.
—R.H. Tawney, M.A.

A few weeks ago there appeared in the *Daily Herald*, the amazing story of how £100 invested in Courtaulds, became £300,000. Now there appears in the Financial Times the record of the Grape Mill Company, Oldham, which is almost as wonderful. The Shareholders are to receive a distribution of reserves to the extent of £70,000, and in addition to this are to be given free, gratis, and for nothing, ten £1 shares for each £5 share now held. This distribution is equal to 1,000 per cent.

When the fact is remembered that the original shareholders only paid £1 for their £5 shares and have been drawing dividend at the rate of 10 per cent. to 20 per cent. each half-year on the £5 for which they only paid £1, it will be seen that the original share holders have had bonus distributions equal to 1,400 per cent. on the original £1 paid for their shares, in addition to numerous dividends. This amazing tale of robbery, for it is nothing short of it, explains to some extent one of the reasons why Bolton cotton operatives cannot get decent wages. In some degree the above statement is the position of a number of industries, and it *does* explain why the Unionist Party and the Press of the country are so anxious to stem the flowing tide of Socialist thought.

Alleged To Be Jokes.

A farmer applied at Antrim Labour Exchange for Harvesters. Do you know anything about threshing he asked one applicant. "Yes!" was the reply. "I'm the father of seven boys."

*   *

Mr. Grouser, an employer with an unsavoury reputation, called at the Labour Exchange to interview John Smith. John was told to get a reference from his last employer, and to bring it to Mr. Grouser's place of business later in the day. John did so, and was greeted by the employer, with: "Well, did you get a character?" "I did", replied John, "I got your character, and I'm not going to work for you."

*   *

When an unemployed man residing in a Rural or Urban District makes a claim for State Unemployment Benefit, the first question usually put by the Committee is "Do you own or rent any land." "Yes!" replied one applicant "a own twa graves in Rocalfin." "What" says the Chairman indignantly. "You have two fields and a calf in them! How dare you apply for the dole."

*   *

The Conductor of a Church Choir was instructing the Choir how to sing a well known hymn. He said, "The tenor singers will sing the first four lines, down to The Gates of Hell, and then everybody will come in."

Employers and the Empire.

"If we look at our own Empire and find the antagonism which exists against us in several markets, the tariffs which have been erected against us, the resolutions which have been passed by Municipalities, that under no circumstances will they take goods from this Country if they can conveniently get them from any other Country— if you examine the Far East, with the rising power of Japan, and the rising power of China, and the hold that Germany is again getting in that vicinity, then I think that you will realise, and have realised right through these conferences, that our hold on the markets of the world has been very seriously impaired, and having been impaired, will suffer diminution in volume and in power." Thus said Sir Allan Smith, Knight of the British Empire, presiding at a special Conference in the Great Central Hotel, London.   10/2/25.

Special Election Number

The Labour Opposition Of Northern Ireland

Vol..1—No.2   April, 1925.   One Penny.

Maxton's Message to Belfast.

It is a great pleasure to me to pay another visit to Belfast and meet the Comrades here. There are many ties which bind together the people of Ireland and the people of Scotland—ties of race, of temperament, of tradition and of historical experiences. When

James Maxton

on my previous visits I have looked around on this great City, I have seen too, other similarities. Here, as in Glasgow, is a great, rich, flourishing community, with its huge shops, its fine Municipal Buildings, its factories, its beautiful parks and gardens, and rich men's houses. But here, also, as there, are the same terrible evidences of the capitalist system—horrible slums, over-crowding, poverty, barefooted, under-fed and poorly-clothed children; haggard over-burdened women, and hopeless men, wandering about in a fruitless search for work. Here, as in Glasgow and in all our great cities, are people at one end of the town, living in the direst poverty and wretchedness, and at the other end, people squandering in idle luxury, the wealth produced by the workers.

Here, as often in Glasgow, I have asked myself, how long will men and women consent to live under such degrading conditions, how long will it be before they realise that they are worthy of better things? But I have hope. Here, as in Scotland, is a race of men who will refuse to suffer for ever the intolerable conditions imposed upon them by the capitalist system; here are men who will combine in their Trade Unions and their I.L.P. branches to work together to overthrow the present mad system, where people starve in the midst of plenty, where men and factories stand idle, while the same men lack all the necessities of life, and to substitute in its place a better system, which will give to each according to his need.

Though there may be points on which you here differ from us, yet we are one in our earnest and steadfast purpose to win for the common people justice, security, and all the things that make life worth living. Socialism is a cause big enough to swallow up all smaller differences, and to bind together peoples of all races and creeds. Socialism is the only hope of the world. It is the only sane message to a world brought to a state of chaos by a system which sets the greed of gain before the service of the community. It is no use looking to others to save us. The working men and women have got to work out their own salvation. Comrades, it is in this task of establishing the Socialist Commonwealth that I urge you to rise up and play your part as never before.

JAS. MAXTON.

Within the Boundary.

BY MARKSMAN.

Northern Ireland has the same area as Yorkshire. Northern Ireland has a population of 1.25 millions.

United States of America has a population of 95 millions. The Chief Justice of the United States is paid £3,000 per annum. The Lord Chief Justice of the Six Counties gets £5,000 per annum. The eight judges of the American Supreme Court draw less than £3,000 each.

In Northern Ireland we are provided with four judges, two with salaries of £4,000 each, and two with salaries of £3,500 each, and an Attorney-General at £2,500, but this is not all. In addition to big salaries being paid to Secretaries and Assistant Secretaries, they are also in receipt of a bonus which varies from 20 to 130 per cent.

Our Houses of Parliament costs £25,584 to run, and they usually sit for about two hours per day extended over a period of three months.

Salaries and allowances to Members cost us £9,500 per annum.

The Speaker's Department costs us £4,713. This includes salaries to Librarian, Editor of Debates, Assistant Editor of Debates, and the salaries of three Chaplains. In addition to the salaries paid, there are also bonuses being paid in the Speaker's Department, to the tune of £1,333, and of course these are *not* bonuses on production.

I should explain that many members of the Commons have jobs of one kind or another. Tom Moles, M.P., has a good job as Chairman of Ways and Means, at a salary of £1,500, and yet Belfast does not pay a salary to its Lord Mayor.

The Members of the Senate are paid at the rate of £2.2s.0d. per day.

Members of the Commons are paid £200 per annum.

The Clerk of the Commons has a salary of £1,300 plus £300 allowance, plus a pension of £881 5s 0d., from the Imperial Government.

The Serjeant-at-Arms has a salary of £600, plus £200 allowance, plus an Indian Army Pension of £850. The Serjeant-at-Arms has at least one well paid Assistant in the person of—Black Rod, who receives £450 plus £225 bonus plus a pension of £597 from the Indian Army. Black Rod also acts as Manager of the Ulster Pavilion at Wembley in his spare time, and receives an additional £250 for this spare time job.

THE CABINET costs £12,669 to run.

The Prime Minister receives	£3,200	per annum
The Parliamentary Secretary receives	£600	"
Permanent Secretary receives	£1,340	and bonus
Assistant Permanent Secretary receives	£1,150	"
Five Cabinet Ministers receive	£2,500	plus
£1,500 each as Heads of Department		

MINISTRY OF FINANCE.—

The Minister receives	£2,000	per annum
Permanent Secretary receives	£2,000	"
The Parliamentary Secretary receives	£1,000	"
The Assistant Parliamentary Secretary receives	£600	"
The Financial Secretary receives	£1,000	"
Two Assistant Secretaries receive	£2,235	and bonus

In addition to the above there are scores of highly paid officials under the control of the Ministry of Finance, who receive salaries ranging from £700 to £1,500 per annum. In what is called the Legal Division, there are five gentlemen in receipt of a total of £3,440 plus bonus. What is true of "Finance" is true of the other departments.

MINISTRY OF LABOUR.—

The Minister receives	£2,000	per annum
The Parliamentary Secretary receives	£1,000	"
The Permanent Secretary receives	£1,413	plus bonus
The Two Assistant Secretaries receive	£2,613	"
Five Principals receive	£3,707	"

MINISTRY OF EDUCATION.—

The Minister receives	£2,000	per annum
The Parliamentary Secretary receives	£1,000	"
The Permanent Secretary receives	£1,334	plus bonus
One Inspector receives	£1,100	"
Two Assistant Secretaries receive	£2,258	"
One Accountant receives	£1,050	"
Four Principals receive	£2,752	"

MINISTRY OF HOME AFFAIRS.—

The Minister receives	£2,000	per annum
The Parliamentary Secretary receives	£1,000	"
The Permanent Secretary receives	£1,320	plus bonus
The Two Assistant Secretaries receive	£2,240	"
The Government Hospitality	£2,000	"
The Secret Service	10,000	"

MINISTRY OF COMMERCE AND AGRICULTURE.—

The Minister receives	£2,000	per annum
The Parliamentary Secretary receives	1,000	"
Two Permanent Secretaries receive	£2,620	"
Two Assistant Secretaries receive	£2,203	"
Four Principals receive	£3,709	"
Three Inspectors receive ..	£2,357	"
Travelling Allowance	£3,765	"

If there is a more costly Parliament in any part of the Globe, I would like to hear about it.

Sam Kyle's Election Address.
LADIES AND GENTLEMEN,

Being nominated by the North Belfast I.L.P., and adopted by the Labour Party, N.I., to contest the North Division in the cause of Labour, I offer my services to you. As a Socialist of many years standing, I am convinced that nothing short of a complete change of outlook will bring about that better day that all parties are anxious to see. In offering my services to you I do so the more readily in consequence of the utter failure of the Northern Government to deal with the growing volume of Unemployment that is sapping the vitality of our Northern life. Further, Sir James Craig and other prominent members of the Government have repeatedly said how necessary it is to have an opposition in Parliament. I agree with them as to the need. If there had been an Opposition we in the Northern area would not have had to carry such a crushing load of taxation. The fact that the Judges in Northern Ireland are more highly paid than Judges in U.S.A. is a glaring example. Office has been multiplied by office until to-day we have a staff of officials enough to govern an Empire, much less a province.

On the subject of the Boundary, the boundary which most concerns me is that between the poor who have no bread, and the rich who have a surplus. Not until the Commission has reported will it be possible to decide whether their decisions are wise or not. As a citizen of

VOTE NO. 1 FOR KYLE!

Belfast I do not desire to see anything that would cause bloodshed or any aggravation of the relations that exist between the North and the South. Sir James Craig has stated that it is a matter that can only be settled as between the contending parties. This is following the lead of Mr. MacDonald, who, when Labour Prime Minister, endeavoured to bring the nations of Europe to agreement on the same lines. Until the Free State is prepared to give the same conditions to Teachers, Old Age pensioners, and Unemployment Insurance as we have in Northern Ireland, we in the North should not permit of any worsening of our positions.

My programme, if elected, will be:— (1) The alleviation of Unemployment (Work or Maintenance). (2) The ratification of the Washington Convention *re* Hours of labour. (3) Economy of Administration— e.g., Sergeant-at-Arms paid as follows:— Salary, £600; Allowance £200; Indian Army pension £850—£1,650; with 12 Assistants. (4) The reduction of the Bank Rate in Northern Ireland. (5) Widows' Pensions. (6) Abolition of the penalty on thrift in Old-Age Pensions Administration. (7) The provision of Houses to let and the continuance of the Rent Restriction Act (1914 rent for 1914 Houses). (8) Government action to reduce the cost of living and prevent Profiteering.

If you agree that the foregoing are desirable, I solicit the favour of your vote and influence.

Yours truly,   **SAM KYLE.**

Waste and Want

Within a week we will be a Party with a new status and a new responsibility, for we shall have sent three representatives of the Working Class to voice their aims and aspirations in the Northern Parliament, and to put a check to that outrageous extravagance that has made our Government the most costly in the world. No one now doubts that the embittered class legislation introduced by Sir James Craig's Ministry was only possible because the Workers themselves had given him a mandate of absolute power. But the times have changed. Go where you will to-day among the Democracy of the Six Counties and you will find that Toryism is tottering and Conservatism is crashing. Even in Belfast, the impregnable fortress of the Tory Ascendancy, the workers have at last realised that if they are to save themselves from utter starvation and ruin, then they must get rid of Sir James and his henchmen, and send their own workmates to replace them. In this matter, Ballymacarrett has spoken with no uncertain voice, while on the Shankill Road, Sam Kyle addresses huge and enthusiastic meetings on the very spot at which our Candidate of last October was refused a hearing.

Who doubts for one moment that Councillor William M'Mullen will win the West? No one! Not even his political opponents. His work on the Poor Law Board and his insistent advocacy of the people's rights in the Council Chamber have opened the eyes of the doubters and shown them what **Independent Labour Representation** can achieve. Alarmed at the appalling state of industrial stagnation that holds Ulster in its grip, and realising his utter futility as a constructive politician, Sir James sought to save himself by erecting barriers and boundaries, instead of providing work for the people. How else can he explain his action of stampeding the electorate into a general election when he had still a complete year to run. If we might paraphrase Robert Burns without undue sacrilege to the Poet of Democracy, we would say that "Craig's incapacity to govern, makes countless thousands mourn." His callous indifference to the Old Age Pensions; his savage legislation in the matter of unemployment benefit; his cold refusal to use £167,000 given by Britain for work in Ulster; his eager acceptance of a million pounds to equip a standing army of non-producers; his squandermania of public funds at Stormont and elsewhere, have all convinced the people of the Six Counties that he might be of use to the Landlords, the Big Farmers, the Property Owners, and the Capitalists, but of absolutely no use whatever to the common people. The "last outpost of Empire" has definitely revolted against semaphore signalling with the flag and has set itself the task of evolving order and security out of the industrial chaos and anarchy into which the Unionists have plunged us.

The clandestine marriage of Sir James Craig and Mr. De Valera in Co., Down, has disgusted and outraged honourable people, while the effort to revive a dying Nationalism in the west, by putting new *spirit* (Publicans) into the Devlin Party, and seeking alliance with the Unionist Anti-Prohibition Party is not calculated to inspire confidence in a man who effaced himself from public life during four years of terrible hardship among the people.

The record of Labour is clean ! ! Its service to the community is unswerving; its integrity is unassailable, and not one single act of public perfidy can be charged against us. The grim experiment of gambling with human happiness in Northern Ireland has ended. The tide is with us in Belfast and after forty years of insistent struggle, we are about to be rewarded by success. Let us go to the Polls with calm determination, and let every man and woman work with loyal zeal in the interests of Labour. Let Humanity be your watchword; Progress your Battlecry; and Justice for all people your eternal aim.

The Boundary Bogey.

BY T. GEEHAN
(Secretary, Court Ward Labour-Party).

Once more we are in the throes of an Election. Sir James has sounded the Clarion call, and all is bustle and excitement in the Tory Camp. The issue is the Boundary, and we are told that it is an issue of vast Importance to the loyal workers of the Six Counties. The old game is about to be played all over again, and the Tory press has started to blaze forth with its Poisonous Dope; dope that is intended to fan the dying Embers of Sectarian Passion in the minds of the Working People: The Wage Slave, the Unemployed, and the thousands of our Destitute people will be told that the only thing that matters now, is that the loyal Province of Ulster must be kept for the Empire; that our liberty must not be interfered with. What does it matter if Poverty and destitution is rampant among the Working People? What does it matter if our Workhouses are full? Or that our Women and Children are starving in the midst of plenty? These things do not matter to Sir James or the Class he represents. Greater issues than the welfare of the People are at stake, and as loyal men and women you should turn a deaf ear to the cries of the hungry children and forget that you are living in hovels that a Landsdowne or a Castlereagh would not stable a horse in.

This Patriotic Game is a great game, when you know how to play it right, and Sir James and his satellites are masters of the Art, for they have played it before with great success. Look how patriotic the Shipping Magnates, the Railway Owners, the Mine Owners, and the Financiers were during the great war. Didn't they lend their money to the Government, to help to beat the Germans? What does it matter if these Sharks demanded exorbitant interest on their money? To them it was a business deal, a chance to make fabulous fortunes out of the blood and tears of a stricken humanity, whilst millions of the workers poured out their life's blood on the far off fields of Flanders, of Mespot, and the Dardanelles. And hearken my loyal workers of the Six Counties to what Winston Churchill says about these dead heroes. Speaking in the House of Commons on the 15th. November, 1915, Winston says—

"The Dardanelles adventure was a legitimate War Gamble, with stakes that we could afford to lose, and it was worthwhile to carry through and with utter disregard of life."

Amongst the stakes we could afford to lose were 26,202 killed; 12,544 missing and 75,809 wounded; 96,683 sick and fever cases sent to hospital. Was your husband or son among the stakes? Did Winston's Gambling Counters mean anything to You? Remember that Churchill is part and parcel of the party you are being told to vote for on the 3rd. of April.

What about this liberty we hear so much about? Liberty is a word that symbolizes Truth and Justice. A word to conjure with; not to vex the ear in empty boastings, for liberty is—justice, and justice is the Natural Law of Health and Symmetry and Strength; of fraternity and co-operation. Where such liberty rises, there virtue grows, wealth and happiness increases. Knowledge expands, and fraternity and co-operation exists among the people.

Is there liberty to-day? The poor semi-starved, hunger-scared souls who live laborious days, who are doomed to silence and to hopeless miserable toil. Have they liberty? No! there is no freedom of choice, no liberty of selection for the social bottom dog.

Civilisation so based cannot continue. The eternal laws of the Universe forbid it. On the horizon the clouds begin to disperse, and a light appears, a light that will ultimately guide us to that promised land; a land where liberty and justice will reign supreme. Where the atmosphere will be redolent with true Christianity. Where poverty and misery will be unknown, and all the better qualities and higher Powers of human nature will have an opportunity for full development. Let us make a beginning in Belfast by voting Labour on the 3rd April.

No Work and No Money.
BY COUNCILLOR WILLIAM M'MULLEN, P.L.G.

We are frequently reminded by those who are interested in the maintenance of the Government of Northern Ireland of the advantages which the people enjoy by having the Government and its departments in our midst, instead of being situated in Dublin or London.

There are, however, very serious drawbacks to a government such as we have which far out-weighs its advantages, and the most serious drawback from many points of view is the smallness of the area over which it functions.

This is well exemplified in the case of the Unemployment Insurance Fund, and is well known to the Minister of Labour and the members of the Northern Cabinet, only it is not judicious on their part to broadcast the fact to their followers whom they have nurtured on the belief that our little statelet is in a prosperous way and is quite solvent.

Off the platform and seated in his sanctuary without Press representatives present the Minister of Labour will unburden his mind, and speaking in analogical language, will inform you that his department is like that of an Insurance Company, having all the property in the six Counties insured, and a conflagration taking place, destroys all the property in that area, the Company could not meet its obligations and would be compelled to go into liquidation while its policy holders would be ruined.

In like manner the Minister of Labour, with unemployment rife over the whole six county area (with many potential contributors such as agricultural labourers non-contributors to the funds), finds the Fund considerably in debt and so jettisons those with moral or legal claims on the Fund. This with a view to inducing the British Government to again take over the Fund while callously disregarding the claims of the individual whose unemployment benefit has ceased and who has no means of obtaining employment to provide himself and his dependents with the necessaries of life.

Many people thought when the 1,600 odd workers were disqualified from receiving unemployment benefit at the beginning of the present year because they had not paid six contributions within the last two years that an end has been put to the disqualification of people for an indefinite period. Now other workers are discovering that they too are being disqualified, and when they inquire for reasons are informed that two years had elapsed from the date since they paid contributions to the fund and that benefit is, consequently suspended.

This brings us to the point as to what the workers intend to do. Are they prepared to accept the implication of this decision that they should have been able to obtain 6 weeks employment during the two preceding years? And having failed in a glutted labour market to obtain employment are they prepared to starve quietly? There is, of course, the Poor-Law, but that is another story.

SHOP!!
If you are a "Shop Assistant or a Clerk," or if you work in an Allied Occupation, you out to join the **National Union Of Distributive And Allied Workers.** The Union is 100,000 strong, and last year paid out £400,000 in benefits. If you want higher wages and better conditions call or write to the Secretary—
J.A. Kirk, 27 Garfield Chambers, Belfast.

Jim Craig's Manifesto.
BY SLUMDOM JACK.

Sir James Craig's pathetic wail to the people of Northern Ireland to give his household and stupid Government a new lease of life is hardly likely to work the oracle. In drawing up such a palpably insincere concatenation of absurdities, Sir James was certainly not moved by any desire to insult the intelligence of the workers, for it must be obvious to any person who perused the precious document, that Sir James and his minions do not credit the workers with being in possession of that specific intellectual commodity.

Obviously the publication of the bemuddled document created no small amount of commotion in certain organisations, but the only effect it had in the Labour Movement was to make us more determined to oust the Tories from that Mutual Admiration Society, euphemistically characterised the Northern Parliament, and no amount of intimidation will succeed in deterring us from putting our best efforts forth in the accomplishment of that object.

A very laughter-producing item in the manifesto is where Sir James says to the Workers of Northern Ireland "Ulster is Yours". Just how much comfort that tit bit of political bunkum is able to convey to the forty-eight thousand men and women in Ulster drawing State Unemployment Benefit can be better imagined than described. And exactly what effect it will have on the thousands who have become ineligible for State Unemployment Benefit through the drastic conditions recently introduced by the Ministry of Labour, Sir James Craig will soon be in the position to know.

Sir James Craig is nothing other than a cunning politician, and he is perfectly well aware that if he deferred the elections till after the findings of the Boundary Commission became public property it would, so to speak, be all U.P. with him and his valiant band of place-hunters.

So Sir James has decided that if he is to have another trick at the wheel, that feat can only be accomplished on the Politico-Geographical myth issue. We in the Labour Movement make it our business to study the psychology of our people, and we are but too well aware that the Educational system, aided by the press and pulpit, has succeeded in creating emotional creatures who take a peculiar pleasure in running after shadows.

We in the Labour Movement recognise one Boundary and of course that is the meridian that separates our people from the things that go to make life worth living, and on that specific issue we shall go the whole hog for the Labour Candidates.

I shall conclude by acquainting Sir James Craig and his followers that the unemployed workers' reply to his manifesto is:-

Soft words a woman's love may win,
Or soothe a maiden's fears,
But hungry stomachs heed them not—
The belly has no ears.

Hits and Misses.
BY MARKSMAN.

I note that a well dressed young woman tried to personate in the South Dublin Election last week. She was sentenced to two months' imprisonment and fined 20/-

* *

Lord Justice Andrews at the Belfast City Commission last month said: "That a person should for all purposes of the laws relating to Parliamentary and Municipal Elections, be deemed to be guilty of the offence of personation who at an election for a County or Borough, or at Municipal Elections, applied for a ballot paper in the name of some other person whether the name be that of a person living or dead, or of a fictitious person, or who having voted once at any such election applies at the same election for a ballot paper in his own name."

* *

I think I have said enough to indicate how serious the crime of personation or attempted personation really is, and I hope that at the forthcoming elections that all policemen, personation agents and presiding officers will do their duty without fear or favour.

* *

Sir James Craig says "Stand Firm," that's right "Sir James" your only desire seems to be to stick in the mud all the time, of course you must have been in the best of spirits in November, 1923, when speaking in Sandy Row Orange Hall, you said—"No matter what happens in Great Britain, I will solve the unemployment problem of Northern Ireland."

* *

Sir James do you realise how tired many of us are of your "We won'ts," "We shants," etc., and when we ask for homes fit for heroes, you talk glibly about new lunatic asylums and a new convict prison.

* *

The unemployed of Northern Ireland, ex-servicemen and civilians should be provided with work or maintenance or if you and your colleagues cannot do this "John M." then I respectfully suggest that you clear out and make room for those who will make an earnest endeavour to do what you and your Cabinet have never attempted.

* *

I suggest to "John M." that this is a blot on the escutcheon of the Cabinet of which he is one of its ablest members.

* *

I have just been glancing at the Estimates for Services, 1924-25, Northern Ireland, and they are a damning indictment against Toryism.

* *

Our Fighting Fund.

We appeal to all friends, sympathisers and wellwishers who desire to see a strong, alert and effective **Opposition** in the Northern Parliament, to send a subscription to our I.L.P. Fighting Fund. Any sum, much or little, will be welcomed, and will be acknowledged with thanks in these columns. Send your "sub." c/o. this Office at 48 York Street, Belfast.
Sam Kyle, Hugh Gemmell.

	£	s	d
Workers' Union No. 1 Branch	£15	0	0
Joint Committee I.L.P.	3	3	6
William Moneypenny	1	0	0
H.B.	0	10	0

Why Women Must Vote Labour.
By MARY H. KYLE.

The die is cast; a General Election is upon us; and our opponents will trot out all sorts of stunts about murder and the flag. But women who have a home and a family to look after, have to face up to hard facts, and practical realities every day, and they are not likely to be carried away by high falutin talk. They will realise that the Labour Party is *their* party, the only party that is going to help them in their every day lives, and hold out a better prospect for them and their children in the future.

What then, are the facts from the woman's point of view, and what are some of the things the Labour Party has to offer them?

First the Labour Party demands adequate provision of *houses* at *low rents*. Women suffer most of all from the shocking housing conditions that exist at present, for they spend most of their time at home. The Labour Party demands more and better houses, planned as working women want them. Give Labour a chance to get you what you certainly want.

Secondly labour stands for much better provisions to secure the *health of the people*. The amount of preventable sickness and disease is appalling, and though low wages and bad conditions are very largely responsible for this, yet at the same time we want more done for the sick. More hospitals and sanatoria are needed, and more maternity wards, for the number of women who die in child birth is very large indeed and has shown no sign of decreasing in the last 30 years. A woman Inspector under the Ministry of Health when reporting on this stated that a considerable number of deaths are quite definitely due to improper or insufficient treatment of the mother when in childbirth. We want more clinics too, for infants and mothers, and the provision of milk where necessary. Then there is the proper medical inspection and treatment of school children, together with meals for those in need. Give the Labour Party a chance to get on with some of these necessary reforms.

Thirdly, Labour demands pensions for widowed mothers and the children dependent on them. The Labour party in the Imperial Parliament has tried to introduce this at least twice, but always the Tories including the Ulster Unionist M.P.'s oppose it. Give Labour a chance in the Ulster Parliament and remove the terrible anxiety that wears away a woman, who loses her husband and is left with children to support.

Fourthly the Labour Party is determined that the cost of food and other necessities must be reduced. This is a large problem demanding the re-organisation of industry and commerce, but we shall never get lower prices until this is done. Give Labour a chance to start on this tremendous task.

Fifthly the Labour Party has long stood for votes for women on the same terms as men, and therefore all young women must support it.

In short the whole Labour programme stands for better conditions in the home, and in the factory, for holding human life of greater importance than property, and women who play such a part in the re-production of life must needs support the Party that sets a higher value on the life they produce. As the mother works unstintingly herself for her family and sees that a fair share goes to each member, so the Labour Party works unstintingly to see that a fair share of the world's wealth goes to each member of the human family. So every woman must vote Labour on April 3rd.

Printed by John Adams, King Street, Belfast for the Proprietors, North Belfast Branch I.L.P., 48 York Street, Belfast.

The Labour Opposition Of Northern Ireland

Vol.1—No.3   May, 1925.   One Penny.

May-Day.

BY IDA BOYD.

"Oft when men and maids are merry
    Ere the sunlight leaves the earth,
And they bless the day beloved, all too
    short for all their mirth,
Some shall pause awhile and ponder
    On the bitter days of old,
Ere the toil of strife of battle
    Overthrew the curse of gold."
            —WILLIAM MORRIS.

On this day, men and women of the working class the wide world o'er, are gathered together, filled with a spirit of Comradeship and Fellowship, to rejoice in life and renew their faith in the International Brotherhood of Man. Even in North East Ulster the Labour and Socialist movement has shown signs of quickening life, and men and women with renewed determination mean to change "this sorry scheme of things", with its chronic penury for the *many* and idle luxury for the *few.* The present order of society that allows preventable misery and suffering to continue, stands condemned, and must be replaced by a nobler and more just system that will permit happiness, love and beauty, being brought within the reach of all. Reformers have always paid for the awakening of new ideas and have ever been the despised and rejected of men. Anything that savours of change and progress is, at first, met with scorn and abuse. New ideas are rather disturbing and therefore unwelcome. Still, we must plod on, heeding not the reverses, buoyed with the assurance that right will eventually triumph and the People's *will* prevail.

Labourers.

These are men who have never been
           honoured,
    Whose voices for ever unheard,
Their portion of wealth is their living,
    The price of their living unshared.
You may count them in limitless
           numbers,
    Far scattered, their multitude grows,
As the grains of the sands in the desert,
    As the flakes that are merged into
           floes;
Yet their labour is world-wide and
           leagueless,
    They claim neither colour or creed,
They are slaves to no languid
           profession,
    They struggle and toil to their need.

Classed by the "trades" as a Gypsy,
    Wanderers, guildless, forlorn,
Yet learned in the arts of commerce
    Before science or trades were born.
Bearing their burden with patience,
    Dumb in their direst plight,
Silent, they swallow their grievance
    While others are bared to the light.
Sons of the soil and the city,
    Reckless, and imprudent, still,
Men who are stickers and doers,
    Bending their backs with a will.

With the pick and the shovel you'll find
           them
    Bedraggled, half naked, unkempt,
With the wealth of a stub on their faces,
    Their clothing all tattered and rent.
In the slush and the slime of the city,
    Knee deep in the mud and the mire,
Defying, cajoling, confronting,
    The iron girt roads in their ire.
Friends of the pick and the shovel,
    Mate to the sledge and the saw,
Learned as were primitive people
    In the muscle and sinew lore.

It is appropriate that Socialists should choose the 1st of May to proclaim their faith in human kind, for that was the ancient feast day—the Feast of Hope—and May-Day is so very full of significance for us. All around, Nature is bursting forth with renewed life, and hope is singing and dancing within us, inspired by love and beauty—the symbolism of Socialism. Stirred afresh, we are caught up in the quest of the *oneness* of Humanity and the "RED" Flag, beautifully symbolises this oneness because the blood—that international bond of brotherhood—of all peoples is red, irrespective of Race, Class or Creed. It is fitting that we, as part of the great International Socialist Movement, should on this May-Day reconsecrate ourselves to the Cause of the People. Pressing ever upwards and onwards towards that time acoming when, under a New Social Order, every human being will not only be assured of **Bread** but also **Roses**.

In the warm weary days of the summer,
  In the sweltering heat and the glare,
Tearing, and rending and mending,
  Hugging the earth like a bear;
Shovel and sledge, and pickaxe,
  Chisel, and hammer, and bar,
Smoothing the roads for the traffic
  With square set, macadam, tar.
Friendless and favourless workers
  Striving an ultimate aim,
Swamped in the depths of their visions—
  What does their energy gain?
       THOMAS CARNDUFF,
       Belfast Shipyard.

Hits and Misses.
BY MARKSMAN.

Congratulations to Jack Beattie, Sam Kyle, and Billy M'Mullen, on their splendid fight and great victory. Each will need all his courage and determination in the great fight which lies ahead. No doubt attempts will be made by opponents to bribe or cajole them. So called friends will attempt to divide them by repeating all sorts of tittle tattle, but I appeal to each of them to remember that they are the standard bearers of the great forces of Labour and Socialism which will eventually sweep away all social evils.

*   *

Sir Robert Lynn in moving an amendment to the address said—"he congratulated Mr. Barbour on his promotion to the Cabinet," "If there was one man who could make an office *which had been no use to the province in the past* useful in the future he was the man to do it."

*   *

There were some stupid things said during the elections, but I think that when the next election takes place Mr. Archdale should be muzzled. He is reported to have said—"I have 109 officials, and, so far as I know, there are 4 Roman Catholics—three of these were civil servants turned over to me whom I *had to take* when we began."

*   *

I am informed that Clause 5 of the Government of Ireland Act, 1920, lays it down that—"Parliament shall not impose any disadvantage or disability on account of religious belief". Might I point out that Mr. Archdale is at present the head of the Orange Institution in Ireland, and he will be prating about civil and religious liberty in a few months time.

*   *

I note that our Canadian friends are very angry at the embargo which has been placed on potatoes; for the first time in history, Canada was able to sell potatoes in Northern Ireland, at a cheaper rate than our own producers. As soon as this state of affairs came about Mr. Archdale's advisers discovered the "Colorado Beetle" with the result that Canadian potatoes are being prevented from entering out ports. Potatoes are now coming from the Continent, so don't be alarmed if you hear about the "Rotterdam Bug," or the "Belgian Cricket," As there are at least 150 different kinds of potato bugs, it is quite an easy thing for a government department to resurrect the bug bogey.

* *

I hope that one of the Labour men will concentrate on Agriculture, it is extremely interesting, and pressure must be brought to bear on the Cabinet to compel them to set up a Wages Board, same as in Great Britain. How many of our readers are aware that Mr. Archdale has committees set up to advise him as to horses, cattle, pigs, sheep, flax and potatoes.

* *

I don't know how many of the 40 or 50 gentlemen who have been appointed are Catholics, but I do know after scanning the list that there is not a single representative of Labour, and this is a matter which should be enquired into by one of our Labour M.P.'s.

* *

I wonder what Mr. Archdale has done during his four years of service to help agriculture. One might sum up his record by saying that he has succeeded in making two nothings grow where only one grew before, but we must not forget his generous contribution of public money to the Farmers Union to be used by them for Educational purposes. One might say that this was "Hush Money".

* *

If Dame rumour is true, another of our stupid Cabinet Ministers was able to avert defeat by the sacrifices made by Thompson Donald, whose friends were appealed to vote 1 for Sir Dawson Bates.

* *

I am glad to see that Mr. R. D. Megaw, Secretary to the Home Office was beaten at the polls in Co. Antrim. This is the official who, more than any man, was responsible for the suppression of Cookstown, Downpatrick and other Rural Councils, and for the jerrymandering of electoral areas and the abolition of P.R. in local government elections.

* *

Mr. Megaw's defeat in Co. Antrim, means that a £20 per week job is vacant, and there is also a £12 per week job vacant owing to the defeat of Harry Burn. There are also two £20 per week jobs vacant owing to the death of Mr. R. J. M'Keown, who was Parliamentary Secretary to the Ministry of Education and the Ministry of Commerce.

* *

Sir Robert Lynn, speaking in the House the other day said—"as editor of an important newspaper he could not conscientiously discharge his duties and at the same time be a member of the Government." I wonder what Mr. Moles thinks of *that* statement! It evidently means that Mr. Moles is a man who has no conscience, otherwise he would be content with his salary of £1,000 from the "Belfast Telegraph" and £400 salary from the Imperial Parliament, without grasping a further £1,500 as a member of the Government of Northern Ireland. Mr. Moles' income is therefore £2,900 per annum. That is to say, Mr. Moles has been in receipt of £56 per week during the last four years. During the last four years the Northern Parliament has sat for 533 hours, or an average of 133 hours per year. Mr. Moles, as Chairman of Ways and Means, at an annual salary of £1,500, has been in receipt of over £11 per hour. Is Mr. Moles worth £11 per hour to us? Can our impoverished people afford it? Evidently the "Billy Dubbs" of South Belfast are quite willing that this legal robbery should continue as they have voted for it.

Labour Men of the North.

Mr. John Beattie, M.P.

The Subject of our sketch this month is a Poor Law Guardian, and the senior member for East Belfast, who won such a sensational victory at the recent Parliamentary elections. As a boy in 1904 he joined the 8th Irish Hussars, returning from South Africa with the rank of serjeant. Interesting himself in his trade union he was appointed Assistant Secretary of the Belfast branch of the Associated Blacksmiths and Ironworkers Trade Union, later on becoming Branch Secretary, also District Secretary and the first G.E.C. Member for Ireland. Appointed as full time official in 1917 he was successful in opening new branches at Belfast, Dublin, Dundalk and Derry—claims that he never belonged to any political party other than the Labour Party and was elected as delegate to Belfast Labour Party in 1917. His splendid work as a Guardian of the poor has endeared him to the poor and oppressed of East Belfast. That he may be long spared to fight the battle of the unemployed and the poverty stricken is the earnest wish of

BOB M'CLUNG.

The Prince of Ballymacaduff.
BY TOM KANE.

Prince Soanso was a naughty Prince, he...well he was naughty. To punish the Prince for his numerous indiscretions, the Queen, his mother, would send him to a remote part of the kingdom, to open a Town Hall, or some such petty function. Nothing the Prince resented more.

"Your conduct will bring the Monarchy into disrepute," the Queen would say. "Here is a town that would be honoured if you would open the town hall." "Oh mother!" The unfortunate Prince would plead, "Please spare me. Bad as I am, don't be so cruel."

When the Queen considered that the conduct of the Prince merited it, she would be insistent.

On one occasion, our friend the Prince was on a visit to the North of Ireland. It came to the ears of the Council of Ballymacaduff that the Prince was to stay overnight at a lordly residence in their neighbourhood. Here was an opportunity not to be missed. Why not ask the Prince to open the New Town Hall? How the dear old heart of Ballymacaduff throbbed, at the pleasure with which the Prince would accept the invitation of this famous loyal town. Whatever might be the thoughts of Ballymacaduff Council, the Prince thought they were taking a mean advantage of him. In a weak moment, however, the Prince promised to open the Ballymacaduff Town Hall.

The little town had several kinds of fits of delight. The people wanted to see the Prince, the shopkeepers wanted to make money, the Council wanted to be snobs. Robes were borrowed and decorations secured. Ballymacaduff was dressed up like a Christmas tree. The great day arrived, the prince did his job. The agony of having dull addresses read to him, patiently submitted to. During the reading of the addresses, the Prince amused himself observing the characteristics of the members of the Council. The Prince had a keen sense of humour. The poor little town went off its head. The Prince had a glorious send off. Ballymacaduff went to rest, in the sure conviction, that no other place knew how to receive a Prince. Poor Ballymacaduff.

That night the Prince, soothed with the expectation of an early return home, entered into the gaiety of the entertainment provided at Obe Castle. When the night had advanced just a few intimate friends of the Prince remained. On such occasions, the Prince usually sang. But as his songs were few, the Prince proposed to give an impression of the behaviour of the members of the Ballymacaduff Council that day, and his mimicry provoked much mirth. The Prince had no mean talents as a humourist, and the loud applause expressed the success he attained that night. Yet Ballymacaduff slept in innocence. The Council never for a moment doubted that the Prince was favourably impressed by them. No power the giftie gie them, to see themselves, as . . . the Prince saw them.

VICTORY!

After such outstanding and complete success at the Polls, Labour in the Six Counties is entitled to do a little shouting. It was a glorious victory, and the "Voice of Labour" has at length been heard in the Northern Chamber. And not alone that, but we are absolutely entitled by the logic of industrial and political evolution to be the official opposition in the House of Commons. The fact that the Nationalist Party numbers 12 as against Labour's Big Three, does not matter in the least. It is not numbers that count; it is principle and policy, and so far as policy is concerned the Nationalist Party is as politically bankrupt as the older group so ponderously led by the Prime Minister. They are both Capitalist Parties, and their entire legislative outlook is dictated by Big Business. Trade, Commerce and "the trade," are an unholy trinity, that never yet introduced a progressive measure unless compelled by an insistent public outcry for reform, or unless they perceived some economic advantage for themselves from its adoption.

Sir James went to the country to get a mandate on the Boundary; he returned to find that Capitalism was on its trial in Ulster and that the paramount questions were unemployment, old age pensions, and an industrial security programme that would enable the workers to get an increased share of the wealth that they produce. Compelled at last to face the real issues, Sir James, loyal to his class interests, proceeded to lead a forlorn hope and wage a bitter "class war" of Capitalism against Socialism, and that is why we are in **Official Opposition.**

But we must not be content with our victory. We must not rest. We must tighten up our internal organisation and extend the scope of our propaganda. Every Municipal Ward in Belfast ought to have a division of the Labour Party as well as a live Branch of the Independent Labour Party, and all the Wards in a Parliamentary Division ought to have an Electoral Committee composed of delegates from the Municipal Wards in order to be ready for every contest. Rule of Thumb and Slapdash are dead, but Science still liveth.

Enthusiasm and sacrifice can win great victories; organisation alone can consolidate the gain and lay the sure foundations of a new social order in Ulster. Speed the day.

Glad Tidings.
BY THE HERALD.

There are 48,917 people unemployed in Northern Ireland. A further 4,636 are on what is called "systematic" short time. Employers were able to exercise their love of philanthropy by giving 22,758 more an extended holiday over the period when we celebrate the greatest event in the religion of Brotherhood. It looks well printed as a "holiday", doesn't it? 76,311 people (not to mention their dependants) in much the same position as the horse which was being trained to live without food. For some unknown reason the horse died, just on the eve of victory, when its rations had been cut down to one strand of hay per day (I've just heard, by the way, that a Scotchman aged 108 who heard this story when he was in "high infants" has written to the "Mail" to say that he believes the horse died of hunger).

Leaving aside the systematics and the "holidayers" we have 48,917 folk who, even if their money was as elastic as a Lloyd-Georgian promise, couldn't make ends meet. But what of that!! All's well. The Cathedral balance is on the right side. Sir James has no time for Socialism, and **The Marquis has been with us.**

Yes, the Marquis, Hamilton of; son, eldest of, the "Governor". The "News-Letter" tells me he is 'in' the Grenadiers. I'm sorry I couldn't let you know sooner in case you wanted to attend some of the "functions held in his honour." He obtained "Special leave" to come and visit us, so you will appreciate how much trouble he takes on our behalf.

And the 76,000 odd workers who couldn't get work because it wouldn't do to interfere with the brainy system under which we live, will be glad to know that the blue-blooded Grenadier was able to manage butter for his bread while he was in our midst. The Lord Mayor of Belfast gave him a light snack in the City Hall, on the afternoon of Wednesday, 22nd April; not a real tuck-in you know, just a matter of 5 or 6 courses perhaps; enough to stave off the pangs until he got to Stormont in the evening, when Sir James entertained him to dinner.

But being a Marquis is not all steak and onions. So far as I can gather nobody took him out on the Thursday at all. Maybe he "signs on" of a Thursday. But if Sir James did him anyway well on Wednesday night and if the Duchess had anything "left over" he was fairly lucky because there was another spread for him on the Friday afternoon. In Derry this time—famous City of walls, gates and noisy Maggies. After stowing away the good things provided our lord stood up and received gifts. The gift-lifting continued on Saturday and Monday.

The 76,000 odd "holiday makers", the old-age pensioners, who have saved a little too much, the widows and orphans to whom pensions cannot be given, the parents who watch their children die for lack of food, and the children who lose their parents because of grinding toil and foul housing conditions, all these will be glad to know that there is not much fear of the bold Grenadier missing his butter ration while we provide his father with £8,000 a year and a room or two . . . maybe.

LABOUR M.P.'S MAIDEN SPEECHES.

Old Age Pensions.
THRIFT DISQUALIFICATION CLAUSES.
REDUCTION OF OLD AGE LIMIT TO 60
(Abridged).
JACK BEATTIE, M.P.

In rising to move this amendment to the Address, I do so because I feel that there has been a wanton neglect of the aged poor in the Six Counties. Now, I say that the privileges of the Old Age Pensioners of Ulster have been lessened as compared with their fellows in Great Britain. It is sad to think that the last Government lived four years and neglected the very people who were responsible for bringing the City of Belfast into the prominent position it occupies today. We in the past in Northern Ireland have been looked upon as a very industrious race. I have heard it repeatedly said to me, "you must think of nothing but work." Work has been the battle cry of the Northerner from his earliest boyhood until his old age. Well, perhaps we have been working very hard, and at the end of our years of hard work we cannot see very much to maintain us in our old age. Now that is the case, and if our hard work has accumulated a little savings for the people of Northern Ireland, I cannot see why their efforts in that field should now be penalised by their being denied the right to pensions at the age as stated in the Act. I would claim that this amendment is a justifiable one as far as thrift is concerned, and proceed to the matter of drawing the age line at 60.

I would like to give a comparison that is running through my mind. Take the persons who are **now** receiving old age pensions. Take a boy of thirteen years of age who was sent into the mill or the factory, or the shipyards in years gone by to earn some money to help to maintain the house. Study that boy growing up until he becomes 70 years of age. I am sure you will agree that boys who enter industry at that age never become the recipients of old-age pensions. I entered the Belfast Rope Works when I was very young. I transferred my services to the shipyard, and I am not very old to-day, but I may say if 20 years more had been spent there I would have been looking for the old age pension, because I would not have been physically fit enough to follow the occupation. Northern Ireland workers have the shipbuilding, they have the linen, they have agriculture. I say these are three industries that tend to wear the worker down more so than any other industry that I could mention at the moment within the confines of the Ulster Government. For that reason I would ask the House to reduce the age from the present standing of 70 years to 60 years.

Let us show the people that we are in earnest in what we preach, when we say we are looking to the welfare of the Six Counties. By our Government ye shall know us; and by the government of the Country will the people of the Country realise that it is a Government of the People.

Our Policy
(Abridged).
SAM KYLE, M.P.

I have listened to the speeches of the Prime Minister and the two Honourable Members who preceded him, hoping to hear from them what the Government's Policy was going to be so far as concerned the continuance of the Rent Restriction Act. I hope every member of the Government will realise that nothing short of the continuance of that Act will satisfy the electorate of Northern Ireland, until such times as there is an adequate supply of houses at low rents—rents that a shipyard worker at 38/6 can pay and rents that a textile worker at 25/- or 26/- for a 48 hour week—when he is working—can pay. We want homes in which we can rear our children, and of which our wives and sisters will be proud, instead of desiring to get out of, as so many of them do at the earliest possible moment.

It is very easy for the representative of the University and for other Hon. Members to say that the policy of the Government should be non-contentious. Go and live up the Shankill Road, the Crumlin Road, or the Falls Road, and you will agree it is high time, whether matters are contentious or not, that these needs should be met to the utmost by the Government. It is the duty of the Government to see that these people are fed and clothed, that they are shod and that they are housed. If the Government cannot do that they should say to the public that they cannot do it. They should openly confess their failure under the present system to introduce measures for the relief of those people who are in such a bad state *now*.

We want to get Wages Boards established in the various counties that comprise our Northern Province so that the wages of agricultural workers will be sufficient to enable them to live more decently. When one remembers that the wage of an agricultural labourer is 25/- a week in some parts of the Six Counties one appreciates the difficulty that he experiences in bringing up his children in the way every Hon. Member would like to see theirs brought up. If it is good enough for our children, the children of the agricultural labourer should get the same opportunity of developing themselves in the fullest possible degree, and the establishment of Wages Boards will help to do something to bring about a better state of feeling on questions of agriculture. I have nothing to say about giving seed

potatoes to people in badly hit districts. I would only say that we ought to give ordinary potatoes to the unemployed people in Belfast; that we might get bread for those people who are hungry. I assure the Prime Minister that the real issue at the election, at least to the people of Belfast, was the boundary line that divides the poor who have no bread, from the rich who have got a surplus. That was the issue in North Belfast and in every district in this city, and I hope this House will get down to doing something for the Unemployed, to doing something in regard to Housing, to doing everything possible to relieve the distress so widespread in Ulster.

Unemployment Debate
(Abridged).

COUNCILLOR WM. M'MULLEN, M.P.

I think it is to be regretted that no definite proposal has emanated from the Government as to how they intend to solve the question of unemployment. The attitude that has been taken up by this and by every other Government up to the moment has been that of ameliorative reform. This Government has worked through the medium of the Loans Guarantee Act, and they have assisted local administrative bodies by granting 60 per cent. of the wages cost in connection with schemes that have the approbation of the Minister of Labour. But I want to suggest that that is only treating with effects instead of causes, and unless the Government are prepared to tackle the question *fundamentally* it means that the problem of unemployment is going to be with us for a considerable period.

In 1923, we had 37,000 unemployed. I now observe that we have 48,600 unemployed in the Six Counties, and, unfortunately this does not fully show the facts of the situation. I elicited from the Minister of Labour that 1,777 people have been disqualified from obtaining unemployment benefit from the start of the present year. I have gone back over the industrial history of the last century to discover when industrial crises occurred, and I find that we are having a recurring cycle of trade depression on an average every seven years. I am going to suggest that there are ways in which the Government can tackle this problem. It does appear to be an anomalous position that our shops and warehouses are stocked with all the commodities that the people who are in poverty and are unemployed require. I met a tailor, the other day, and asked him why he was unemployed. His clothes were threadbare, and he suggested that he was unemployed because there were too many suits produced. Shoemakers are barefoot, because too many boots have been produced. Agricultural labourers are unemployed and in poverty at the moment, presumably because there is too much foodstuff produced in this country, (laughter). Honourable members can afford to laugh because *they* are in comfortable circumstances. They can jeer and sneer when certain statements are made on the floor of this House. I want to suggest that there is any quantity of land idle, any amount of industrial capital in the way of machinery idle, and any number of workers idle. We have got 48,600 unemployed and, so far as I have been able, with a limited intelligence to observe, these are largely the things required to produce wealth.

MIDGLEY v GREGG.

The debate in the Ulster Hall, on the 20th April, was an enormous success, and friend and foe alike agree, that the Socialist position outlined by Councillor Harry Midgley was unanswerable. Mr. Gregg, no doubt, did his best with the material at his disposal, but the truth is becoming widely realised that Capitalism as a System of Life is doomed and dying and must soon yield its place to the superior organisation of Socialism.

The Perpetual Problem Of Wages
by C.J. M'CRYSTAL.

To speak of wages theoretically, politically—economically is a dry subject—or to quote Carlisle, "a dismal science." Nevertheless we should interest ourselves in the economic law which regulates our Social Life.

There is trouble to-day about wages; there was trouble a hundred years ago about wages; and it depends on human evolution, materially, mentally, or spiritually, whether that trouble shall be a lasting inheritance. Political economists define wages as that portion of wealth paid in exchange for labour and regulated by custom, necessity and competition. However fair this definition may be, yet no mention is made of a *living* wage. Is it a fair exchange for the human labour power expended and absorbed in the production of commodities? Half a loaf may be better than no bread, providing it is sufficient for life and health. Is it? Besides, is there no other way open for the workers to secure a more economic foothold in the world?

If we trace the growth of Trade Unionism, we find that economic necessity forced the workers to combine and resist by industrial action and strikes, etc., a system which accelerates the mental and physical deterioration—tending towards vagabondage, disease and crime. The action taken by the employers on the other hand, took the form of lock-outs, and out of this pitiable clashing a curious psychology develops; that is to say, both desire the maximum of profit, leisure, etc., at the minimum exertion. Take for instance a national calamity—wars, earthquakes, etc. The Capitalist, with psychological exactitude grasps the situation and then proceeds to reap the huge profits which the circumstances had created. On the other hand, the worker, in a perspective relative to his position, sees himself in a new light. Supply and demand; higher wages; higher standard of life. All these things meet the capitalist and worker with that peculiar force, which makes each realise his own importance. Oh, but what a division of humanity!

In the old times before the earth civilised itself to private property owning or to capitalism, there were no employers or wage earners. Every family helped itself to the earth's store; cultivated a patch of ground; hunted, fished and thus lived. but, for "better or worse" that state of affairs has been transformed; the earth and its stores and products, and the machinery of our manufacturing age are now in the hands of a comparative few, who have acquired their possessions by exploiting the energy of the masses.

Our quarrel is not directed against the accumulation of wealth. It is when that wealth is utilised to produce more wealth with profitable intent—at the expense of the workers—yes, there our quarrel lies—and the remedy? It is this: just so soon as the workers acquire possession of the tools of production; just as soon as those tools are manipulated in producing for use only—then, just so soon shall the perpetual problem be solved.

OUR FIGHTING FUND.

We appeal to all friends, sympathisers and well-wishers who desire to see a strong, alert and effective **OPPOSITION** in the Northern Parliament, to send a subscription to our I.L.P. Fighting Fund. Any sum, much or little, will be welcomed, and will be acknowledged with thanks in these columns. Send your " sub." c/o. this Office at 48 York Street, Belfast.

SAM KYLE,
HUGH GEMMELL.

			£	s.	d.
Joint Committee, I.L.P.	..	..	£3	16	9
Wm. Moneypenny, senr.	..	..	0	10	0
P. T.	..	..	5	0	0
Mrs. Moneypenny	..	..	0	12	6
J. & G. Scanlin	..	..	0	10	0
M. Caulfield	..	..	0	5	0
S. Bradley	..	..	1	0	0
J. H. Gilliland	..	..	0	10	0
R. G.	..	..	0	10	0
W. Wilson	..	..	0	10	0
S. Moneypenny	..	..	0	10	0
J. Banter	..	..	0	2	0
J. Banter	..	..	0	5	0
Alex. Caawford, Lecke, Ballymoney	..		0	1	0
Loco Men, per W. Reid	..	..	6	0	0
Mrs. M'Mullan	..	..	0	2	6
J. Malcolm	..	..	0	10	0
J. Collins	..	..	0	5	0
Mr. Ryan	..	..	0	5	0
S. Geddis	..	..	0	5	0
R. Beattie (Barrow)	..	..	0	10	0
J. F. H.	..	..	1	0	0
Wm. Murphy	..	..	0	2	6
D. Brady	..	..	0	2	6
C. W.	..	..	2	2	0
J. C.	..	..	5	0	0
Selkirk, per T. Bolster	..	..	4	0	0
Fred Carson	..	..	0	5	0
Mrs. and Mr. Barter	..	..	1	0	0
L. Dell	..	..	0	5	0
R. Levin	..	..	0	5	0
J. A. Kirk	..	..	0	5	0
N.A.C., I.L.P.	..	..	40	0	0

The Labour Opposition Of Northern Ireland

Vol.1—No.4   June, 1925.   One Penny.

WHY I AM A SOCIALIST.

BY REV. A. L. AGNEW, B.A.

(Rev. A. L. Agnew, B.A., who contributes this article is a native of County Down. He was educated at Belfast and Oxford, and served on active service in France. During the short time which he has been in Belfast, he has proved himself a fearless and outspoken preacher and the fact that, labouring under many handicaps he has already built up a large and increasing congregation, including many who do not agree with his views on all points, proves that with more ministers of his stamp the church would regain some of that respect which it is so obviously losing to-day.—*Editor*.)

Why I Am A Socialist.

To give one's reasons for being a Socialist in a short space is difficult, dangerous and verging on the impossible. It is difficult because one would first have to define Socialism, and that cannot be done in a few words, and were one to fill a few volumes it is doubtful if one would succeed. The task is dangerous because of the peculiar way in which toleration, broadmindedness and Christianity are expressed in this part of the world towards any one who calls himself a Socialist, by those who do not even know that the stones they sometimes throw are provided by Socialist enterprise, or that the religion of peace and goodwill over which they shoot one another is Socialist in Principle, if a trifle materialist and capitalist in practice. The task moreover verges on the impossible, because men do not act from reason, though they may think they do. Were the writer reasonable, this article would not go to press, the *fence* being a more reasonable place for him to sit on than the particular side he has chosen.

A socialist is understood by the majority of Belfast people to be a wild man whose only desire is to pull down the mighty from their seats, divide all wealth amongst those who agree with him, and get a soft job for himself. Incidentally, a Socialist is an Atheist, a friend of Russians, Germans and foreigners, and one who is out to ruin family life, nationalise women, and provoke riot and bloodshed the world over. Now with this kind of Socialism I have of course no sympathy. It is far too near to various other "isms" in this City which are opposed to it. The difference between a Socialist as above defined and another "ist" who goes to no church unless paraded there, who buys rifles and revolvers from Germans to shoot his fellow Christians, who eagerly reads Divorce Court News and shows his disloyalty by opposing his Majesty's Forces, when they try to prevent him looting some poor neighbour's house and dividing the spoil there, is hard to perceive even in the providing of soft jobs for its advocates. Socialism as above defined comes too near to the other local "isms" to attract one who desires to see something different.

The Socialism to which I owe allegiance goes much further. Its proud boast is that "it shoots nobody", that it is concerned more with present day matters, housing, education, wages and peace, than with the past doings of the Prince of Orange or the future policy of the Pope of Rome. It takes no concern with theology or with churches, being content with the fact that the ends to which it works, Universal Peace, the Brotherhood of Man and a Better World, are Christian Ends. It does not believe in leaving politics to its leaders, but that every member should understand or try to understand for himself, politics, economics, citizenship and history. Education is its watchword, and ideals are its driving forces. It numbers amongst its adherents an ever increasing number of earnest, thoughtful, studious young people, many of whom instead of having "soft jobs" have to suffer for their principles, and do so.

This Socialism is non-dogmatic. It cannot be defined, its members hold different views as to the practical solutions of the problems of life. Not being a politician, I cannot deal with these, nor would I, had I space. Socialism is a movement. When I compare it with other movements in the City, movements based on appeals to prejudices and hatreds which have led time and time again to ruination of trade, the suffering of thousands and loss of life, movemments supported by a misleading press and saddest of all by what passes for the Christian Religion, I feel it a duty to support it. So long as the Movement is true to its principles, nothing but good can come out of it. When it takes a different course then will be the time to leave it. As for religion, socialism can do it no harm. Those who harm the Christian religion are those who have made the name of Belfast something which can be hurled by the heathen in the face of those Missionaries which Belfast so abundantly sends abroad, or those who in its name, attack those who strive only for the people's good. If the people of Belfast devote themselves as much to the service of their churches as they do to those movements which are supposed to defend them, the church will survive and revive even under socialism. **"Why am I a Socialist?" It would be more reasonable to ask others why they are not!**

Hits and Misses.
BY MARKSMAN.

Do we pay too much for Law and Order? Yes!

Our total revenue is £13,000,000.

The R.U.C. cost us £862,771.

The "Specials" cost us £1,143,500.

Total cost for policing Six Counties, 2 millions.

Are our policemen overpaid? No!

But our labourers and artizans are *underpaid*.

Are our Judges overpaid? Yes, decidedly — Lord Chief Justice Dennis Henry receives £5,000.

Lord Chief Justice in Free State receives £4,000.

Lord Justice Andrews receives £4,000.

Justices Brown and Wilson receive £3,500 each.

Minimum wage for our Judges, £3,500 per year.

Five Free State Judges are paid £2,500 each.

The Free State is going to economise further on the administration of the law. The Northern Bench is not only overpaid, but overmanned, yet our Government does not intend to sack a Judge or close a Court.

We pay exactly one-third more per head for police than the Free State.

The cost of a single R.U.C. Unit is £285 per annum, or £5. 10s. 0d. per week. Our constables receive a minimum of £3. 10s. 0d. per week in wages, and a maximum of £4. 15s. 0d. A Sergeant in the R.U.C. begins at £5 per week rising to £5. 12s. 6d. A Head Constable starts with £6 and finishes with £6. 16s. 6d. A District Inspector begins with £7 per week, and finishes with £13 per week. A County Inspector begins at £14 per week and finishes up with £18 per week. In addition to salaries there are all sorts of allowances, such as rent, uniform, boots, clerical, subsistence, separation and personal.

A Constable in receipt of the maximun £4. 15s. 0d. per week, is also allowed his clothes, quarters, a boot alowance of £3. 18s. 0d. per year, and medical allowance of £1. 17s. 0d. per year. An Inspector has a minimum allowance of £2 per week, and may also have a rent allowance varying from £1 to £2 per week. How do these salaries compare with the old R.I.C.?

The old R.I.C. cost us £136 per head in the year 1913, or a total of £1,400,000, for a force numbering 10,260 of all ranks.

A correspondent asks me about Sir Dawson Bates' relatives. This family receives £5,300 of public money each year. Sir Dawson receives £2,000 as Cabinet Minister; an Uncle receives £1,500 as Recorder of Down; a Brother receives £1,200; a Sister £600.

The Government is economising (Moryah). I hear that the 6d. per night allowance to policemen on "watch" duty is withdrawn, and that the 2d. per day allowance for "point" duty has also been withdrawn.

The cost of Governing Northern Ireland is £10. 11s. 10d. per head. The cost of Governing Denmark is £4 per head. The cost of Governing Belgium is £2. 15s. 0d.

Our revenue is £13,000,000. The revenue of New Zealand is £28,000,000. The cost of Ministerial Offices in Northern Ireland is £21,900. The cost of Ministerial Offices in New Zealand is £12,300.

Ministerial Offices, Quebec £10,000 per year, yet Quebec has twice our population. Ministerial Offices, New South Wales, £17,000 and New South Wales also has twice our population. Victoria, population 1,625,000; Revenue £21,000,000; Ministerial Salaries £9,000. South Austra-

lia, Salaries £7,750. Queensland Revenue £13,000,000 Salaries £9,300.

A wink's as good as a nod to a (politically) blind man.

Bradford has erected houses by direct labour and has effected a saving of £58 per house.

When you want anything done right, do it yourself.

Lurgan Municipal Gasworks produced over five million cubic feet of gas last month, at a cost of 3/5 per 1,000 cubic feet; sold at 5/6 per 1,000 cubic feet; profit £50 per month. Socialism pays.

Lisburn proposes to build 101 labourers' cottages to be let at 3/7 per week.

Whitehead has been raised to the dignity of a Township and nine merchants have been elected as Town Commissioners. Bangor can elect Labour men, why not Whitehead?

Cookstown hiring was held on the 9th. May, and human beings were hired in the market like cattle.

Ballynahinch half-yearly hiring fair was held on 7th. May. Prices ranged as under:—

Good Strong Men £19 to £26 for the six months.

Good Strong Boys	£12 to £17	" "
Small Boys	£6 to £8	" "
Good Strong Girls	£12 to £15	" "
Small Girls	£5 to £7	" "

Newry still gets its scavenging done by contract. Shame Newry?

In Northern Ireland there are 53,000 people anxious and willing to work and cannot get work to do.

Some people are drawing the dole and they are not entitled to it. For instance:-

Queen Alexandra	£70,000 per annum.	
Duke of Connaught	25,000	" "
The King of England	470,000	" "

I think if the above persons were summoned to the Court of Referees, they might have trouble in proving their claim to Free Benefit.

In addition to the three dole drawers named, I have before me a big list of Lords, Dukes, Generals and ex-Judges, who should be asked to prove that they are "genuinely" seeking work," and "normally in insurable employment."

The Linen Thread Co., of which Mr. Milne Barbour, M.P., has been Chairman of Directors, has decided to start a new mill for the production of linen goods at a small town near Genoa, Italy. Who said Patriotism? eh! No wonder the Milfort Company went bankrupt, and no wonder our Textile Workers are idle.

The well-to-do class of Great Britain has invested £6,000,000,000 abroad. "God Save the King."

There are 137 persons in Great Britain who admit that their net income is over £100,000 a year; £2,000 per week, or £36 for every hour of an eight-hour day.

Some well-to-do persons died last year. One man left over four millions. Two men left over three millions. While another two left over two millions. One millionaire dies every month, and a fool is born every minute.

Labour Men of the North.
BY BOB M'CLUNG.
Alderman George M. Donaldson, Belfast.

The subject of our sketch was early attracted to the Labour Movement by the speeches of the late Willie Walker. When only a boy he stood outside the "Telegraph" and cheered the Labour victories in the year 1906. He got an early training in Trade Unionism, as his father was a superannuated member of the Amalgamated Woodworkers' society. Joining the Plumbers' Association in 1909, he was made a Committee man when only 21 years of age, later becoming Auditor. He was appointed full-time Secretary and Delegate in 1917, a position which he still holds.

Many of the older labour men will remember how Donaldson worked like a Trojan in Court Ward in an endeavour to return Robert Gageby, as M.P., for North Belfast.

In 1920 he was Official Labour Candidate for St. Anne's, winning the Aldermanship as nominee of the Plumbers' Association. In 1923 he again won S. George's Ward as senior Councillor receiving almost 2,000 clear majority votes, and later when claiming his rights as Alderman on the vacancy created by the death of Alderman Boyd, was again successful in defeating all the forces of Toryism. He was a member of the Railway Commission, and along with S. Kyle, M.P., presented a minority report in favour of National Ownership and Workers' Control. He is at present a member of the Industrial Commission and has reported in favour of the community owning and controlling the coal industry. He is a man of high character and pleasing personality and a credit to the Labour Party.

Truth, Greatness And The Press.
BY ENOES.

"A Nation's greatness depends upon the education of it's people," said a great Irishman. And on the authority of Mr. Baldwin, the greatest educational force in modern life is a clean and truthful public press, meaning the Tory Press of course.

So now you know, the secret of greatness is out. Read their press! That glorious organ of truth, and stout defender of the liberties of the people. Read the manly sentiments of your local leaders of political thought, learn how your mighty forefathers fought and died in defence of their civil and religious liberties. "Eh, what, where are they?" I don't know, but can't you read about it anyhow. And if you don't feel a lump rise in your throat and your eyes do not grow dim, then Sir, I say you are not a true patriot, you are a cowardly white livered "sosh" (vide press), whose only idea of liberty is to rob the frugal and industrious mill-owner of the fruits of his industry, and despoil the kindly landlord, or worse still, you would crush the poor tax-ridden whisky magnate out of existence. Henry, how could you be so cruel, so envious and so greedy. I think of their poor wives and little children, how their hearts would ache if they had not their simple comforts like little trips to the continent. How would they cure father's lumbago. Ask yourself that. You would deprive them of their bread-winners. And Henry, would you also take away their motor cars, and make them walk like you and I? Then I suppose you would demand the right of entry to the Universities, and expect to be treated as an equal. If that should happen do you realise that it would endanger the whole commercial and economic structure of society. "Rot, nonsense!" you exclaim. It's perfectly true my man, use your reason. Surely you would not be a political hun, or worse still a Russian Bolshie, a wrecker of homes and destroyer of the sanctity of the marriage vows. 'Don't butt in with tactless remarks about Society Scandals, draw your dole, and be thankful, sir." But we are not beaten yet. James of Stormont has said "not one inch" and he is a man of his word, in some things. At least he will never give way one inch to your selfish and ignorant demands for equality. Depend on James. He has also said that "Ulster is right," and so it is, for James and the aforesaid industrious and patriotic gentlemen whose case I have endeavoured to plead, I fear me, with but scant success. "What the H——," hush Henry Dubb, don't swear it isn't done in good society, unless, of course, when you take a mighty and solemn oath in defence of things as they are. And now to decide a very momentous question. Should the great loyal hearted men of Ulster be named with the dull stupid toilers of other lands? I say no. Let them be named apart. Not Henry Dubb, but Billy Mugg.

Despite all this you might still remain one of those who believe with John Wheatley— "That it is a mistake to think that Capitalists have hearts as well as pockets." If you are, then education will teach you to ignore what does not exist, and concentrate on the realities. Read the Press, but . . . think!

The Next Step.

The Labour Opposition in the Northern Parliament has made the pace so hot for the Government that the Official Unionists no longer dare to absent themselves from their duties. This is a great change from the slippered ease and slothful indifference that characterised their attitude in Parliament during the last four years, and is a first class testimonial to the success of Labour's shock tactics. They used to open a lazy eye when Labour prodded them, and then slumber peacefully on. Nowadays, they have been punched and jabbed into a snarling virility that does not stop at the Labour Opposition, but is carried into their own family quarrels. Harry Mulholland, M.P., even went further than mere snarling, and in a most intemperate and violent speech gave it as his considered opinion that the Independent Unionists should be "kicked" out of the country. That is not a very statesmanlike utterance and displays neither good taste nor good judgement, but it certainly is consistent with the man who, during a very serious debate in the House, took it upon himself to inform us that he kept goats.

Frankly, the Government is afraid, and is becoming alarmed at the widening gulf that separates the Official Clique from the Independents. Neither men nor Governments dare to stand still, and the Independents must either go back penitently to the fold, or they must progress further, and publicly declare themselves in wholehearted sympathy with Labour's Policy and Programme. Every day strengthens the position of Labour in the Six Counties, and while a successful contest in South Belfast might have been doubtful a month ago, there is no longer any doubt whatever that we can win that bye-election. Information from the rural areas shows the same swing to

Labour, and it is time that our Organisers and Propagandists set themselves the task of forming active units of the Independent Labour Party and of the Labour Party of Northern Ireland, and get them linked up with the centre in Belfast. Five separate fingers on a hand might be very useful to point the way, or to illustrate a lesson, but the five fingers need to be "closed up" into a hard fist to give the K.O. to Ulster's Capitalist Government. The people are with us and are ready and willing to come our way, but we must not hope to win victories with scattered forces or loosely knit units. We must tighten up and during the incoming months we should conduct a forward drive from the one end of the Six Counties to the other. The Belfast Divisions are enrolling new members daily and conducting a vigorous open air propaganda in every part of the City, and we turn now confidently to the Country to support us in our effort.

TO OUR CORRESPONDENTS.

"Pat Macken".—Kindly send your name and address.

P.E.P., Newry.—Thanks, hardly just suitable for a monthly, but notes, articles and scandals always welcome.

Thos. Canning.—Not our style. Have another try.

Coleraine.—Received O.K., and passed it on.

Enquirer.—Certainly, always open. But be bright and brief and say it with a kick.

Our Fighting Fund.

We appeal to all friends, sympathisers and welwishers who desire to see a strong, alert and effective OPPOSITION in the Northern Parliament, to send a subscription to our I.L.P. Fighting Fund. Any sum, much or little, will be welcomed, and will be acknowledged with thanks in these columns. Send your "sub." c/o this Office at 48 York Street, Belfast. *Sam Kyle, Hugh Gemmell.* Previously acknowledged: £76 6 9. Mrs. M' Veigh 2/6; John Gorman 10/-.

The Farmer's Confession.

"This brings me to what I consider to be the root of all our troubles, and it is **want of Education**! Farmers, as a rule, are an uneducated class, trying to carry on a very complicated business. They are very conservative also, and seem to think that what the rest of the world is doing is no concern of theirs."—p.4.

"We must from this on, start and farm, with our brains."—p.15.

"There are two other important Ministries which I would like to congratulate, but I cannot in their present unclean condition. I, in the near future, if they cannot be induced to part with their black spots, may, in the public interest, state definite charges.

"I refer to the Educational and Home Affairs Departments."—p.15

"The profits of Ulster Agriculture in the last twenty years—a period including both the wartime inflation and the postwar depression—were greater than ever before. They were greater than the profits of agriculture had been anywhere in the world before until then."—p.17

These extracts are from *The Irish Breeder,* May 1925. The back cover contains an advertisement for Diamond Rings at £50 each. The poor, distressed Farmers also got £128,000 from the Government of Northern Ireland, in relief of rates. The farm labourer got nothing, not even unemployment benefit, as he is not in an insurable occupation. The Farmer has his Union. It's time the Labourer was in his.

The Tragedy.

Over 1,300 disabled ex-servicemen in Belfast quite fit for work, but unable to obtain it. Will you *remember* these men by providing them with employment? Casual or permanent. For particulars apply to the Secretary, Local Employment Committee.

And The Reason The Boss Gives

"It never occurred to us that the little jobs we did about the place could possibly be botched by any human being. We got our eyes opened, however, when we tried to train an *ex-soldier* who had been a city mill worker.

"The 'creature' was keen enough and earnest enough, but every time we left him he did something terrible. Dug up borders, ruined the verge of the lawn, even when a sample drill was made for him in the garden. On our return he had made drills three feet wide and at the angle of a dog's hind leg. We also had a sample of the same type of 'Tommy' in Egypt. What can be done with them?

"Mr. Lloyd George and Mr. Lansbury talk glibly about idle men and idle land. But we or any other farmer who has tried *them* could tell a different story. It would cost more to watch *them*, and instruct them, than *their* labour is worth."

That's what Captain Gregg, O.B.E., thinks of the Ex-Service men, and he says so in the editorial of *The Irish Breeder*, May, 1925. This is the 'old block' whose 'young chip' Councillor Harry Midgley knocked out for the count, in the famous Ulster Hall debate on Socialism.

A grateful country will never forget you. Anyway, it didn't forget the big bugs, because they got so much money for nothing that they didn't need to work.

Admiral Beatty got £100,000; Field Marshal Haig, £100,000; Admiral Jellicoe, £50,000; Field Marshal French £50,000; Field Marshal Allenby, £50,000; Field Marshal Plumer, £30,000; General Rawlinson, £30,000; General Byng, £30,000; General Horne, £30,000; Lieut.-Col. Hankey, £25,000; Admiral Madden, £10,000; Admiral Sturdee, £10,000; Rear Admiral Keyes, £10,000; Vice-Admiral de Roebeck, £10,000; Commander Tyrwhitt, £10,000; Field Marshal Wilson, £10,000; Air Vice-Marshal Trenchard, £10,000. Total, £585,000, or more than half-a-million pounds between 19 men.

Last week an ex-soldier dragged himself into the Railway Goods Yard at Omagh, and died there. He left a wife and family. He had been summoned from his home to come into Omagh for inspection by the Doctor, in an effort, I presume, to reduce his pension.

Cut this out and hang it on the wall. It will tickle your memory for the next war, and will do you more good than a calendar of dates. **Hotspur.**

Branded.

The experience of all ages and nations, I believe demonstrates that the work done by slaves, though it appears to cost only their maintenance, is, in the end the dearest of any."

Adam Smith. **Wealth of Nations.**

One day recently I was musing on the passage of time and reflecting on the changes recorded by written history.

In particular I was thinking of the days of Chattel Slavery when the slave had an iron collar fastened round his neck and the name of his master clearly engraved upon it. These were galling and oppressive days and in our school books we were tutored in the pathetic misery of "Uncle Tom's Cabin," and proudly taught that "Brrrr...it ons never, never, never, will be slaves."

It is true that slavery was officially abolished in Britain by Act of Parliament about the year 1826, but if we are no longer Chattel Slaves we are very much wages Slaves, and tied very definitely to a Class even if we are free to move from one individual employer to another. Nor are we free from the galling and insolent branding of our masters, because only yesterday I met a handsome young member of the working class garbed in an attractive blue uniform and on his collar, branded in plain letters so that all who run might read was the name of his owner

"Thomas Cook & Sons." Like a far flung flame of flashing fire the searing thought of the slave's iron collar swept through my mind; the ages were spanned in an instant and I realised that society still rested on an unfree class, fettered to the productive machinery of modern times, and bearing the brand of the owner. It was a dreadful discovery and I immediately looked around me to discover any fresh evidence of our slave condition. I went into Liptons and there behind the counter were a dozen slaves, all branded on their collars with the name of their exploiter.

From one place to another I went, seeking for freedom and individualism and everywhere I went I encountered hordes and droves and crowds of slaves, many of them in the uniform of their lord and master, and most of them with the infamous badge of their servile state. In the shipyard and factories I found a deadly uniformity, but no uniform, unless the dongaree be considered as a uniform, but on inquiry as to why they had no uniform supplied to them I was sarcastically informed that the work was so dirty and severe on the clothing, that the employer considered the expense of upkeep too great and therefore imposed the burden on the wage-slave, but, said my informant, we are branded all right and producing a brass check from his pocket he showed me his number and told me that that was the brand of his master and that he gave it to a timekeeper to hold for him while he produced wealth for his employer and that if he tried to escape work without taking his badge of servitude with him he would not receive any money and therefore no food, clothing or shelter.

Later as I wended my way among the crowds in the street I encountered numerous men in a blue uniform and on their collars, a letter and a string of numbers. These men were tall and strong looking, walking about leisurely and casting eagle glances at the people around. These I was told, were favourite slaves and were given special conditions and privileges to remain loyal to the employing class whenever they were threatened with danger by a revolt of the hordes of less favoured slaves.

Others too, I encountered, dressed in uncouth garments of khaki colour, and these were men of swift movement, alert, virile and purposeful. They were called soldiers and were gathered together in a barracks and drilled and disciplined into an effective fighting machine, and armed with lethal weapons, on which they affixed a long sharp blade of steel called a bayonet which could disembowel men. These men I was informed, were the real bodyguard of the Lords of Wealth Production and often used their murderous weapons to shoot and maim the workers when they revolted against their servile state and attempted to gain some measure of Freedom. This was known as a strike and the workers had preserved a long list of butcheries, from Peterloo to Featherstone, when the employers had used their soldier slaves to shoot down their productive slaves.

These were terrible discoveries to make in the year of Christ, 1925, and it seems that we have no real freedom at all to-day despite the platitudes and assurances of the hireling hacks of King Capital

Yet freedom cannot be far distant and once free the worker slaves of to-day cannot enslave another class because there is no social stratum beneath them, and when Democracy reaches out to grasp the prize of liberty which all the ages have striven for in vain, their act of justice will disrobe them of their uniform of slavery and strike the hated collar of servitude from their necks.

"The Solemn League and Covenant
Whiles brings a sigh and whiles a tear;
But Sacred Freedom, too, was there,
If thou'rt a slave, indulge thy sneer."
BURNS.

Ulster Industries.
Minority Report Of Development Commission.

(This report, together with the majority report, was sent out to the Press. The Boss's report was boosted, our's was "busted". We need at least a Weekly Paper, to keep pace with their perfidy.—EDITOR)

"We assert that it is highly desirable that the community itself should own the mines. If the State is to undertake exploratory work and is also to render financial assistance in the early days of the industry, it is only reasonable that the community should reap the full reward of its activities by securing all the gain that may accrue from the industry rather than that private individuals should reap most of the profit, while not prepared to take the initial risks. Again, it is admitted that it will be necessary to recruit miners of experience and skill from other countries and that they must be assured of satisfactory working conditions. We maintain most emphatically that the only way in which satisfactory conditions can be secured is by the community taking the whole responsibility in the industry. Private enterprise will undoubtedly fail, and we accordingly contend that the industry should be owned and controlled by the State.

"Further, there is the fact that the amount of profits and royalties derived from the coal industry during the past ten years has been more than double the amount of capital invested, but even more important, from our point of view, is the fact that in 1923, 1,297 workmen were killed in the coal mines of Great Britain, or an average of almost four every day of the year. In addition to this ghastly loss of life, there were, during the same year, 212,256 accidents to workmen which involved incapacity for work for seven days or upwards—a casualty total affecting an average of 680 persons each day of the year.

"It is because we believe that Nationalisation of the Mines would tend, inter alia, to reduce this fearful toll of life and limb that we now make a strong recommendation for its adoption.

"Northern Ireland has just commenced its life as a separate entity, and it is of outstanding importance that we should take advantage, in every possible direction, of the experience of other countries in order that our social life may be built upon a proper foundation. We are confident that this note of ours expresses the opinions held by an ever increasing number of people, and we accordingly consider it to be our duty to tender to the Government this expression of our opinion as to the advisability of nationalising the Coal Mining Industry."

Signed,
Geo M. Donaldson, Belfast.
Wm. Logue, Derry.
R. M'Clung, Belfast.

The complete minority report can be had from the "OPPOSITION OFFICE", post free, for threepence in stamps.

Picked From Our Post bag.

A CHARA,

You can send me on five dozen Oppositions. I can dispose of them. Henderson may thank the **Opposition** for his Election for Co. Antrim. I not only posted the Cartoons "which were fine," but had on sale at each of the five polling booths round here on election day our grand paper, and strange to say the **Farmers** went wild to get it. Well I need hardly say how pleased I am at Labour's success in Belfast, and you can please convey my congratulations to Brother Kyle, M.P., also Comrades M'Mullen and Beattie, on their splendid success. Jimmy Craig talked about **Stable Government,** well, thank heaven our three Labour men will see to it that Jimmy keeps his **stable clean.** If I'm spared from this on, through the **"Opposition,"** I will do my bit to have at least the worker educated so that when the next Election comes we will be able to return men of our own class.

Mise ve Mess Mop. [Sic.]
James J. Tate,
Cranfield, Co. Antrim.

The Editor, Labour Opposition

Dear Comrade, received the dozen copies of your paper for which I thank you. Please send me four or five dozen by return of post and reserve me one hundred copies of next month's issue. This district is now ripe for an I.L.P. Branch; I have a J.P., a School Teacher, a Roman Catholic Town Councillor, and the Master of an Orange Lodge ready for Socialism. This is owing to my lending my copy of the Glasgow "Forward," so our flower of Socialism is planted at Ballymoney, and there are more than a dozen readers of the "Forward" who lend their copies several times over. It was unknown in this district when I came home from the war, so like the Apostle of old we invite you to come over and help us to water the little seed so that it may grow to cover the whole earth where the beasts of the field as well as the human family, may have shelter under its Branches.

Yours in Comradeship, *A. Crawford.*

A Word of Cheer,
by Mary Jackson, Belfast.

Dear Comrade,

Good luck to your gallant little paper, I wish it enduring success, in the days to come. It was much needed in this City. May all who write for it be inspired with the true spirit of brotherhood and service, in the glorious cause; may all bitterness and strife and malice and evil speaking be put away, be ye kind one to another.

"The Labour Opposition."

It's an honest proposition, and a pleasing composition;
Buy the Labour Opposition—help the Cause.
It's our determined mission, by active opposition,
To realise transition—change the laws.

Taking up our right position, to fulfil our great ambition;
By the Total abolition—of the poor.
It's by ruthless competition, we are heading towards perdition;
Hence the Labour Opposition—make it sure.

Charles J. M'Crystal

The **Dock Ward Labour Party** General Meeting was held last week in 122 Corporation Street, and Tom Kane presided over a splendid attendance. The members were addressed by A. Ellis and Wm. M'Mullen, M.P. Their representative, Jack Beattie, M.P., gave a most encouraging report of his activities in the Northern Parliament, and gave wise counsel for future organisation. 50 new members were enrolled.

The Labour Opposition Of Northern Ireland.

Vol. 1—No.5   July, 1925   One Penny

The Menace of Unemployment.

BY MARY H. KYLE.

The growth of this menacing problem has at last compelled "the powers that be" to sit up and take notice. It is very significant that the Lord Mayor, on behalf of a Corporation that only a few years ago denied the fact that there was an unemployment problem, and J. M. Andrews on behalf of a Government whose Commander-in-Chief declared in November, 1923, that *he* would solve the unemployment problem in Ulster, have called for the help of representatives of employers and workers in an attempt to suggest remedies or palliatives for the unemployment problem.

It was at the instance of a Labour man of course, that this conference was called, just as it has always been left to Labour men and women to force this problem on the attention of those in high places. Ever since Keir Hardie first entered Westminster as the "member for the unemployed," labour has gradually attracted more and more attention to unemployment, until at last it has become *the* question in politics.

But while we have succeeded in forcing it to the forefront, we have not yet been equally successful in convincing our opponents—the comfortable ones—that the truth is that as long as production for profit is the first principle of industry there is no remedy, and to bring this home a supreme effort has now to be made. They are prepared to call us in to try and help them smooth things over, make the rough places plain, but anything drastic, anything big cannot be attempted. It is too expensive, the risks are too great. And

yet what are the risks if we let things drift on as they are—are not the dangers ahead as great nearly as any that faced us during the so-called "Great War." Then the nation was called to fight against the foreign enemy, now we have an equally deadly enemy at home to fight against. But our friends in power—the Unionists—are such babes they cannot face it. Cannot visualise the devastating results to the human race and to civilisation, so called, of this long drawn out period of stagnation and death, yet if we stop to think of what the effects are going to be the prospect is appalling enough. We are sorry enough creatures as it is, but with the continuation of starvation and want and idleness, what sort of beings shall we become. What sort of babies can mothers bring into this world under such conditions, what chance have the children of developing into healthy human beings, and worse still what chance have the adults of to-day of recuperating from the deadening effect of not having enough food and not having enough work. The latter fact is almost as serious as the former for we all know from experience that if we do not use our faculties or our skill in a particular direction, they become rusty and decay.

So indeed the crisis is a vital one, and yet the Government and the capitalist class generally meet it in a lethargic and timid way. The employers seem to just hope that the tide will turn, and the Government find every proposal too expensive. If there was a war on they would squander 10 times the necessary amount of money on shells and guns and other things that only serve to blow human beings to powder. We want the same effort made, not to produce things to destroy human life, but to help it to live. Let the Government spend money on seeing that their fellow country-men are fed and clothed and housed. They have been careful enough to see that they get more than enough of these things themselves, let them now turn their eyes further afield and consider those whose well-being they are sent to Parliament to consider. Aye let them even look further afield than to provide mere material things, for our civilisation is not so wonderfully high that we couldn't do with more ample provision for education, more ample provision of those things that go to enrich our leisure hours.

So we call on the Government to produce big schemes of work, for use and not for profit. With exports and imports decreasing rapidly these last two or three years, the prospects for the carrying trade are not good, and shipbuilding may never be what it was in Belfast. With the world on the verge of bankruptcy what prospect is there for a luxury trade like linen—so new avenues of employment must be found, and instead of trying to bolster up industries whose prime is past, the Government must be challenged by labour to put Socialism, the only practical remedy, into practice. The resources of the nation are behind it, and if the appeal made is earnest enough, or the compulsion used strong enough, the foundations can be laid now in this time of crisis for the building up of a prosperous, well developed and happy nation.

Hits and Misses.
BY MARKSMAN.

During the past month the Irish Free State Government has sacked—26 Resident Magistrates; 23 Crown Solicitors; 12 Local Government Board Officials; 305 Petty Sessions Clerks. When is our Northern Government going to economise on "Lorandorder?"

* *

Governor-General Tim Healy is in receipt of £28,000 per annum, this is a scandal which the Labour Party in the Free State should tackle at once. U.S.A. with a population of 115 million people pays its President £15,000 per annum. The Viceroy of India has £16,000 per annum, but the other policemen (the natives) are paid from £10 to £16 per annum.

* *

There are 5,000 British troops in Northern Ireland at an estimated cost of £900,000. 35,176 A. B. and C. policemen cost us £1,934,000. In the Free State the Army and Civic Guard cost 4½ million pounds for 24,887 men.

* *

Scotland with a population of 5 million persons pays 2 million pounds for police. Glasgow pays £711,438 as her share of the police force. Under a properly organised system of society every person would be as well fed and as well housed and clothed as the members of the Royal Ulster Constabulary.

* *

Glasgow Corporation has assets amounting to 43½ million pounds and liabilities amounting to 28 million pounds. Moral—vote for municipalisation of the public services. And Glasgow is the "RED" City too.

* *

"Profits of £64,961 and £48,103 for Belfast's Municipal Electricity and Gas Undertakings were made last year," says the *Daily Mail* "in spite of the fact that consumers received their lighting and power at prices comparing favourably with the lowest in the kingdom." And yet the *Daily Mail* opposes labour candidates who are pledged to vote for Municipal ownership and control. I will be charitable and say nothing about the local press.

* *

Leeds municipal trams have made a total profit of 1½ million pounds. The profits from Leeds municipal undertakings have reduced the rates by 9½ d in the £. This "Leeds" us to the sincerest form of flattery.

* *

Bradford municipalised its gas supply in 1871. Belfast in 1874. Lucky Bradford and lucky Belfast.

* *

There are 4,000 patients resident in our asylums in the six counties. The annual cost amounts to £221,934. For the annual cost of our Northern Parliament, refer to our April number.

* *

In 1923 fifteen Britishers died leaving £40,000,000. In the same year 400,000 British died leaving nothing of value. An expedition is being despatched to discover where the 15 "rich" men ultimately landed. ". . . as a camel to pass through the eye of a needle."

* *

The W. D. & H. O. Wills' tobacco combine have paid out 35 million pounds in dividends during the past ten years and have built up assets worth 74 millions. Gallaghers and Murrays of Belfast must be packing the profits away in barrels, as they are paying exactly 20/- per week *less* to male adults than the firm of "Wills." We in Belfast are either fat . . igued or fat . . headed. Anyway, we suffer from "Fag."

* *

312 Companies owned and controlled by private enterprise made a total profit of 139 million pounds in the year 1924. The workers' difficulty is the employer's opportunity.

An Apology.

WE APOLOGISE to our readers for the delay in the last issue. The trouble was an article by Hugh Gemmell dealing with an hospital scandal. Our printer would not allow this to go out, and as most of our staff were at cross channel Conferences, it took some time to get the matter put right. Finally, an article which had already appeared in the *Voice of Labour,* was inserted and the *Opposition* was published. The suppressed article subsequently appeared in the *Daily Herald.*

When you've read "The Opposition," please pass it onto a pal.

* *

Iceland codfish is being landed in Hull at 2 3/4d. per lb., and sold in London at 1/6 per lb. These are facts and not codology.

* *

Burmah Oil Company paid dividends of 22 1/2 per cent. for 1924. Total profits for 1924, £2,257,157. God bless Winnie for reducing the super-tax.

* *

The income of the Crown Prince of Italy has been fixed at £20,000 per annum and when he marries it will be increased to £40,000. I respectfully suggest that 2/- per week be fixed for each child.

* *

Last year all the big boot firms paid dividends ranging from 10 to 22 1/2 per cent. and at the moment 50 per cent of our people are wearing defective boots. And the price of brown paper has become abnormally high.

* *

Gt. Britain's five big banks reaped a net profit of eleven million pounds last year. And the Canal Banks also reaped a rich harvest—of suicides.

* *

In 1923 Gt. Britain lost 26,227 skilled farm workers and 24,724 engineering workers. They emigrated. No . . . wonder.

* *

There are 258,000 insured persons in Northern Ireland, and 54,000 of these are unemployed.

The rest of us do not live, but only fail to die.

BALLYCARRY

Ballycarry and back, together with Lunch and Tea, and a light discursive lecture by A. Ellis, the Irish Organiser of the N.C.L.C. and all for **4/6**, is a proposition that ought to attract many workers to visit the historic spot on the 12th day. The Gobbins Cliffs, a Sandy Bay; a strip of green sward and abundant time to ramble and play should provide enough variety to make a memorable day. Have a look at our other columns for the details.

Labour Men Of The North.
BY BOB M'CLUNG.

Alex. Stewart, Belfast.

I don't know if I can do justice to our comrade in the space at my disposal. On reading a copy of the *"Belfast News-Letter,"* dated 3/9/93, I find that a great meeting of 3,000 persons was held at the Customs House Steps, presided over by Alex. Stewart. I have been in the Socialist movement since 1905 and Alex. Stewart has always been prominent and now at 71 years of age he is the same optimist that we have always known him to be, so I take my hat off to our comrade. Alex. is one of the founders of the I.L.P. and won the first independent labour victory at Newcastle-on-Tyne, in 1889, when he was elected to the School Board by 42,000 votes.

He was born at Glasgow in October, 1854, and educated at a "private adventure school" as he terms it, identified with the Scottish Free Church. He served his apprenticeship to pattern-making and was elected as their delegate to Glasgow Trades Council when only 21 years of age. For years he was chairman of the Scottish Land Law Reform Association and as Chairman of the Glasgow Land League he attended conferences at Glasgow, Manchester, Leeds and Dublin.

In Dublin he took part in a strike, won the strike; formed a Labourers' Union and . . . was put in jail. He was also a member of the Parliamentary Committee of the Irish Trade Union Congress, and put in some very constructive work on that body. I wish good health and happiness to my old comrade.

A New Recruit.
BY DOL(E)-OR-(O)US.

Sir William Turner speaking at the opening of the Conference on Unemployment in Northern Ireland said to the Members "they had to tackle a great work, a good work, and if they meant to be successfull they *might have to smash something that at present existed."*

We agree. It is a great and good work to release men from the curse of idleness; women from the heart-breaking task of trying to provide for a family on insufficient means; children from early starvation that lowers their vitality and stunts their growth. It is a great and good work to release all from the yoke of hypocrisy and idolatry.

Is Sir William going to help us to expose the falseness of those glib-tongued alleged leaders who prate so easily of Ulster's greatness while 60,000 of her true men and women slowly starve? Does he mean to cry out against the system that compels the noblest of our fellow-beings to stifle in filthy streets and hovels while the mis-named 'upper' classes, decked in paradise plumes and osprey feathers 'strut an' stare an' a' that' round the grounds of Stormont and Mountstewart at Garden Parties? Will he denounce, with us, the absurdity of overdressed women congregating to raise a few pounds for charity, when the money spent on their clothes for one week would equal all they collect in months for charity?

Will Sir William join his voice with ours in demanding from Sir James Craig the fulfilment of his promise to solve the unemployment problem, or his acknowledgement that it was an empty boast? Can we depend on Belfast's Lord Mayor to ask the Northern Ministers to cease their I-am-so-weary-as-my-job-on-your-behalf-is-such-a-strain-but-though-it-kill-me-I'll-go-on prattle, and either start to show they can fill their jobs or else get out?

Sir William is a plain man of the people; he knows their worthiness and simple honesty; he knows their struggles. He knows also now the tinsel show that passes for dignity in the ranks of the well-off. Let him then help to teach the workers to appreciate their own dignity and ability, and to shun as they would a plague the cringing, servile attitude of slaves. If he does this he will have truly filled with a manly dignity the office of honour he now holds.

Arise, Sir William, and swing your sledge.

The Coming Clash.

The Capitalists of Great Britain have embarked upon the opening phase of an unscrupulous and determined assault against the working class, and those who cannot see the Class War, are likely to get their eyes opened within the next six months. It is going to be a protracted and bitter struggle with lock-outs, strikes and demonstrations, and the customary shooting of the Workers that has accompanied every crisis. The stage is set and the method of presenting "The Circus" to the world is the same now as it was in 1912, 13 and 14. We have the same industrial struggle at home, the same struggle for new markets abroad, the same secret arrangements with the Capitalist Governments of other countries that will ultimately plunge us into a fresh international conflict and kill off the young men who are revolting today against the economic insecurity of Capitalism.

That is the Employing Class's idea of Peace, and in Ulster, Sir James Craig advances the same poisonous doctrine to divert the Working Class stomach from its hunger. He will defend the border ! ! Utterly unable to find work for one single man, and thoroughly incompetent to legislate an improvement in the industrial situation, Sir James calmly shuts down his Parliament and shirks the responsibility of his office. And this despite the boast he made in 1923 that *he* would solve the unemployment problem in Ulster. The Braggart! Yet the Workers of Northern Ireland should not grumble. *They are getting what they voted for.* Sir James and his Class are not workers. They are unemployed by profession. It is unnatural to expect them to be anxious about work, and if the *Workers* want something done, they will have to do it themselves. There is no other way. If the Workers willed it they could solve the problem to-morrow. They built the ships and they could use them. They make the clothes and they could wear them. They grow the food and they could eat it, and all we need is a clear understanding of this simple basic truth. Meantime we are starving, and unless the Government pays heed to our condition, they will be faced with an upheaval that is likely to be more vocal and more *fundamental* than the "44 week" in Belfast.

N.C.L.C. & Belfast Trades Council!
A.A. Purcell.
He is Coming to Belfast.
Look our for further announcements and get your Ticket early.

Knaves and Fools.
The Education Controversy.
Lord Londonderry's spoof.

As we go to Press we see a reported settlement of the Education controversy. "The teachers in the schools will be required to give this instruction as a condition of their appointment, or of their continuance in appointment, but provided they give this instruction bona-fide, the Ministry of Education will uphold the appeal of a teacher against dismissal by the Education Authority on grounds connected with the efficiency of his teaching, of the *undenominational* religious programme."

Really it is too funny for words. The above has been accepted by that well-known Educational expert the County Grand Master of Belfast, who, we presume, gained his knowledge in determining how much could be lent with safety on a guaranteed silver lever watch. But joking aside what do the clergymen and Sir Joseph Davison take the people of the six counties for, do they think that the ordinary man in the street is such a num-skull as to believe that the above formula of words will settle the controversy. That is presuming the protagonists are in earnest, but are they? Everybody knows that what the clergymen were after in this controversy was to compel the teachers to do their work for them! And to have the right to dismiss them, if they didn't teach in the Sunday School, sing in the choir, play the organ or harmonium, take part in raising funds for the churches, running bazaars, sales of work, cake fairs, whist drives, etc., etc.

In fact the clergymen can not get used to the idea that they no longer are to have the power of being the petty tyrants that so many of them were and are in this connection. And we congratulate Lord Londonderry on having again and yet again shown us how really stupid "educated" men can be. Just fancy a Church of Ireland clergyman—and a Bishop at that—Presbyterians and Methodists all agreeing to *undenominational* religious instruction. Shades of the thirty nine articles not to mention the Westminster Confession of Faith, it really is too funny for words.

100,000 PENNIES.
Court Ward Divisional Labour Party.

We are out to win Court Ward for Labour. We want to build a Hall as a centre for all our activities. We want it right now, and YOUR PENNIES can do it. We appeal to Trade Unionists, Labour Men, and all who sympathise with us to subscribe to this fund. Any sum, much or little, will be welcomed and acknowledged in these columns. Send your "Sub" to . . .

Tommy Geehan, 15 Tyrone Street, Belfast.

J. M'Ilroy,	240 pennies = £1
Miss Sarah Walsh,	120 pennies = 10/-
Miss Alice Walsh,	120 pennies = 10/-

SOCIALIST MAXIMS.

The world is my Country; to do good is my Religion.

What is socially produced, ought to be socially owned and controlled.

The only way by which one person can get a thing without earning it, is for some one else to earn it without getting it.

He who will not work, neither shall he eat.

If all wealth is produced by Labour, then all wealth ought to belong to Labour.

You would not trust your Boss as your representative in negotiating higher wages or improved conditions. You know perfectly well that his interests are opposed to yours. Why then, do you vote for him on Election day, and trust him to make your laws.   **HOTSPUR.**

What of To-morrow?

BY STUDENT.

You readers of this Labour paper and all workers and toilers, described as the working class. You can reason and think as well as, or perhaps better (more honestly I would venture to say) than those who pose as your guides, philosophers and friends in the higher altitudes of society. Listen to what I am going to quote to you from one of our noblest writers and greatest thinkers who lived some fifty years back. I mean Thomas Carlyle, "the sage of Chelsea." He says—"Two men I honour and no third. First, the toil worn craftsman that with earth made implement, laboriously conquers the earth and makes her man's. Venerable to me is that hard hand, crooked, coarse, wherein notwithstanding, lies a cunning virtue, indefeasibly royal, as of the *Sceptre of this Planet.* Venerable too is the rugged face, all weather tanned, besoiled with its rude intelligence, for it is the face of a man living manlike. O! but the more venerable for thy rudeness, and even because we must pity as well as love thee—hardly-entreated brother! For us was thy back so bent, for us were thy straight limbs and fingers so deformed; thou wert our conscript, and fighting our battles wert so marred. *For in thee too lay a God created form,* but it was not to be unfolded, encrusted must it stand with the thick adhesions and defacements of labour; and thy body like thy soul was not to know freedom. Yet toil on, toil on; *thou* art in thy duty, be out of it who may; thou toilest for the altogether indispensable, for daily bread."

Now I think no greater tribute could be given to the worker than the foregoing and with an abundance of wisdom in it that should be good for every worker and Labourite to keep before them. And why shouldn't we be acknowledged as a Party that has as much moral and material right to have a voice in the affairs of our nation and a fit proportion of the products and harvest of our toil. Herein is the whole gist of our claim as Carlyle has so ably told it, but we are now 50 years in advance since he wrote the above and this should even justify our existence more strongly if by our unceasing toil we make wealth for the nation without the chance to develop our faculties beyond this, the more reason why we should look for our share and be given our share of the comforts as well as the bare necessities of life. As Labour men we can and ought to feel that the country and the nation at large, owes you something more of the fruits of industry than they ever seem very willing to concede you and if we still keep going on and reinforcing the ranks, the time cannot be far distant when Labour shall have more of this world's comforts and a little bit to live on (not exist only) which as our "Sage" tells us is the result of "the toilworn craftsman." Let us keep in view the character this great man gave you over 50 years ago, and with steadfast purpose to fight on and uphold it and in the end will the victory surely be yours. The fight has been a long one for those who have been the champions of it from its infancy, but they will reap their reward in the consciousness of having done a noble work, and will, I hope, be found to live in the hearts of those whom they have led to victory, and that is a more lasting reward than stone effigies.

To Our Correspondents.

Labour Men of the North."—Yes, we are looking for short biographies of active and genuine Labour men. Send along the facts of his life, together with a photo block or a photograph, and we will fix it up for you.

J.J. Derry.—All that was wrong with your article was that it abused your fellow-workers. Try it on the Boss for a change.

"Worker," Coleraine.—Quite correct. A Branch of the I.L.P. was formed there last week. Get in touch with the man you mentioned.

Bread, Booze, and Banking.

BY HUGH GEMMELL.

During the past month bankruptcies that total over a million pounds have been listed in "The Gazette" and these refer chiefly to the Textile Trades. The self-styled Captains of Industry who own the engineering and shipbuilding works in Belfast can neither pay a wage nor pay their way and they ought to get out and work.

But in the matter of Bread, Booze and Banking, the Belfast Bosses score heavily with big dividends as the following list will show. The dividends are all recent. Northern Bank 17.5%: Ulster Bank 21.25%: Hughes Bakery 20%: Inglis Bakery 20%: Guinness 24% and the previous one 40%: Dunville 21% and along comes Sawers with 13%.

Bread in Belfast is dearer than it is across the water and in these bad times the Workers generally eat more bread in an effort to keep down the butcher's bill. The Bosses say, produce more and the price of living will fall and here we are producing more bread and the price goes up. With the money it is the same. Money is dear in Northern Ireland and its price has been blamed repeatedly for our industrial stagnation. In Ulster we seem to suffer always from the Busy B's, Bread, Booze and Banking. We need to use another "B". We need to use our Brains and sack the profiteers.

Don't be selfish! When you have read the 'Opposition" pass it on to another Worker who is not yet converted. If you must **keep** a copy, then buy another for your neighbour.

*   *

Every new reader of "The Labour Opposition" is another nail in the coffin of Capitalism in Northern Ireland.

Application Form

If you wish to join the North Belfast Branch of the Independent Labour Party, and you agree with the principles of the Party, then sign your name and address underneath and post the form, together with a P.O. for 1/- to the Secretary, North Belfast Branch, I.L.P., 48 York Street, Belfast. It will be attended to at once.!

*Name,*_____

*Address,*_____

THE BRAGGART!

Speaking in West Belfast Orange Hall on Wednesday, November 28th., 1923, Alderman John Graham in the Chair, Sir James Craig said :-

"He welcomed the bold and courageous step taken by Mr. Stanley Baldwin in going to the country and asking the people to help him to solve the terrible and increasing difficulty of unemployment. (Hear hear). He knew the minds of the people of Ulster, and he would not hesitate to take the same step as Mr. Baldwin took, and he said to them that whether the election went right or wrong on the other side of the Irish Sea, *he would solve the problem here in Ulster himself.*" (Loud applause).—The Northern Whig—9/11/23.

And this is how he did it. Unemployment in Ulster is greater now than at any time in our history and with a population of a million and a quarter, we have 60,000 unemployed. No wonder the shutters are up on his Parliament. The workers ought to move in.

Unemployment—Its Origin and Remedy.

BY JAMES MAC.

The student of economics must not assume that men are animated solely by the desire to accumulate the material wealth of the world. Wealth may be described as—whatever men secure by labouring for the satisfaction of human needs. The source of all material wealth, whether it be food, clothing, or shelter, is the land. It is only potential wealth, however, whilst it is in the land; and only becomes capable of satisfying human needs when labour power has been applied to the land to extract it. The prime essentials, therefore, in the production of wealth are Land and Labour power.

The earliest economic activities of

man were principally concerned with obtaining food. In the hunting stage, they hunted in groups to slay animals for food. In the pastoral stage, they began to breed animals, and drove their flocks from place to place as the pasturage became exhausted. A considerable advance in the progress of man was marked by what is known as the husbandry stage, or *settlement* upon the land as a cultivator of cereal.

In this stage, the principal forms of wealth were cattle and crops, while seeds and rude agricultural implements were the means of production. After the Anglo Saxons settled in Britain, there were two types of agricultural organisation; (1) Scattered homesteads with surrounding fields; and (2) the open-field estates cultivated jointly by tenants living in a village in the centre of the fields . This was known as a Manor, at the head of which was the Lord of the Manor. The Manor and the scattered homestead settlement were both entirely self-supporting, and there was little connection with the outside world. The tenants of the Manorial system did not pay rent in money, or work for wages. They had the right to cultivate a certain amount of land and retain the produce, in return for which they worked for a certain number of days a year on other land, *the produce of which went to the Lord of the Manor.* The manorial system was not, of course, from our economic point of view an ideal organisation, but it is instructive to know that **production was for use**, and there was **no unemployed problem**.

The manorial system gradually broke down. Money rents were substituted for service rents. The number of trades in the few towns increased, and men made their way to the towns to follow these trades. In agriculture, money rents and money wages became common. Production which had previously been for **use**, now became production for **profit**. This involved anticipation of other people's wants,

and the consequence was the risk and uncertainty that created the **beginnings of the unemployed problem**.

In the limited space at my disposal, it is impossible for me to comment on the "trade guilds" and the Domestic and Factory systems which prevailed in the textile industries in the eighteenth century. The important fact we have to keep in mind is, that production for profit still obtains in the twentieth century, and that is the root of **all** our problems of unemployment. How are we to **permanently** remedy the evils of the existing capitalistic system?

Fawcett in his "Political Economy" says that "no improvement of the working-classes can be permanent, unless circumstances prevent an increase of population." That is true if we consider the question of working-class improvement under the present system. If, however, the present system of production for profit, were superseded by production for use, there would be no necessity to prevent an increase of population. In production for use there would be sufficient for all. State control of the agents of production (land and labour power) would strike at the root of the unemployed problem. The word "Socialism" is unpopular amongst a large section of otherwise intelligent workers. If they do not like the name, let them call it by any other they wish. It is the **thing** that matters, not the **name**.

East Belfast Labour Party.

Since securing the premises at 5 Mountpottinger Road, in November last, we have enrolled members at every business meeting, until now we have over 200. We have the only Labour Club in Belfast, and it has been a huge success financially and is a living testimony of the hard work put in by the Recreation Committee. Our open air propaganda meetings are doing well, for we have received earnest and enthusiastic crowds of listeners. We purpose continuing them right through the summer months, and our places of meeting will be announced at "the steps" on Sundays.

Boy Scouts. A Viewpoint.
BY THE EMANCIPATED SCOUT.

The greatest activity of Boy Scouts is camping. No matter where you wander, be it wood, meadow, or country lane, you see them studying nature and learning the art of woodcraft. They are there to enjoy by observation and use, the great and varied joys which the earth has to offer. Their laws and rules of conduct are simple and plain, and are not strictly compulsory, a lot being left to the sense of honour of the individual. Before any number or group of individuals can carry on successfully, they must have some sort of code of honour, and also a democratically appointed leader. That is the Boy Scout method and success is assured in that deprtment.

The Scouts' Constitution, with all its faults of detail, is collectively speaking, very good and highly idealistic. When you see Boy Scouts marching along in a procession with flags flying, bugles playing, and a military individual at their head, you see them in their very worst aspect, and unfortunately the people of the town see most of them in that manner. The method and manner of Scout training is largely decided by the Scouter's conception of life and to a great extent by circumstances.

The great love of youth is for games and manly rivalry among one another, and this instinct can be greatly played upon for good and is in the Boy Scout movement. Through the medium of games, the team spirit of co-operation and self-sacrifice is developed, while the body is improved and mentality quickened. We must remember the motto: Mens sana in corpore sano. A Healthy Mind in a Healthy Body. At school the boys learn reading, writing and arithmethic. In the Scout movement they are taught manliness, independence of thought and consideration for others. When we get the boys of to-day thinking, the men of to-morrow

will see a great change in life. By their camping activities many economic laws are learned in a practical manner. They see land over which some Lord, Duke or Earl holds sway, and they ponder as they admire the stately beeches and tall pines, or listen to the music of the bubbling brook. How does it happen that this glorious land can be dominated by one individual; did he make it? No, decidedly no! Having thought thus, he realises the iniquity of our present system of private ownership. The Scout movement causes youths to use their eyes and their brains, and they thus use the greatest weapon against the present capitalist system.

Starters For The Great Human Race

You should support the following meetings and buy the literature on sale—

Sunday	at 3 p.m.	City Hall.
Sunday	at 7 p.m.	"Steps."
Monday	at 8 p.m.	East End.
Tuesday	at 8 p.m.	In Dock Ward.
Wednesday	at 8 p.m.	Library Street.
Thursday	at 8 p.m.	Not Fixed.
Friday	at 8 p.m.	Carlisle Circus.

The North Branch I.L.P. is conducting a special mission in the North Parliamentary Division, while George Donaldson is touring the South Division. There is a meeting **somewhere**, every night of the week and you ought to come along and help in the great work.

The Labour Opposition Of Northern Ireland

Vol. 1—No. 6 August, 1925 One Penny

BURST!

Belfast can no longer lay any claim to Civic Pride or Commercial Greatness, for its industries are bankrupt and its Civic Enterprise is warped and jaundiced. Our shipyards are derelict, our linen is dormant and the Captains of Industry who exalted private enterprise are whining to the Government for a "dole" to subsidise and conceal their failures. The nett wage for unskilled labour in the shipyards is 37/4 per week and even at that starvation level the Belfast Bosses cannot get orders or show a profit. **Private Enterprise has failed in Belfast!** Our Municipal Undertakings, on the contrary, pay £2 11s per week to their unskilled labourers, and over a year's working showed a profit of approximately £140,000.

Unfortunately for the workers, the Town Council has an overwhelming majority of "Bosses" and the profits that ought to have gone to reduced tram fares, reduced gas and reduced electricity has largely gone to reduction of rates. That is nothing short of plundering the workers' pockets to reduce the upkeep of our idle factories and shipyards, but when the Socialists expose these scandals they are voted out with contemptuous ease. Grave scandals exist in our local hospitals; the timber exposure has made our name a hissing and a bye-word among the Nations, while our Sunday Music hypocrisy stinks in the nostrils of all **religious** people.

The Unionist Majority is a danger and a menace to the community and no time should be lost in depriving them of the power they have enjoyed so long.

WHY IT DOESNT BALANCE

COST OF LIVING

SURPLUS PROFITS

Our Next Three Numbers will deal specially with our three great staple industries, viz.; Linen, Shipbuilding and Agriculture. They will contain informative and illuminating articles by technical experts, together with helpful guidance from our local Trade Union Leaders and Politicians. Make sure of your copy.

Vote Labour Next Time!

Hits and Misses.
BY MARKSMAN.

I have been asked by a correspondent are any profits being made out of beer. The answer is yes!

Company	Breweries. District.	1923-4 per cent.
Robinson's	Burton	35
Mann, Crossman	—	30
Ind. Coope	—	25
Cameron	Hartlepool	20
Showell's	Birmingham	15
Hammond's	Bradford	15
Brickwood	Portsmouth	16
Huggins & Co.,	London	15

In 1923-24 Messrs. Mann Crossman and Paulin made a net profit of £359,683. "Here's luck."

* *

Investors are advised to put their money into Booze, Bread or Beef, and Tea is also a safe investment.

* *

London Shopkeepers are doing well. Harrod's Stores made £1,761,280 net profit in 1920-3. Ordinary dividend 50½% less tax. Selfridges made £1,410,485 in 1920-3 ordinary dividend 40% tax free. The Home and Colonial Stores paid 70% 1920-22. "Good old Middleman."

* *

Portland cement is a good investment. Last year the profit amounted to £600,000. In the four years 1919-20-21-22) they 24 per cent. dividend. "Up Magheramorne."

* *

Eastwoods, Ltd., brickmakers and dealers in building materials made a profit of £126,070 in the four years to 1924. The paid up capital amounts to £287,100. Dividends aggregated 31 per cent. A bricklayer who can lay 1,000 bricks per day is not as well off as a director in Eastwoods, Ltd.

* *

Eastwoods, Ltd., are a public company. Local brickyard concerns do not publish the amount of their profits. Price of bricks per 1,000, Belfast and London are as under:—

	Belfast.	London.
Perforated Brick	£5 7 6	£4 17 0
Solid Brick	5 0 0	4 5 0
Stock Brick	3 5 0	2 17 0

The Pre-war price of brick in Belfast was 25/- per 1,000. What has Sir Crawford got to say about our local profiteers?

* *

British Shipping Companies are charging 38/- per ton for carrying goods from Newport to Calcutta, but the same companies carry goods from Antwerp to Calcutta for 13/7 per ton. This proves who is anti-British.

* *

Cheap transport is one of the reasons for great general prosperity in Queensland. This is why railway directors don't like the working people voting Labour. At the moment, Queensland has only 4.9 per cent. unemployed; Northern Ireland has 24.9 per cent.

* *

It costs 26/10d. to maintain a poor person in Aberdeen Parish Council Home, yet a man, wife and two children receive only 2d. more than that from the State Unemployment Fund in Belfast.

* *

The Minister of Labour in the Imperial Parliament proposes to steal 6½ million pounds from the unemployed of Great Britain, at a time when the numbers on the register are leaping upwards, and Mr. John Andres murmurs "parallel legislation."

* *

New Zealand sought a loan of 7 million pounds on the London money market, but the financial British Patriots said No! and yet New Zealand is our biggest purchaser per head of population, but the same rich patriots (?) who refused to help New Zealand have subscribed £2,000,000 to a Hungarian milling and sugar refining company.

* *

In 1924 Industrial companies to the number of 1,411 increased their profits by more than £8,000,000. That's why we are poor.

* *

Courtaulds of Art Silk fame are doing well. The Capital has been increased from 2 million pounds in 1904 to 20 million pounds to-day. Had you been a fortunate holder in 1904 you would have got 1,200 per cent. last year.

* *

In 1924 Germany asked for a loan of 40

million which was subscribed ten times over by hard faced British Capitalists. Who said "Huns," eh?

* *

It is certainly a crime to be poor and the Lisburn Magistrate who sent a 17 years old girl to prison for fourteen days for wandering abroad and having no visible means of support should be knighted. Please note, I said Lisburn *not* Moscow.

* *

Mr. Neville Chamberlain says — "Birmingham Municipal Bank was started in 1916. To-day there are 167,000 depositors while the deposits are upwards of £5,500,000. The Bank has not cost the ratepayers a penny from start to finish and has a reserve of £58,000." I respectfully suggest that our Belfast Labour Councillors get their heads together and push these facts home to the Council.

* *

Labour Men of the North.
BY BOB M'CLUNG.
Senator Bob Dorman.

If it be an honour to be elected to the Senate of Northern Ireland, then I don't know of any one more deserving of the honour than Bob Dorman.

Many of us suffered for our opinions during the years 1920-21-22 and were very dilatory in coming out into the open-air to declare our faith in the Socialist Cause; not so with our Comrade. 1923-24-25 has found him at the Custom House Steps, Belfast, preaching the Brotherhood of Man and the Fatherhood of God. Sunday after Sunday finds him stating his belief in the coming of the Socialist Commonwealth.

Born in 1859 he joined the Navy as a boy and was invalided and discharged from the Navy in 1880. After the formation of the I.L.P. in 1893 he acted as Secretary of the Dublin Branch.

As inspector for a life insurance company his duties took him to all parts of Ireland, and he has been identified with the local labour parties in Galway, Waterford and Cork, where

Henry Ford pays 105 dollars as a monthly minimum wage in his trans-Atlantic vessels, his competitors pay 60 dollars only. Come on all ye private traders, try high wages as a cure for bad times. There is another way to get good wages. Let the wage-earners organise 100% and they can make their own terms and conditions of Labour.

* *

Last month I told you about Leeds trams. Hull Municipal Tramways are also doing well, they made a profit last year of £28,390. It has been decided to allocate £12,000 to relief of rates. The total profit, despite the introduction of cheap fares, was over £33,000.

* *

Last year True Form Boots Co., Ltd., made a profit of £172,949. Stead and Simpson made £72,450 out of selling boots and shoes.

Senator Bob Dorman.

his voice and pen were always at the disposal of the rackrented tenants, the poor and the oppressed. Returning to Belfast in 1912 he at once threw himself into the work of the I.L.P. and becoming a member of the North Branch, he assisted in forming a Socialist Sunday School, and in 1916 became Superintendent and endeared himself to the young people of the North I.L.P.

Has contested Court Ward in the Poor-Law and City Council elections and during his three years work as a missionary of Socialism at the Custom House Steps has received scores of threatening letters. But inside the Socialist and Labour ranks everybody loves Bob Dorman.

The White Scourge.

I have been privileged to read the report of Dr. P.S. Walker who is in charge of the Municipal Sanatorium at Whiteabbey.

During the year 1924, we find that 490 cases were admitted into the Sanatorium and of these 81 were children. Dr. Walker reports that "Children respond to treatment much more favourably and rapidly than do adults, so that the clinical and physical pictures usually show steady improvement from the day of admission onwards." He also mentions the necessity of a covered playground for the children, as at the present time they are confined to the wards in inclement weather. Another regrettable thing is that *economic* circumstances compel adults to leave *before they are sufficiently cured*, the reason being that they want home to earn something to keep the home together. Dr. Walker pays just tribute to a Belfast man, Dr. Henry MacCormac, who was a pioneer of outdoor treatment for consumptive patients, and he was often summoned for breaking windows in houses where he visited the sick, if he found that the windows would not open. Might I draw Dr. Walker's attention to a namesake of his who was also a pioneer and spent years of his life in the interests of the sick poor. Twelve years before the passing of the Health Insurance Act, Willie Walker the Socialist, at a meeting of the Belfast Poor Law Guardians proposed, "That a special Committee of six be appointed to consider and report as to the desirability of purchasing a site whereon an hospital adapted for the treatment of consumption can be erected." This proposal of Walker's in July, 1899 was defeated, only Dr. J. Stewart and Mr. J. Harrison voting for it, but Walker was a fighter and persisted in bringing his motion forward time and again until the Guardians acquired the site at Whiteabbey, and to me the "Abbey Sanatorium" is a monument to Willie Walker, the Socialist Poor Law Guardian of Belfast. We of the I.L.P. fully appreciate the good work which is being done by Dr's. Trimble, Bailie, Walker and Malcolm, and their assistants, but we believe that most people take consumption because they are herded together without fresh air and do not get an opportunity to live the life that God and Nature intended human beings should live. We believe there is little use in having an ambulance at the bottom of the cliff trying to cure the unfortunate people who fall over, unless our public representatives erect a barrier at the top to prevent the disaster. Dr. M'Cormac wrote in 1855. "Consumption is in every case preventable" and if that is true why don't we prevent it by re-organising society so that every child born into the world will have an equal opportunity with every other child. We can produce enough to ensure that everyone will have enough food, clothing and shelter, and opportunities for enjoying good air and sunshine which are just as important as good food.

If Socialism means anything it means equal opportunity for all the sons and daughters of men.

Emigration

Victoria,
Australia,

Dear Comrade,

Good luck to your wee paper, a copy of which has reached me here in Victoria. I want you to issue a note of warning to the unemployed of Northern Ireland and let them know that this is not a land flowing with milk and honey. If there are any jobs vacant in the town they are snapped up by the "Aussies" (Australians). Immigrants are coming every week and are called "Pommies," they are sent to work for "Cockys" (Farmers). They work from daylight until dark for £1 per week.

I was a Tradesman in Harland & Wolffs before I came out here, and now I am a Farmer's boy in Australia, Oh, what a life! Did you milk Rosie and Biddy? then go and feed the pigs and don't forget to chop the wood. I think the following bit of doggerel sums up the position here:-

"I'm a well-to-do 'Cocky' with plenty of
land
And to till my broad acres I needed a hand;
And they sent me a "Pommy" just fresh
from the boat;
A wonderful Pommy just six feet in length,
Could eat like a horse though he hadn't
much strength
His wages were small but he did what he
could
In cutting the thistles and chopping the
wood;
In brushing the horses and digging the
drains,
In welding and mending the links on the
chains;
And when the time came for raising his pay
I said 'I was sorry" and sent him away."

Signed "Ballymacarrett Billie."

Book Reviews

"The Great Drama Of Nature' by *Frank Nolan* price 6d. from all Booksellers appears at an opportune moment, because it is all about Evolution and tells us about evolution in the Solar World, the Animal World, and the Social World. In language of exquisite beauty and simplicity, the author unfolds an enchanting story of birth, growth and decay, and leaves the mind refreshed by its contact with the wide spaces of human development. We enjoyed the book.

Two New I.L.P. Pamphlets.

In **"The Black Man's Rights"** (I.L.P. Publication Department, 14 Great George Street, S.W., price 2d.) Mr. Charles Roden Buxton deals with the importance and significance of what is called the Native Races question. He explains the implications of British possessions in Africa, and points out how the exploitation of the Black Man will lead sooner or later, to the degradation of the white worker also. Mr. Buxton weighs up in a calm, judicial fashion the harm and the good done by the exploitation of the Native Races and shows how the natives are fleeced in connection with lands, forced labour and taxation. He advocates that the International Labour Office should be entrusted with devising a Code of Native Rights and securing its adoption in all territories where needed.

"Banks Prices And Unemployment' by John MacLeod, (I.L.P. Publication Department, 14, Great George Street, S.W., price 2d.) is a simple and readable statement about the Bank Rate, Bank Credits, the effect of Money upon prices of commodities, depreciation, price level and the effect of prices upon wages—the pamphlet is to be highly commended. It will help you to understand why prices are forced down when the amount of Money in circulation is increased, and why when the value of Money is reduced your food costs you more.

Short, trenchant articles are always welcome. All MSS. must be accompanied by the Name and Address of the Contributor, though not necessarily for publication. Unsuitable MSS. will be returned ONLY if a stamped addressed envelope is enclosed.

Address all communications to The Editor, 48 York Street, Belfast.

N.C.L.C. Summer School
At Ballycarry.

Last month at Ballycarry saw the first Summer School in Ireland to be held under the auspices of the N.C.L.C.

The site of the school was admirable. A large Hut perched on top of a cliff overlooking the sea, with a background of green-clad hills.

Comrade Ellis was the principal lecturer, choosing for his subject a series of lectures, beginning with the Economic Condition of Pre-War Europe and ending with a brilliant outline of the effects of the Dawes' Plan on the workers of Europe. I would strongly advise the young and old men—especially the latter—to take a course of economics as taught by the N.C.L.C. in Belfast.

Other speakers were Wm. M'Mullen, M.P., and Hugh Gemmell. Comrade M'Mullen spoke on the "Irish Labour Movement" and demonstrated quite clearly the urgent need for the Labour Movement in Ireland—whilst not neglecting the International side of the movement, to concentrate more and more on the problems that are confined to Ireland.

Hugh Gemmell delivered, as is usual with him, a well-reasoned speech on "The Basis of Correct Thinking," warning his audience against taking anything for granted. As true Plebeians he asked us to question everything, an advice which we certainly intend to follow, even to questioning Labour and Labour Leaders.

Not the least important lecture delivered at the school was one by Frank Nolan, "On the Need for an International Language." Nolan put forward the claims of Esperanto, showing clearly that it was the only medium that could serve, and be accepted by the Nations of the world.

The students who attended the school were not asked to listen all day to Lectures, but were allowed to enjoy themselves to their heart's content with swimming, boating and rambles. In the evening before turning in, Comrade Ellis read to us Upton Sinclair's Play, "The Singing Jail-birds," and Ernest Toller's Masterpiece, "Masses and Men".

Altogether a great week was spent at Ballycarry and despite the efforts of Wm. Grant M.P., I am confident that we will long have the Hut at Ballycarry where Labour men and women can retire in order to study and play.

On behalf of the students, I am asked to convey our thanks to Comrades H. Cleeton, Tom Dickie and the others who, under great difficulties, procured and erected the Hut and made possible the holding of the School. Also to Comrades Hugh Gemmell, Wm. M'Mullen M.P., and last but not least Comrade Ellis. Regret was keenly felt by all the students at not having Comrade H. Midgley lecture on the Linen Industry. No one knows more about this important Industry than does Harry, and I hope that it is his intention to deliver the Lecture at an early date. — *Dick M'Connell.*

The Latest Convert.

Sir Malcolm Macnaghton, Ulster Unionist M.P. for Londonderry, speaking in the British House of Commons on Tuesday, 14th July, proclaimed, though rather inadvertently, his conversion to the fact that Ireland is a nation. Are we to take it that he believes in the unification of the Government of his nation? **Truly a straw may show how the wind blows.**

100,000 Pennies.
Court Ward Divisional Labour Party.

We are out to win Court Ward for Labour. We want to build a Hall as a centre for all our activities. We want it right now, and YOUR PENNIES can do it. We appeal to Trade Unionists, Labour Men, and all who sympathise with us to subscribe to this fund. Any sum, much or little, will be welcomed and acknowledged in these columns. Send your "Sub" to . . .

Tommy Geehan, 15 Tyrone Street, Belfast.

Prev. acknowledged	480 pennies	£2
Wm. M'Mullen, M.P.	120 pennies	10/-
Rev. A Agnew, B.A.	60 pennies	5/-
A Friend	27 pennies	2/3
Miss L. Geehan	36 pennies	3/-
G. M'Bride	120 pennies	10/-

South Belfast Vacancy.

What the Labour Candidate (Alderman G. M. Donaldson) would do with the Railways as taken from the Railway Commission Minority Report presented by him and Mr. Sam Kyle, M.P. for North Belfast on the 30th November, 1922.

1. The Northern Irish Railway system is unremunerative and does not attain the standard which we consider to be urgently required in the public interest.

2. The causes of the present state of the Northern Irish Railways are to be found to some extent in the economic conditions of the country, to some extent in the wastefulness of a system under which 1,259 miles of railway are controlled by thirteen different administrations.

3. The wages and salaries paid by the Northern Irish Railway Companies have already been cut to a minimum nor can any further reduction be contemplated.

4. The amalgamation or unification under private management of the Northern Irish Railways while it would mitigate the wastefulness of the present system, would not secure that the railway system would be run primarily in the interests of the community and would create a private monopoly inimical to the public interest.

5. The nationalisation of the railways of Northern Ireland would secure substantial economies in respect of reduced directors' fees, more economical methods of renewals and repairs, better utilisation of rolling stock, standardisation of the light railways, with a view to their eventual change to standard gauge, and more economical methods of raising capital.

6. The nationalisation of the Northern Irish Railways would further secure that the primary purpose of the railway system would be to promote the economic and industrial well-being of the community, would make possible extensions and developments which are beyond the scope of private enterprise, would relieve the baronies of their liability for the railways in their districts, and would insure that liability for any deficit upon the railways would fall upon the authority charged with their control.

7. The Northern Irish Railways cannot be satisfactorily organised otherwise than as an integral part of a nationalised railway system covering the whole of Ireland.

8. In the event of the Southern Irish Government being agreeable to such a course, an arbitration tribunal should be appointed by the Northern and Southern Parliaments to decide upon terms of purchase of the Irish Railways.

9. This tribunal should have regard to the capital value of the Irish Railways as reflected in Stock Exchange prices.

10. A joint Commission, appointed by and responsible to the Northern and Southern Irish Parliaments should be responsible for the general control and policy of the nationalised railways.

11. A representative national railway council should be appointed to advise the Joint Commission on matters of policy, including questions of wages and conditions of service of the railway workers, and to be responsible for the actual execution of the Joint Commission's decisions on matters of policy.

12. The decision of matters affecting the wages and conditions of service of the railway workers should rest with a joint meeting of the Joint Commission and the National Railway Council.

13. In the event of the Southern Irish Government not being agreeable to nationalisation and joint working of all the Irish Railways, the Northern Irish Government should acquire the railways wholly situated in Northern Irish territory, and should operate these through a Minister of Transport assisted and advised by a representative Railway Council.

14. During the period which must elapse before the nationalisation of the Irish or Northern Irish Railways can be effected, wages and salaries on the Northern Irish Railways should be stabilised at their present level, and the Northern Irish Government should guarantee the Northern Irish Railways a sum equal to half that guaranteed to them by the English Government during the period of war control.

Every Socialist, Labour man and Trade Unionist should rally to Donaldson's assistance in the fight for South Belfast.

Men and money are urgently needed.

Britons Never Shall Be?

BY JAMES MAC.

In Howitt's "Aristocracy of England" there is told a story of an Indian and a Kentuckian who once made an agreement to hunt in company, and divide equally the game which they might chance to kill. Unfortunately, a crow and a wild turkey were all they shot. "Well," said the Kentuckian, at the end of the day, "as we are to divide equally, you take the crow and I'll take the turkey." "How's that?" enquired the Indian. The Kentuckian in rapid accents repeated his proposal, to which the Indian, after a blank and puzzled look, consented, but with the remark:- "It sounds all very fair; but, somehow or other, *you* always get the turkey, and *I* always get the crow."

This is a good illustration of the manner in which the capitalists in all ages and countries have dealt with the working-classes. Under the iniquitous system of Production for Profit, they have invariably contrived to keep the turkey, and put off the poor bamboozled people with the crow. To-day Capitalism is plotting by underhand methods to reduce wages and lengthen the number of hours of labour. The recent parrot-cry of "speeding up production" in order "to restore our lost trade," is only a part of the insidious campaign.

An increase in the efficiency of labour increases the amount of wealth produced; but labour does not—and never did— under Capitalistic production, receive its just proportion of the increase resulting from greater efficiency. The motto of the workers to-day should be "educate and organize." If they do not educate themselves in that part of Economics which comprehends labour problems, and their solution, they are liable to be deceived by the powerful forces arrayed against them—

LIFE.

Life, eternal problem—striving on
    To overcome environment, towards death;
Cheating itself ever and anon,
    By mingling joy with pain in ebbing breath.
Though life remains the same, yet outlooks alter;
    A hideous nightmare or a pleasant dream;
We either walk robust, erect, or falter,
    In misery doomed, or think what might have been.
What strange perspective causes us to give
    Reaction to our feelings as we write;
Recording all the things for which we live,
    Lifting the veil of darkness, seeking light.
Our minds in agonising torment yield
    To every cursed ordeal in this sphere.
Disappointments, doubts, sans mental shield
    To repulse danger, or resist our fear.
Like petty insects crawling in the slime;
    Struggling to obtain a better grip
Impulse urging us perhaps to crime—
    Reaching out to grasp the Master Whip;
Buffeted, kicked, or shouldered to the wall,
    In wretched grief, each fighting for his share;
Responding not to weaker Brother's call,
    Each for himself—reck not how others fare.
In harmony the universe revolves;
    While nature decorates our Mother Earth;
Yet mankind's destiny remains unsolved—
    Condemned to struggle from his very birth;
Live on! live on! to find a parallel,
    By which our Social Life to regulate;
Live on! live on! and just remember hell
    Was never meant for earth at any rate;
Accelerate our progress in the North;
    Foundations lay to speed the coming day,
Reflecting all of educative worth,
    To mould the workers in a finer clay.

—C. J. M'C.

Capitalism and Aristocracy. It was the economic ignorance of the French peasant, in the eighteenth century, which led to his political subjugation by the nobles.

In France, previous to the great Revolution, the whole burden of taxation was borne by the working-classes. In fact, one of the *immediate* causes of the French Revolution, was the immunity from taxation enjoyed by the French nobles and clergy. In Britain, after the Revolution of 1688, the first step of the Aristocracy under William 111 was to secure possession of *all* the land by "cajoling the crown out of its private estate, and flinging it as *a pauper on the people*." Then, with consummate cunning, they divided themselves into two belligerent, political parties under the names of Whig and Tory, and assumed the real Government of the country. Until within recent times, they kept up a fierce struggle for the reins of office. It did not matter which party won; *the workers had no direct representation*. It is time for the workers to wake up and not be misguided any longer by the modern capitalists' appeal to their "patriotism."

In the eighteenth century, the great Dr. Johnson (England's first lexicographer) defined "Patriotism" as "the last refuge of a scoundrel." Seventy-five years ago, Thomas Carlyle in one of the "Latter Day Pamphlets" said, that the population of England was "twenty seven millions, *mostly fools*." Since then the population of Britain has increased to a very considerable extent. It is now approximately forty-four millions The question is: are they still "mostly fools?" Are the working-classes still content to take the crow, whilst the wily capitalist quietly appropriates the turkey?

Dealing with the working-class conditions of eighty years ago, Howitt says (in his "Aristocracy"):—

"Free do we call ourselves, while we stand in the eye of Heaven shaking our chains, and the very angels blush at the ignominious spectacle." These quoted words might well apply to our own time. We have been slaves in the past. Let us now arise, cast off our chains, educate, organise and prepare for the great opportunity which is certain to come in the near future When that time comes, we will then be in a position to successfully translate words into action by putting a strong Labour Government in power.

Dock Ward Labour Party.

It is quite a pleasant business to transform into a report the expanding activities of Dock Ward Labour Party. Historically typical of Labour's progress, it has been developed by steady propaganda, and the result is reflected in the workers' anticipation of meetings which are held every Tuesday night (8 p.m.) at the corner of New Lodge Road and North Queen Street.

Following close upon the Municipal triumph of Councillor Midgley, Dock Ward Labour Party was formed to cement the reaction against Capitalism, by the untiring efforts of Comrades Kane and M'Allister—efforts which have been prolific in the production of a sturdy party which will respond in the future and oppose those who are incapable to represent our class.

To Our Correspondents.

We regret that many articles are crowded out, owing to lack of space, while others arrived too late to allow any time for consideration. Frankly, we need a much larger paper and a full time staff, but in the meantime, we must all work heard to push the sales of *The Opposition,* and thereby get a weekly instead of a monthly. If every Comrade would get us a new subscriber we could obtain a weekly very soon.— ED.

The Workers' Union

desire to draw the attention to the following list of **fair employers.**

Picture Houses:
The Picture House, Royal Avenue.
Classic Picture House, Castle Lane.
Clonard Picture House, Falls Road.

Hotels:
"Kensington," Gt. Victoria Street.
Montague Arms, Portstewart.
N.C.C. Hotel, Portrush.
Donard Buildings Hotel, Newcastle.

Cafes:
Imperial Picture House Cafe, Belfast.
Trocedero Cafe, Ann Street, Belfast.
The Picture House Cafe, Royal Ave., Belfast.

Belfast Hairdressers:
Hoffman's High Street.
Rottger's, Bedford Street.
M'Mullan & Chappell, Donegall Road.
Coulter, Donegal Street.
Rea, Donegall Street.
Coulter, High Street.
Ferguson, Lombard Street.
Thompson, Ann Street.
M'Gowan & Lyness, Ann Street.
Higginson, Ann Street.
M'Grath, Ann Street.
M'Cullagh, Ann Street.
Graham, Chichester Street.
M'Guffin, Great Victoria Street.
M'Coy, Rosemary Street.
Doherty, Great Victoria Street.
De Vito, Skipper Street.
M'Alevey, Donegall Road.
Cahoon, Donegall Road.
M'Aleeman, Antrim Road.
Murray & Co., William Street.
Dollaghan, William Street South.
Watterson, Ormeau Road.
Rea, Ormeau Road.
Cinnamond, Ormeau Road.

Corrections or additions to the above list will be made on application to District Secretary, 13 Skipper Street, Belfast.

"And it is important to remember that we fearlessly accepted an entire change in the present structure of our social system, by which the present community shall own and control the means of life for the benefit of all as against the system whereby the few profit and the majority suffer." A .A. PURCELL.

CONGRATULATIONS!

To Councillor Harry Midgley on his enthusiastic re-election as Organising Secretary of the Irish Linen Lappers and Warehouse Workers Trade Union. Harry tops the bill, and fills the bill.

To Robert Dorman, of the North Belfast I.L.P., hereinafter, and for the purposes of the Act for the next eight years *at least*, to be referred to as Senator Bob Dorman. Some people get an upper cut and the K.O. Bob got the upper chamber and it's O.K.

To A. A. Purcell, M.P. who won Forest of Dean for Socialism and is coming over to tell us all about it. He is a big man, physically and mentally, and his smiling eyes are dreadfully deceptive of the tremendous vitality that lies in the brain behind. You should go to hear him.

"The Opposition" is steadily growing in Power, Circulation and Influence. What we need now is a Weekly, and every new reader and every fresh subscriber is a definite step towards that goal.

Starters For The Great Human Race

You should support the following meetings and buy the literature on sale—

Sunday	at 3 p.m.	I.L.P.	City Hall.
Sunday	at 7 p.m.	"	"Steps."
Sunday	at 8 p.m.	Lab.Pty	John St.
Monday	at 8 p.m.	" "	East End.
Tuesday	at 8 p.m.	" "	New Lodge Rd.
Wedne.	at 8 p.m.	I.L.P.	Library Street.
Thursday	at 8 p.m.	I.L.P.	Ardilea St.
Friday	at 8 p.m.	Lab.Pty	Carlisle Circus.

The Labour Opposition Of Northern Ireland

Vol. 1—No. 7.   September, 1925.   One Penny

What Purcell Thinks Of Belfast.

"And it is important to remember that we fearlessly accepted an entire change in the present structure of our social system, by which the community shall own and control the means of life for the benefit of all as against the system whereby the few profit and the majority suffer."

A WONDERFUL EVENT.

On February 6th, 1919, was held at Belfast a demonstration of Solidarity, an event I have always regarded as unique in Working Class history. The City and surrounding districts were in the throes of what it has been my good fortune to refer to in many parts of England and the Continent of Europe as a highly important page in our Working Class struggles.

The struggle commenced in the Shipyards; it then spread to every employing establishment for miles around, until practically all workers, excepting sections on very short hours of work, were involved.

But the Demonstration was the thing. I think it was a Thursday. Hour after hour the processions swept along the Grosvenor, Falls, and Shankill Roads, Donegall Place and Royal Avenue; Queen's Bridge was a seething mass of surging humanity, as the procession coiled round and round in upon itself, until it formed a solid mass encircling the beautiful island building, a noble edifice, expressing good workmanship—the Belfast City Hall.

I have witnessed demonstrations in big cities like London, Berlin, Vienna, Leningrad and Moscow, but in no instance have I witnessed higher discipline than that displayed by the tremendous mass on that February day

(To Page 2, Column 1)

A Word To Mothers.

BY MARY H. KYLE.

Each day, we housewives are vitally concerned with the cost of food, and the nearer we get to the end of pay week the more urgent does the problem become.

We are apt to think it is all a question of good wages and good house-keeping—a family affair in fact, but we have got to realise that it is partly a political question too. Until we become good politicians (Socialists of course) we shall never be good housewives. The present capitalist system means robbery, and the housewife must pay in high prices for the booty that a few lucky individuals reap. The price of food is a woman's question first and foremost, and women must take the lead in fighting for the abolition of the present system of exploitation and high prices. If they do not, why should anyone else help make them make ends meet?

Once we realise the facts we must act, and act together. The facts are obvious, and although we could quote illustrations of the high profits made out of the necessities of life of the people, we think that those of some of the Tea Companies are sufficient.

Take the following items and think them over.

S. India Tea Estates, 1924-25.—Ordinary Dividend 45%.

Alliance Tea Comp., Ceylon, 1924—Ord. Div—45%.

Ceylon Tea Plantations, 1924—Ord. Div —50%.

A 100% Share Bonus was distributed in 1919.

(To Page 2, Column 2)

in 1919, when the Belfast Workers opened its far-flung mass to enable a funeral cortege to pass through, with due reverence, then instantly close up again to proceed with the "orders of the day."

I have always held that Belfast would "come back".

It will not fail, it may delay. Industrial Organisation is a weathery sort of thing in its march, but it does not default, some stages are larger and swifter than others.

Thus it's grammar, and it must win through because it cannot lose. It is the destiny of our Class to be so, it has its own logic and persistency.

A. A. PURCELL.

Chubwa Tea, 1923-24,—Ordinary dividend, 50%.

A 100% share bonus was distributed in 1924.

Standard Tea of Ceylon, 1924.—Ord. Div—80%.

Quite a nice little sum of money to be made out of shares in tea evidently, and yet we are told we must have competition as a safeguard against exploitation.

No, we must have Socialism and secure good and cheap food for our families.

Hits And Misses.
BY MARKSMAN.

"The Six Counties may adopt Prohibition, a policy to which he (Sir James Craig) is opposed though *he is himself a teetotaller*." Herald and County Down Independent 25/7/25.

Well, now, a joke's a joke.

* *

"On his retirement (from the Premiership) he (Sir James Craig) will be offered a peerage and will no doubt return to England, for it will be recalled that *he had no home of his own in Ulster*, when he became leader in succession to Sir Edward Carson." Herald and County Down Independent 25/7/25.

Belfast alone is short of 10,000 working-class houses, not to speak of other towns, yet the workers of Ulster bought and paid for Stormont Castle and installed Sir James in regal magnificence. Let us think of ourselves in future, for charity begins AT HOME.

* *

Questioner at the "Steps" last Sunday. "How would you treat old age pensioners in Northern Ireland?" Speaker . . . Monkey Glands!

* *

Now that a tax on Bachelors is proposed in the Free State, all the eligibles will be taking a single ticket into the Six Counties. Joking apart, the Capitalist Class regard it as a crime for a worker not to marry. If all

the workers were to remain unmarried there would be no children to carry on industry at a profit for the bosses, and that would end Capitalism.

* *

What is behind all this Russian propaganda in Belfast? First we had the Russian Cabaret in the Ulster Hall, Belfast, and then the Russian Cossacks in the Balmoral Show Grounds. Why, our Linen lords will be demanding flax from Russia next!

* *

Dr. W. C. Dawes, lecturing at the Savoy Hotel, London, said, "Don't cook your food, eat it raw. At one unfired six course dinner, Mrs. Dawes had 39 articles of food on the table." Lucky man Dr. Dawes; I know one family of unemployed workers who had 2 articles of food on the table each day. Porridge and buttermilk for breakfast, dinner and tea.

* *

Londonderry warns A. J. Cook of the consequences of revolution. Oh, what a joke! Remember 1912.!

* *

According to Belfast Harbour Commissioners: "During the six months ending 30th June 1925 we exported 73 asses and did not import any" There are plenty of asses in Belfast yet, and you will find them voting for the Tory candidate at election times.

* *

The population of Ireland is about 5 million people. Yet we are cursed with 46 different railway companies.

* *

BELFAST—Ropework Company Ltd., have declared a dividend of 7 per cent. less income tax for the half year, £15,000 being placed to reserve. Not quite bankrupt yet you see!

* *

DERRY—County Councillor Christie, speaking on August 8th, 1925, said, "If they went into one of the Government offices in Belfast, the number of officials found there was a disgrace to any civilised country. They were as numerous as rats." Most unkind of you Mr. Christie!

* *

LARNE—Urban Council "yearns for a return to the practical commonsense and prompt methods of the old Local Government Board and condemns the Ministry of Finance, N.I., for defective organisation and lack of sympathy." Resolution passed 7/8/25. Disloyal sentiments these!

* *

CLONES—On Monday 3/8/25, the people of Clones enjoyed an excursion to Warrenpoint. Orange bands, Foresters and A.O.H. bands marched together in procession. That's the stuff that smashes up Bigotry.

* *

PORTADOWN—At a meeting of the Town Council held recently, Mr. Locke reported "that a house in Quarry's Row was not fit for a pig to live in. The woman who occupied the house had hanging on the wall two certificates of sons who served in the war and who he thought were killed in the war." Where are the hard faced profiteers who told the Portadown people they would get "Homes fit for heroes?"

* *

LURGAN—had 1,909 unemployed workers, and 784 on short time on 3/8/25. At the corresponding period last year, the number of persons totally unemployed was 277 and on short time 23. And Sir James Craig promised that he would solve unemployment in Ulster. Oh! the Braggart!

* *

CANADA—Mr. James Simpson, Secretary of the Canadian Labour Party says that last February there were 30,000 unemployed in Toronto alone. Yet Shipping Companies are crying out for more and more labourers for Canada.

* *

ABERDEEN—Municipality own 105 trams, 8 motor buses and 7 motor coaches, and have made a gross profit of £38,555. Socialism pays every time.

Johnny Walker (Distillers) 1924-25 paid a dividend of 21½ per cent. and the shareholders are not grumbling. Of course, some people are easily pleased . . . when they get all they want.

* *

A battleship of the Rodney class costs for upkeep £432,960 annually. And that is *one* of the reasons why the poor are poor!

* *

There are 60,000 people in Northern Ireland anxious and willing to work and cannot get work to do. In January, 1925, the figures were 23,000. Now that Sir James Craig has defined his personal position with regard to booze, he will perhaps, make an effort to redeem his promise, for Mr. Grant, M.P., says that Sir James never breaks a promise.

Our Visitors.

Ellen Wilkinson, M.P., comes on the 16th October.

Davy Kirkwood, M.P. comes on the 30th October.

And Frank Smith, W. Lorimer and W. Sherwood come on September the 26th.

It looks like another heat wave!

TOMMY GEEHAN, Secretary of Court Ward Divisional Labour Party, goes to Canada next month. That means a very distinct loss to us, because Tommy was a hard and uncomplaining worker, and it was under his Secretaryship that the Division made its great forward drive.

In his new home we wish him health and happiness and we hope that he will write to tell us all about it.

And we know that our loss is Canada's gain.

Labour Men Of The North
BY BOB M'CLUNG.

Councillor Harry Midgley, Belfast.

I can remember "Harry" presiding at an I.L.P. meeting at the "Steps" when he was 14 years of age, and even then he was a ready speaker and keenly interested in public affairs. He served his apprenticeship as a joiner in Belfast Shipyard, and assisted in the building of the Langley Street I.L.P. Hall after the foundation stone was laid by James Keir Hardie.

He assisted in two of the early parliamentary fights in North Belfast, joined the British Army in 1914 and was demobilised in 1919. Recommenced work in Harland & Wolff's as a joiner and was appointed Organising Secretary of the Irish Linen Lappers and Warehouse Workers Trade Union in October, 1919, reappointed 1922 and 1925.

Acted as Secretary of Labour Party, N.I., for over two years. Has been parliamentary candidate on three occasions. In 1921 he stood as candidate for East Belfast at a time when it was considered dangerous to label oneself Labour or Socialist; contested West Belfast in the elections for the Imperial Parliament in December, 1923 and again in October, 1924, his opponent being Sir Robert Lynn, Editor of "Northern Whig". Midgley polled over 21,000 votes on each occasion; was elected Councillor for Dock Ward in January, 1925; is a frequent contributor to the Labour Press and a merciless critic of Capitalism by tongue and pen, and he has also found time to write a fine collection of poems which are on sale entitled, "Thoughts from Flanders." Of a cheery disposition, Harry has hosts of friends and I feel sure he will play a big part in the bringing about of a new and happy Ireland.

When you've read *"The Opposition,"* **pass it on to a pal.**

Councillor Harry Midgley, Belfast.

Notes and News.

Friendly rivalry is a splendid thing, and Court Ward Divisional Labour Party is ahead of the others with propaganda, distribution of leaflets, sales of literature, sales of "Oppositions" and canvassing for the register. They're a lively bunch and no error. Now, Divisions, what about a spurt to catch up.

Glad to see the "West" awake again and beginning to kick out. The penalty of being a pioneer is, that while you are consolidating your advance, the next "division" carries on the attack.

Would like to hear more from the "South-West." But perhaps you are "boring from within" as Daniel De Leon would have said, and making steady progress. Anyway, the South vacancy is a great opportunity for active propaganda, and should be exploited.

Dock Ward is very steady, and so is the East Belfast Labour Party. Their propaganda is very effective and they "mind their own business" by directing attention to local needs and local abuses. We need a great deal more "stay at home" stuff.

Coleraine I.L.P. reports steady progress, and new members at each meeting. Under the urge of John Nevin, James Forsythe and George Simpson, Coleraine should soon be a centre of Fellowship, Education and Organisation.

We want a MAN in Lurgan, one in Banbridge, one in Ballymoney, and one in Richhill with enough enterprise, intiative and "brass neck" to get a Branch of the Independent Labour Party started in each of these districts. Who will be the pioneer? Drop a line to the Editor and all particulars will be sent by return. And if you want a Speaker, we will send one anywhere, provided you pay his rail fare and give him his food. You must be courageous, and determined, and you must do the thing yourselves.

Clifton Branch I.L.P., Belfast, is the latest recruit to our movement and well over 30 names on the books bids fair to growing up strong and big. On behalf of the entire Movement we send our greetings and sincere wishes for success and long life.

The Joint Committee of the I.L.P. Belfast is having a strenuous time, and Propaganda is conducted at white heat. All the Speakers and Chairmen are rallying to the "big push" and if you have not yet joined in the game, then come along and report and we will fix you up good and plenty.

The Fellowship Movement in the I.L.P. is tremendously popular, and on every Fellowship night the hall in York Street is crowded. Fellowship and Music makes the time swing merrily round, and when the I.L.P. Dramatic Club gets thoroughly going we will have nights of memory. For Education, Fellowship, Culture and progressive politics, the I.L.P. leads the field.

—HOTSPUR.

COUNCILLOR ELECT.

Comrade Jack M'Mullan, Slumdom Jack—has been chosen by Court Ward to contest the Corporation Vacancy in January. He is an out and out Socialist, a member of the I.L.P. and if his popularity is any criterion of victory, then in January he will be— COUNCILLOR ELECTED.

100,000 PENNIES.

Court Ward Divisional Labour Party

We are out to win Court Ward for Labour. We want to build a Hall as a centre for all our activities. We want it right now, and YOUR PENNIES can do it. We appeal to Trade Unionists, Labour Men, and all who sympathise with us to subscribe to this fund. Any sum, much or little, will be welcomed and acknowledged in these columns. Send your "Sub" to . .

Paul Carleton, 6 Concord Street.

Prev. acknowledged

	843 pennies	£3	10	3
PER—				
M'Tier Street	30 pennies	0	2	6
Ballysillan	42 pennies	0	3	6
Hugh Baxter	60 pennies	0	5	0
D. Lundy	60 pennies	0	5	0
T. Cain	30 pennies	0	2	6

WOMEN'S SECTION
(Labour Party Northern Ireland.)
ELLEN WILKINSON, M.P.
Is Coming To Belfast
ON 16th October, 1925.
Secure Your Ticket Early From Any
Member Of The Above Section.
Sixpence Each.

How The Ulster Linen Lords Made Their Wealth.
By Dawson Gordon.

The Spinning and Manufacture of linen goods is one of the oldest in the British Textile Industries. Linen was made in Scotland in the year 1600 if not before. Dundee has always been the great centre of the Linen manufacture in Scotland, and was engaged in export trade before the end of the 17th century.

About the end of the 17th century Leeds became the centre of the English Linen Trade. Although the power loom was invented in 1785 it was not until 1821 that the first really successful linen power-loom factory was established.

The first Irish Flax Spinning Mills were started about 1828 one in Belfast by Messrs. Mulholland (now the York Street Flax Spinning Co., Ltd.); one in Castlewellan by Messrs. Murland, and one in Cork.

The linen thread trade was established in Scotland about the year 1722 by a lady named Christian Shaw. She excelled in spinning flax by hand and the idea occurred to her to twist the yarn into thread for sewing and lace purposes. She then had a 12-bobbin hand machine brought over from Holland. With this she produced a fine thread superior to the Dutch, and the Scotch thread soon became famous. Mills were established at Johnston, Kilbirnie and Beith.

The Irish linen thread was established by a Paisley gentleman named Barbour at Hilden. Soon afterwards a Mr. Dunbar started a thread mill at Gilford, and it is interesting to note that the new linen Thread Combine consists of these two mills and also includes Stewart, (Lisburn); Messrs. Hayes of Banbridge; Messrs. Knox, Kilbirnie; Finlyson of Johnston and Beith in Scotland; Cleator Mill in Cumberland and the Linen Thread Co., New Jersey, U.S.A. The Irish Linen Industry is centred chiefly in Northern Ireland. Until the middle of thee nineteenth century the industry was more or less of a domestic character, and very little progress had been made in the application of power to the various processes employed in the trade, but the American Civil War and the consequent shortage of cotton goods gave the needed impetus to the industry which was also further helped by the temporary removal from the field of competition of two of the principal rivals by the Franco-Prussian War. For a time afterwards the industry enjoyed great prosperity but a reaction set in and it became evident from the employers' point of view that output had more than overtaken the demand. To remedy this a number of Belfast Spinners bought up a few of the weaker firms, thus establishing for the first time, on a small scale, control over production. Since that period organisation by the Employers has been brought to a fine art with the result that to-day production by the industry is regulated by the Employers' Associations. This goes to prove that even the employers do not always believe in unrestricted production.

The following table is given to show the number of spindles and looms in 1915 as compared with say 38 years ago:—

Country.	Spindles.		Looms.	
	1877	1915	1877	1915
Ireland	922,322	951,942	19,611	37,335
England	291,735	49,941	4,081	4,424
Scotld.	*275,119	*160,085	16,756	17,185

*Includes Jute Spindles.

The foregoing table will show at a glance that during this period the number of spindles and looms increased in Ireland by 29,620 spindles and 17,724 looms. While the decrease in Scotland was 115,034 spindles and an increase of only 429 looms. In England the Spinning Trade during this period went from bad to worse as the decrease in spindles totalled 241,794 though looms increased by 343.

The industry is largely dependent upon foreign sources for its supply of raw material, only about one-eigth of Ireland's requirements of raw Flax being produced at home. The best Flax comes from Belgium which, together with Russia, furnished the bulk of the supplies. The following table will show the principal sources of supply:-

Items.	Country.	Value of Imports.
Flax Dressed	Russia	£2,806,829
and Undressed	Belgium	1,262,141
	Russia	503,160
Tow or Codilla	Belgium	65,335
	Germany	12,050
	Belgium	769, 297
Yarns	France	139,118
	Austria	122,977
	Total:	£5,680,907

The total value of imports from British possessions during the same period was as follows:- Flax £1,347; Tow, £3,152; Yarns, £12.

It will be noticed from the above table that the great bulk of raw material was imported from Russia, therefore it behoves each textile worker to take an interest in the question of

Peace With Russia.

so that in the near future the industry may obtain that which is necessary to carry on.

The imported raw material was converted into finished goods either in the form of Linen Yarn, Thread, or Piece goods and **exported to other countries,** and the total value of these exports amounted to almost $9_{1/2}$ millions sterling. The principal market for Piece goods is the U.S.A., Australia, Canada, Argentine, Cuba, Brazil and British India. Yarns were exported to Germany, Belgium and the U.S.A. The value of the total output of the Industry is estimated to be about 15 million sterling per annum, and these figures deal with the industry up till 1913. During the War years the industry was chiefly engaged in the making of war material such as Aeroplane cloth, and it is estimated that the total output of this material was about 93 million yards.

I am sorry I am not in the position to give you either the profits or losses made by any firm during the whole period under review but I apppend a few balance sheets showing the profits made during the **War Years**, and I am sure these will be of great interest, especially to those employed in the textile industry, when they remember that it was in November, 1915 that they received their first advance in wages—namely: Men, 2/- per week and Women 1/-, although the cost of living at this time had increased by 32 points.

York Street Flax Spinning Co., Ltd.		Messrs. Brookfield Linen Co.	
Years.	Profits.	Years.	Profits.
1914	£68,048	1914	£32,796
1915	74,475	1915	29,753
1916	84,273	1916	32,115
1917	88,649	1917	55,294
1918	107,459	1918	80,609
1919	137,079	1919	63,136

Messrs. Richardson & Owdens.		Linen Thread Co. Ltd.	
Years.	Profits.	Years	Profits.
1914	£122,411		
1915	132,657	1915	£257,418
1916	151,218	1916	276,064
1917	174,046	1917	284,192
1918	202,899	1918	288,509

Some Aspects of the Linen Trade.
By Councillor Harry Midgley.

There are many phases of the Linen Industry about which I would like to write. For instance, it would be instructive to deal with the question of output per head for both the post war and pre-war periods. We might thus discover that the arguments of employers for cheaper production through increased output had already been met by the volume of output to-day.

We might also collect valuable data as to whether the available productive plant is being utilised to the best advantage, and I think our investigations would prove that this important industry is many years behind the times in the matter of scientific production.

Another aspect of the question which we might study with advantage is this, what methods do we propose to adapt to stabilise existing markets, and where shall we seek to develop new markets? In pre-war days America was our largest customer, the annual exports to that country alone amounting to approximately 65 per cent. of our total. This, added to our exports to the Argentine, Cuba, Brazil, the Colonies and European countries outside of Britain, absorbed practically our whole output of linen, for it must be remembered that the *consumption of linen on the home market was very low indeed.*

When the war came with its blockades, "U" Boat activities, and the increasing demand for linen fabric as a war material, a form of "protection" or "Tariff Reform" was imposed upon this country. Produce which formerly went abroad was consumed at home, and other countries had either to do without or use substitutes. Hence it is that to-day, though we have gone far—much further than some industrial magnates will admit—towards recovering our American trade, yet the cold fact must be faced that the war caused us to lose some portions of our foreign market permanently; and we will never again enjoy a monopoly in those spheres. The question, therefore, is this: How do we propose to repair the ravages of war? Will we seek to develop a greater demand in the home and Colonial Markets, or embark on a mad scramble in the Competitive world with those who are out to undersell us, and in this way inevitably make the lot of the worker more degraded?

These are, briefly aspects of the linen industry which might be discussed in an article such as this.

I propose, however, to deal with an altogether different aspect in the hope that I may focus attention upon the greatest weakness in the industry from the workers' point of view.

Organisation in the Linen Industry.

Let others, whose forte it is, write about the technicalities of the Industry, I mean this to be a clarion call to the workers employed in the industry, or who would normally be employed but who are now tramping the streets looking for the job that isn't to be found, and to those who are privileged to be officials in the various Textile Unions.

The industry employs between sixty and seventy thousand workers, and during the boom period immediately following the Armistice the number of workers organised in the various Unions reached a higher level than ever before, but alas, since the trade depression the tide has receded, until now the trade union ship in the sea of difficulty threatens to become high and dry.

I sometimes wonder if it is realised that there are less than ten thousand workers ORGANISED throughout the whole industry. That is to say, that from Scutching to Weaving, and from Weaving to the packing of linen Goods for export, *only one out of every six or seven is Organised.* To speak of Organisation whilst this continues is indeed grotesque. What we should talk about is the Disorganisation in the Linen Trade. I write in this strain because I feel most strongly on this matter, though I did not belong to the Industry. Nevertheless, without trying to detract from the value of the work performed by those who strove to rouse the textile workers from their apathy, I think the time has now arrived when we must frankly admit that the best, up to the present time, has not been good enough, and that we must all join in a grand crusade to organise the textile workers Industrially and Politically.

In this crusade, neither workers, nor leaders who stand in the way of unity should be spared. The rank and file of each Union should be frankly informed that we have too many Unions and not enough unity. The rank and file should not permit any official bound by hoary tradition to prevent the Union from taking a step towards the affiliating and amalgamating of kindred interests. To-day we witness the melancholy spectacle of many Unions' representatives attending a Wages Conference without even first having had a preliminary discussion as to their attitude on the matter to be raised at the Conference.

What is Needed.
The need of to-day in the Textile Industry is Amalgamation into a class-conscious unit of all the forces at present kept divided by the craft stupidity of some Unions, and by the suspicions and jealousies of others. With a welding together of all the component parts into an efficient amalgamation, sub-divided into sections which would speedily utilise our power to remove the reproach that only one in every six is organised. To this end every man and woman in the linen Industry should work through their own Unions, and hasten its achievement.

No finer rallying cry could be sounded throughout the textile industry to-day, than this:- "Workers of the Linen Industry Unite on the Industrial and Political fields, you have nothing to lose but the horrible nightmares of the past, you have hope, love, joy and freedom to gain."

Labour Defeats The Government.

27th November, 1923, Sir James Craig boasts that **HE** will solve Unemployment in Ulster. 27th Nov., 1923, till June, 1925, Unemployment doubled in Ulster and now totals 70,000 on the live Register, and God knows how many J. M. Andrews struck off. In the meantime, murder, suicides, starvation, Corporation Scandals and Bankruptcies galore. 9th June, 1925: Northern Parliament goes on Holiday, full pay, after sitting three months. Labour warns the Government: Government laughs. Meantime matters get worse; Labour Party calls a Conference on Unemployment and says what it means to do. Wireless S.O.S. sent by Cabinet to Deauville, Riviera and other dug-outs of the Rich, to return at once and pacify the people. September the 1st: Parliament meets one month before its scheduled time.

. . . . ? Collapse of Tory Government. Labour takes control.

The Linen "Slump."
BY SAM KYLE, M.P.

Linen is about the oldest textile recorded in history, fine linens being mentioned several times in the Bible. The plant from which it is obtained grows in every continent, and Russia up to 1914 supplied the mills in Ireland with very large quantities at fairly reasonable rates. But with the advent of the Soviet Republics and the growth of Co-operative agencies in the Baltic States; (which formerly belonged to the Russian Empire) with the increased and increasing standard of life amongst the Peasants, and the avowed determination of the Soviets to develop and maintain a higher standard it will be appreciated that this field of cheap supply will no longer be available, particularly when the stupid, insensate policy of Coalition and Tory Governments is taken into account.

The slump in the trade at present has not been lessened by the action of the British Government in reverting to the Gold Standard which means in effect that our prices for Linen, already too high for business in bulk to be done, are increased by a further 10%. This *plunge* was taken by Winston Churchill and the Tory Government; but Winston has a penchant for "Gambles," and whether it is lives on the Dardanelles or British trade, it does not seem to matter a great deal to him.

The very latest idea is to get a tax placed on flax, and it will be interesting to learn how *that* is going to cheapen Yarns to our manufacturers.

The facts of the matter appear to be that our Spinners and Manufacturers have been content to carry on their business in an Empirical fashion. So long as profits were maintained, very little experiment and next to no research work was done to enquire and experiment to the end that the ever-changing fashions and customs might be catered for.

The very large number of Middle-men connected with and living off the trade has long been notorious, and the fact that all their business premises and their salaries (often out of all proportion to the service performed) add to the cost of producing Linen, and produce prices that are outside the reach of all save the well off people in the community. Despite the undisputed fact that Linen is the most difficult tentile to produce and calls for more skill and experience than any other, the wages of linen workers have always been low and not in keeping with the skill and experience necessary in these workers. Of course, the wage paid is in direct ratio to the amount and intensity of *the Trade Union Organisation of the Workers.*

But when that is said it does not fully explain the fact, that the workers in the Linen Trade are the lowest paid— on the average—of all the Textile workers in Great Britain and Ireland. This can only be remedied by BETTER TRADE UNION ORGANISATION, and by every worker in the trade feeling it is up to him or her to belong to a trade union.

It was not until the year 1917 that anything approaching Trades Unionism was general amongst the workers. In that year the Irish Textile Trades Federation was formed, and was able through the pressure of war time exigencies to hale the linen employers before the Committee on Production, and through this pressure was able to get the workers considerable advances in wages. About the year 1919 the hours of labour were reduced from 55 1/2 to 48 per week, and in the Bleaching Trade from 58 to 49 1/2. Both these reforms were got by direct negotiation with the Employers' Associations concerned, and in the writer's opinion these are the real benefits that Trade Unionism has brought to the workers in the trade.

Another very desirable object was obtained in 1920, when a Schedule of prices was established for the weaving trade, making a uniform price for all operations in that end of the trade, and ending the anomalies that had existed from very early times, the principal anomaly consisting in the fact that almost every factory had its own scale of prices, and this caused endless friction. Since the big slump set in, some Employers have taken advantage of the workers in certain badly organised places by reducing the prices on the list. The workers in these places, not realising that it was only through constant activity on the part of the Unions that a Schedule of Prices was obtained, and that the advantage gained by Trade Union organisation can be lost by the lack of the same factor, were taken advantage of by the Employers' superior organisation. Eternal Vigilance is the price we have to pay for Liberty.

"The Opposition" is steadily growing in Power, Circulation and Influence. What we need now is a Weekly, and every new reader and every fresh subscriber is a definite step towards that goal.

The Northern Parliament Wakens!

The Northern Government is summoned to meet on Tuesday, 1st September at 3 p.m. This entirely warrants the criticism by the Labour members on the 9th June, at the adjournment. Mr. Sam. Kyle on that occasion told the Government that unless they (the Government) were prepared to take more interest in, and concern for the situation, so far as Unemployment is concerned, that a very serious state of affairs would be the result of this negligence. The crisis is upon us! Nothing has been done! And we call upon the Government to (1) immediately re-impose the 6d. on the income tax taken off in their Budget, and to retain the £400,000 thus obtained, for relief of unemployment. (2) To immediately raise the school-leaving age to 16, or to compel employers to pay full contributions for all their Juvenile workers from 14 to 16. (3) To immediately take action to secure, for the relief of Unemployment, all profits paid by Employers to their dividend warrant holders of more than 5%. (4) To immediately institute an inquiry into the effects of a subsidy to the Linen Trade. (5) To immediately lower the pensionable age to 65 with the hope of lowering the age to 60 in a subsequent year. (6) To immediately re-impose the Death Duties lifted in 1925.

Drastic Diseases Require Drastic Remedies!

Short, trenchant articles are always welcome. All MSS. must be accompanied by the Name and Address of the Contributor, though not necessarily for publication. Unsuitable MSS. will be returned *only* if a stamped addressed envelope is enclosed.

Address all communications to The Editor, 48 York Street, Belfast.

The Labour Opposition Of Northern Ireland

Vol. 1—No. 8.   October, 1925   One Penny

What Is Socialism?
BY HUGH GEMMELL.

There is no longer any doubt that the political issue in Ulster is Socialism versus Capitalism, and thousands of workers who formerly voted for the Boss are now embracing Socialism as the only way out of their difficulty. The word Socialism comes from the Greek, "Socious", a companion, and the full significance of Socialism is the International Brotherhood or Comradeship of Man. That is why we call each other Comrade.

All human life is based on the need for food, clothing and shelter, and to obtain these, man must engage in the production of wealth. Under Capitalism all wealth is socially produced and distributed, but it is privately owned, and Socialists argue that what is socially produced ought to be socially owned and controlled. The Land is the great storehouse from which all wealth comes. From it we get coal for light, heat and power; we get clay for bricks, slates for roofing, and stones for our roads. From it we get the ores and minerals that provide the raw materials for our industrial processes, and on it we grow the corn, wheat, barley and other cereals that feed ourselves, and the animal creation that gives us milk and meat, and from which we get our woollen clothing and our leather bags and boots. The Land is the great mother of all wealth, yet no man or group of men created it, and Socialists say that the Land should be free to all, without rent or profit, or interest, and should be owned in common to promote the common good. Half a dozen big landlords in Ulster own the biggest portion of the three million acres that comprise our territory. They did not make the land, and they do not use it to promote the well-being of the people. As a matter of fact, there is documentary evidence which proves conclusively that their ownership is a barrier to progress.

After Land, we require the application of man's labour power in order to obtain the bounty of Nature. To sow, plough, harrow and harvest requires the labour of men and women working socially together, and in our industrial undertakings the same elementary logic manifests itself. Without the labour power of the working class not a factory would be built, not a ship built nor a railway laid. Without the skill of the workers applied to modern machinery, not a wheel would turn, not a thread be spun, nor a yard of cloth woven. The working class produces all wealth and the Socialist says that all wealth ought to belong to those who produce it.

The last great factor in wealth production is "Capital" and the capitalists claim that no wealth can be produced without "Capital". That is not true. Capital is only a portion of wealth already produced by the workers, that has been set aside for convenience in producing more wealth. What is called Capital, viz., Ships, Railways, Factories, Mills, and Machinery were all produced by the workers, and under Socialism it would be called "means of production."

The workers need not fear Socialism. Socialism will free them from unemployment, starvation, ragged clothing and slum houses where they do not live but only fail to die. Socialism will not destroy Religion, but free it from the sordid trafficking with Mammon that is the disgrace of the world to-day. Socialism will not destroy home life or family life, we leave that to the "Rich" who flaunt their filth in the gutter presses of Capitalism.

Socialism would bring peace and security to a war weary and a stricken world and your obvious duty now is to embrace Socialism and help us in our fight. A hundred religions have come and gone, a thousand creeds lie shattered in the dust; Empires and Thrones have blazed and been forgotten, but not the destiny of the working-class. Through the blood and tears of Slavery and Feudalism we have come, marching from defeat to defeat, until to-day we are massed for the final struggle that will break our bonds and make us free. We call you, we need you and we want you to play a man's part in the great struggle for human freedom. Be loyal to yourself, loyal to your wife, loyal to your children and loyal to your class. Put out the drones and the slackers who steal your produce and squander your wealth in debauchery and idleness. Rise up off your knees and face the light of truth and help us to make the world a place fit for honest people to live in.

COME !

Hits And Misses.
BY MARKSMAN.

The *Belfast Telegraph*, 15/9/25, reports the case of a Belfast Harbour Board employee aged 79 years, who obtained the Old Age Pension by making a false statement to the pensions officer. Prisoner said his wages were 38/- per week, and he had a daughter and grand-daughter in bad health. Fined £25 with the option of four months' imprisonment, and given one month in which to pay. As he is only a labourer, and cannot make ends meet, he must go to jail.

Now read the next paragraph and see what happens to one of the *employing class*.

* *

The *Belfast Telegraph*, 15/9/25, reports a similar offence at Warrenpoint, but in this second case the defendant was a well known resident of Scarva and Warrenpoint. Fined £25 and 20/- costs, the Chairman said that but for the defendant's age he would have sent him to jail. "But would he?" In this second case the defendant could well afford to pay as he had monies invested as under:-

Arnotts, 15 shares; Goldring Bros., Ltd., 20 shares; White, Tomkins & Courage Ltd., 350 shares; Lever Bros., 100 shares; Imperial Tobacco Co., 120 shares; Northern Bank, 30 shares; York Street Spinning Co., 200 shares. These are all gilt edged securities.

Jails were built for the *working class* to be punished in, and those who live on Rent, Profit, and Interest, are only sent there when money cannot get them free.

* *

Bangor.—The Unionist Weekly paper called *North Down Herald*, 12/9/25, says— "Mr. Megaw, who has been appointed to enquire into the Belfast Housing Scandal, has not the monopoly of brains, and the Home Office should select some other competent person." This is a bit rough when you consider that Mr. Megaw was Parliamentary Secretary to the Ministry of Home Affairs, from 1921 to 1925. How these Unionists love one another.

* *

Armagh Co. Council has been informed, that in future Malone Reformatory will charge 43/7 per week for each youthful offender placed in their charge. Yet Armagh Co. Council want their surfacemen to maintain themselves and dependents on 27/6 per week.

* *

Toomebridge.—The Irish News, 15/9/25, reports a case which was heard at Toome, Co. Antrim. John Dunseith, 91 years of age, was found guilty of stealing a hen from Alexander Allen, 92 years of age. Allen said "he had the hen for a pet all his life." Poor old hen, also 92 years of age. There must be some gay old "birds" at "Toomebridge".

* *

Lough Neagh fishermen are being refused the dole, and now we learn that Captain O'Neill has sold the eel fishery rights to the Toome Eel Fishery Company, who have decreed that eel fishing in Lough

Neagh and the River Bann is in future to be prohibited, thereby depriving 2,000 people of their means of livelihood. First they stole the land, next they steal the waters, and next, they will bottle and sell the air we breathe.

* *

Cookstown Poor Law Guardians are advised by Mr. John Mitchell, P.L.G, to cut down the sums paid to recipients of outdoor relief. John Mitchell's motto is—"To Halifax with you, Jack Dubb," as John M. is alright, and nice and comfy too.

* *

North Down Herald, 5/9/25, says— "Blackmen would like to know why they are addressed by non-blackmen at public meetings." No! dear reader, this has nothing to do with Minstrel Troupes, but is a dig at a well known Cabinet Minister.

* *

Mr. Rowley Elliott, M.P., is a terrible fellow. He is going to raise the question of Sunday desecration by members of the Government. Yes! The Home Secretary actually tours the *Border* on Sundays, and the Minister of Agriculture actually took the South African Farmers on a char-a-banc trip round the country on Sunday August 2nd, 1925. Sure everybody knows why people visit the *Border on Sundays!*

* *

Clogher Board of Guardians have entered into a contract with P. M'Caffrey, who undertakes to supply steak at 7¾ per lb. "Marksman" cannot buy half-a-pound for 7¾d!

* *

Omagh Poor Law Guardians are in clover; they have a credit balance of £1,509. By refusing to pay a generous scale of outdoor relief, they are able to pack the money away in barrels.

* *

Cookstown Rural District Council have accepted the tender of Mr. Hampsey, who undertakes to light Stewartstown for £19 during the winter months. Mr. Hampsey will not make his fortune out of this contract. Trim your lamps and be ready, Hampsey.

* *

During the past month, 6 milk vendors have been summoned for selling new milk deficient in fat, two were fined, and the others dismissed. In one of the dismissed cases, evidence showed that the milk was 41 per cent. deficient in milk fat, and contained 4.8 per cent. of added water. Eight well known J.P.'s adjudicated, in addition to Mr. H. Toppin, R.M. The J.P.'s were mostly well known Unionist public men.

* *

8,617 branches of Trade Unions and 1,018 Co-operative Societies are banking their monies with the Wholesale Bank.

The Co-operative Wholesale Society produced and sold £13,500,000 worth of goods during the past six months. Who says we can't do without the capitalist?

* *

Three more Sugar Beet Factories are to be built in Gt. Britain. The Irish Free State has decided to encourage the building of a factory. But our fat headed Minister of Agriculture says "No factories here as we have no money." No, he did not say no brains! he said no money. As a matter of fact Dutch Capitalists have offered to erect a factory in Ulster.

To our Correspondents.

Once again, many articles have been crowded out owing to lack of space, and among others an article by James Mac, for which we hope to find room later.

J.F., Coleraine.—Many thanks for papers, useful.

John Murphy, Milwaukee.— Greetings, and delighted to hear of your progress.

"Red Flagger." —If broken legs and mangled bodies were infectious, the Master Class would have the Hospitals nationalised to-morrow. That is why the Fever Hospitals are under public control.

"An Interested Reader."—Thanks for the compliments. We don't want to increase the price, and more pages can only come with increased circulation. Will dress down the Landlords later.

J. M'A.—Very welcome and acceptable if you would make it more economic and political. Say it with a kick.

Fighting Fund

One Guinea from a few workmates, per R. Y.

Labour Men of the North.
BY BOB M'CLUNG.
Sam Kyle, M.P., Belfast

I find it rather difficult to write about Sam Kyle, as we have been close friends for 18 years, and as comrades have been working together in the same Trade Union Office for 7 years past. We hear a lot about loyalty in the North and Sam Kyle has been always loyal to his comrades, to the I.L.P. and to the working class generally.

A consistent member of the I.L.P. since 1907, he has acted as Branch Secretary to the North Belfast I.L.P. since 1910. He was Secretary of the Workers Educational Association in Belfast for many years and maintains that the W.E.A. ideal of the broad highway of education is the proper one, while also agreeing that for the making of propagandists the National Council of Labour Colleges' policy is one that every worker may consider worth while.

He has been a leader in every forward movement in the textile trade since 1916, having stated the case for every advance which has been gained for the various associations in the textile industry. He stood as Official Labour Candidate for the Imperial Parliament in 1918; was appointed as full time official of The Workers' Union in January, 1919; was elected as Alderman for Shankill Ward in 1920; was defeated in 1923; was Chairman of the Northern Labour Party in 1924; was elected to the North of Ireland Parliament in April, 1925 and was appointed Parliamentary Leader of the Labour Party, a position which he has filled with credit to himself and to the satisfaction of the Labour Movement in Northern Ireland. He is a fearless critic of the Capitalist System wherever he finds himself. He has numerous friend everywhere, being a delegate to the I.L.P. Conferences on many occasions, and having spoken for the Socialist movement in Great Britain. He was

Sam Kyle, M.P., Belfast

invited recently to be a Party agent in a cross Channel constituency, but he prefers to work for the advancement of the cause in his native town.

DINNA' FORGET ! The Socialist Demonstration in the Ulster Hall on October the 30th. The I.L.P. is bringing David Kirkwood, M.P., and he's ginger right up to the top.

Notes And News.

The September Opposition was completely sold out. And the Staff is done out.

Our biggest "hit" this month is our smallest "miss," because "Ellen" is "the little lady of the big house," and she will easily fill the Y.M. on the 16th.

The British T.U.C. adopted a resolution to extend the use of Esperanto, and Belfast Comrades should note that a class is commencing now at 109 Donegall Street. The N.C.L.C. Winter Programme is now complete, and numerous classes are announced for Belfast. A P.C. to THE OPPOSITION will bring particulars by return.

Congrats. to Willie M'Mullen, M.P., on the acquisition of a second little daughter.

The Building Trades Federation Conference at Nottingham decided to form a Regional Council for Northern Ireland, and the Annual Conference of the B.T.F. is to be held in Belfast next July.

Country Comrades are doing some remarkable work in selling OPPOSITIONS.

The "Kirkwood" tickets are available. They are hard to get, but well worth looking for. The Belfast Labour Movement is now running 30 propaganda meetings per week.

Don't walk on the footpath on the 6th October. Walk on the street, hold your head high, and . . . be a **Man**: Bring the women and children, and let the Bosses see our misery and our determined will.

The November OPPOSITION will be a rather remarkable affair, with some really startling features. It will probably be double-size, and double price, but sixpence wouldn't buy a copy the week after publication.

To the Editor, Labour Opposition.

Dear Sir,

Allow me through the column of your widely read paper, to return my sincere gratitude to the Labour representatives on the Belfast Board of Guardians (particularly Mr. Philip Wilson) Falls Ward Representative. Through their medium, I have been fitted with an artificial limb and all accessories to suit. As I am only a mill employee, you can understand that I could not have provided same personally.

Trusting you will give this the publicity it deserves.

Thanking you in anticipation,
I remain, dear Sir,
Yours faithfully,
MRS. GRAHAM.

Short, trenchant articles are always welcome. All MSS. must be accompanied by the Name and Address of the Contributor, though not necessarily for publication. Unsuitable MSS. will be returned *only* if a stamped addressed envelope is enclosed.

Address all communications to
The Editor, 48 York Street, Belfast.

100,000 PENNIES.
Court Ward Divisional Labour Party.

We are out to win Court Ward for Labour. We want to build a Hall as a centre for all our activities. We want it right now, and YOUR PENNIES can do it. We appeal to Trade Unionist, Labour Men, and all who sympathise with us to subscribe to this fund. Any sum, much or little, will be welcomed and acknowledged in these columns. Send your "Sub" to....

Paul Carleton, 6 Concord Street.
Received to date   1,060 pennies
£4 3 4

Mr Ewing	20 pennies	0 10 0
W. Belfast, A.E.U.	120 pennies	0 10 0
Belfast, A.E.U.	120 pennies	0 10 0
Mr. M'Ilhagga	120 pennies	0 10 0
George M'Bride	120 pennies	0 10 0

Still Required 99,000 pennies Hurry up!

Northern Ireland Labour Party
(Women's Section)
Miss Ellen Wilkinson, M.A. M.P.
Is Coming To Belfast To Speak On
"Mother's Pensions,"
In The Y.M.C.A. (Large Hall),
On Friday 16th October, at 8 p.m.
Doors open at 7-30 p.m.
Admission by Ticket, Price, 6d. Each.
On Sale at all Labour Meetings.

Christian Civilization Meetings,

(Customs House Steps East.)
Speakers For October.
Sunday, October 4th.   Mr. S. Geddis.
"The Failure Of Capitalism."
Sunday, October 11th—Mrs. Ida Boyd.
"Women And Labour."
Sunday, October 18th.—Mr. S. Kyle, M.P.
"Labour And Parliament."
Sunday, October 25th.—Mr. Dawson Gordon. *"Textiles And Trade Unionism."*

Chairman—Senator Robert Dorman.
All Meetings commence at 3 p.m.

Is Belfast Shipbuilding Down And Out?
By Harry Spiers
Secretary, Belfast District Committee;
Engineering and Shipbuilding TradesFederation.

Has the Shipbuilding Industry— once the pride and support of many thousands of Belfast's population— reached a stage of depression where not even a glimmer of the dark cloud's silver lining is to be seen, and all hope of its recovery abandoned? To the unfortunate unemployed Shipyard Workers undoubtedly it may seem so, but in this article let us examine some facts of the situation and draw our conclusions therefrom. In the first place we will examine Lloyd's Register as to the comparative total of World's tonnage afloat 1913—1924.

June	Gross Tons.	Surplus over 1913.	% Surplus over 1913.
1913	47.0 Millions	—	—
1922	64.4 Millions	17.4 Millions	37%
1923	65.2 Millions	18.2 Millions	38.7%
1924	64.0 Millions	17.0 Millions	36.2%

Thus the world tonnage was in June 1924, 36.2% in excess of the pre-war figure. This included some 5.3 million tons of vessels which on account of age, or because they were built under special conditions during the war, could not be considered serious competitors for the carrying trade of the world. 13.5 millions were 20 years old or upwards, and 7.4 millions, 25 years or over. Also 4 million tons of American shipping built under special conditions (wood) could not be regarded as serious competitors. How far the remaining surplus can be regarded as dead is a matter on which opinions will differ, but it will be agreed that, eliminating obsolete and uneconomic vessels, we will be near our 1913 tonnage. Another factor to be considered is the claims made for the Marine Diesel Engine. If these are substantiated (and there is every likelihood that they will), we shall witness a more rapid conversion to this form of propulsion, and vessels which would otherwise remain in service longer will certainly become obsolete. Assuming a pre-war volume of trade, one would be forced to the conclusion that the Shipbuilding Industry was not as bad as it is pictured, but the truth is of course, that actual trade is far below pre-war years, and thus our chief and foremost efforts should be to restore world trade, not to pre-war level but far in excess of that level. How can that be done? Did someone say Russia? Well, why not take Russia as one means of restoring trade essential to the re-employment of thousands of our Brothers and Sisters, who through no fault of their own, have been compelled to tramp the hard pavements of our City looking for work that does not exist, with the constant dread that at their next court they will be adjudged N.G.S.W. (not genuinely seeking work). The irony of the situation is, while loud mouthed Tory or Liberal politicians who received thousands of working class votes, give lip-service to the desperate position of the unemployed, their actions in Parliamentary legislation are dead against any improvement of their cruel lot.

The Trade Agreement with Russia promoted by Labour when in Office being ruthlessly turned down by the combined Tory and Liberal Vote, without even an attempt to show a just or proper reason. It is truly said, Russia is a vast country requiring a considerable amount of agricultural machinery, locomotives, tools of all descriptions, scientific apparatus, ships for their waterways and canals, and boots, clothes and such things. Why not be honest with ourselves, it is no concern of ours what form of Government the Russian people choose, but it is our concern and our duty to explore every avenue and adopt every proposition that will reduce the number of our unemployed. By diplomatic recognition of Russia and the adoption of trading facilities we will be on the road to the ultimate achievement of that end. What effect would this have on shipbuilding? Well, in the first place, they need ships for their own waterways, that would not be competing with World Shipping Trade. Again, the manufacture of their other requirements in Great Britain would necessitate their removal to Russia by ships, thus increasing our seaborne trade which is essential to shipbuilding prosperity. Again, Russia has vast Wheat and Flax growing areas and the shipment of these raw materials to this country would not only increase seaborne trade but provide us with the means of producing cheaper food and clothing and allow us a splendid opportunity of entirely capturing the American linen trade. India, China, Japan, South America, Argentine and the British Dominions are also factors if properly handled by an honest Government that would result in supplying their quota to the revival of seaborne trade.

Profits And Efficiency.

In the second place we will examine this Country's ability from a financial and efficiency standpoint to retain her place as the premier shipbuilders, and a perusal of the profits of a few of the shipbuilding firms will show that we (sic) have no cause to be down hearted from that source, and from the efficiency side sufficient evidence has been produced to show, that while there is room for improvement in equipment in some of the Yards the workmen are as highly skilled and efficient as any in other parts.

We will take John Brown & Co., Ltd., who are to a large extent interested in the firm of Messrs. Harland & Wolff.:—

Year Ending March.	Net Profit.	Ordinary Dividend.
1914	£377,493	10%
1920	£378,609	12$_{1/2}$%
1921	£331,921	10%
1922	£210,407	5%
1923	£212,294	5%
1924	£212,230	5%
Cammell Laird & Co., Ltd :—		
1913	£169,126	2$_{1/2}$%
1919	£303,006	10%
1920	£260,642	7$_{1/2}$%
1921	£170,487	5%
1922	£145,906	5%
1923	£70,054	—
Swan Hunter :—		
1913	£280,717	7$_{1/2}$%
1919	£447,748	10%
1920	£397,139	8%
1921	£415,399	8%
1922	£411,277	8%
1923	£398,494	8%

From the **Shipowners** standpoint, linked up as Shareholders in most cases with the **Shipbuilders**, the "Financial Times" shows that the Court of Directors of the Royal Mail Steam Packet Company had succeeded in building up a very powerful position during a period of unprecedented difficulties and unforeseen developments. During the period from 1910 to the close of 1921 the issued capital had increased from £1,500,000 to £6,800,000, the reserve from £80,000 to £1,600,000 and the investment fund from £22,600 to £291,000 in the same period, while during the eleven years 1911-1921, the total amount of the rate of dividend on the ordinary capital amounted to 65%.

The Elder Dempster Steamship Company's total rate of ordinary dividend amount to 103%. during the years 1911-1921, the reserve fund was increased from £250,000 to £1,325,000 while in addition 10,000 management shares were merged into ordinary in the year 1921. The debenture shareholders meeting of Messrs. Workman & Clark's, in a statement of approximate accounts, showed that a profit of £937,442 was made for the sixteen months ending December, 1920. £591,317 for the year ending December, 1921, and £312,336 for the year ending December, 1922, so apart from insecure speculation and re-investment dealings, sufficient profit was still being made in the Industry to ensure a fair return in the way of profit to the shareholders and a fair wage to the workers.

The Path To Progress.

I will finish up with a few words about organisation [in] the yards and shops. It is a well known fact that things are not as they should be, many non-Trade Unionists being employed while loyal Trade Unionists are walking the streets, so it is up to every man to do his bit to get his section 100 per cent. organised, as it is only by proper and efficient organisation (each section standing solidly together in some form of Federation), that we will be able to improve the present unsatisfactory position of our shipyard members.

Socialise The Shipyards.
BY ALDERMAN GEORGE DONALDSON.

I was introduced to Shipbuilding 23 years ago, when I was apprenticed to the plumbing trade. For 16 years I went daily to Harland & Wolff's, leaving home at 5-15 a.m. and returning at 6-20 p.m., and those early years moulded my political opinion and gave me some knowledge of shipyard conditions.

Changes have taken place in the Belfast Shipyards, though the only apparent change in the interest of the worker was the departure from the 54 to the 47 hour week.

In every department, speeding up of output is taking place to-day and this can easily be confirmed. It can partly be attributed to more up-to-date machinery, but largely to the additional numbers of Foremen and Managers, and Charge Hands, and the economic position the workers are placed in; living as they do in daily dread of being paid off; induces a speeding up in the hope that their period of employment (and Profit making for their Employers) may be longer than their fellows. Nothing deprives a man of independence and individuality so much as the spectre of unemployment.

The position of the wage earner and manual worker in Belfast Shipyards is to-day such that they cannot, on present wages, maintain a decent standard of living. Why do I say wage earner and manual worker? Because, when sweeping reductions were made in their wages, the Management and Executive Staff were not cut pro-rata. It is an astonishing truth that when one of the Local Shipyards (at present claiming to be in a bad way) can *pay one of its directors a fee of £7,000 per annum*, and other Directors are credited with receiving beyond this, and when we consider that one local shipyard could, during 1920-1921-1922, divide a profit of almost Two Million Pounds (£2,000,000), we wonder why it was necessary to force the workers to accept starvation wages, and then blame it on sheltered trades having so high a rate.

I had, during my term of office as President of Belfast District Committee of Engineers and Shipbuilding Federation, the unpleasant experience of negotiating on wages, knowing full well that such negotiation had only one result and that was a reduction, as the National Federation had at this time accepted the principle of reduction in the hope (as the Employers promised) of an increase in orders for ships. But the iniquitous War Treaty prevented this. During the whole local negotiations it was argued from the workers' side of the table that *wages must be a first charge on Industry*, and failing that Industry being unable to meet such charge then it could rightly be regarded as of no value to the community and should cease to exist. All Political Economists declare that "Any Social condition in which the Development of Wealth involves the misery, the physical weakness, and the degradation of the worker is absolutely and infallibly doomed to collapse," and one of the factors that weakened negotiations, was the large amount of non-Union Labour in the local shipyards. Admitting the fact of the difficulty in organising unskilled and semi skilled workers, the trouble lay most with *craftsmen* and still exists to-day. Our own section was faced with 50 men refusing to remain in the Union, and we forced these men in by a strike covering a period of four days, resulting to-day in 100 per cent. organised workers amongst plumbers.

I know it is not popular to state that other Craft Unions are only partly organised, but however unpopular it is, it is nevertheless true; and the whole forces of Trades Unionism should be employed to combat this evil. This should be followed by a merging of unions catering for one class of workers, and ultimately arrive at one Union for all workers. Money would be saved that is spent on demarcation questions and other minor matters, while officials would lose their jobs. This appears to be a big factor in preventing solidarity and my experience is, taught that very often officials stood in the way of linking up with other unions.

Having done this we have prepared the way for political action, and we must work and vote for the complete overthrow of the system that gives to the few the power to take from the workers a huge portion of the product of their labour. This ceaseless labour of the workers continually enriches those already rich, until extreme wealth enables a minority to live in careless luxury.

It is my considered opinion that Individual Ownership of Shipyards and Factories and other means of Production shall give place to Collective Ownership.

In a few years at most, essentially National services such as Coal Mining, Railways, Canals, etc., will be run for the benefit of the whole Community by the will of the whole Community. Shipbuilding could therefore be regarded as essential and should be owned and controlled by the State. Ships would no longer be produced for profit, but for use, and the misuse of capital in the hands of individuals would be swept away.

To those who suffer, I appeal! That time is fast approaching when capital can be made public property, no longer at the disposal of a few, but owned by the community for the benefit of all.

The power is in your hands; chances of using that power are within your reach; neglect those chances and you and your children will remain the victims of competition and Capitalism for decades to come.

The Bogus Pensions Bill.

BY MARY H. KYLE.

The secret is out, and after many conflicting rumours in the Press, we at last have an official announcement that the Government is to introduce a Widows', Orphans' and Old Age Pensions Bill during the next Session. It will, we may assume, be exactly the same as the Act passed in Great Britain last August.

Labour's Attitude.

What is Labour's attitude towards this Bill, and more particularly, what have Labour Women to say about it? I hold that we should do our outmost to resist it, making it perfectly plain that this contributory proposal is **no pensions scheme** as Labour knows it, but merely an insurance scheme, and a bad one at that. Considered on its merits as an insurance policy, it must rouse profound dissatisfaction in the heart of every Labour man and woman, for the allowance of 10/- to a widow, 5/- for her first child, and 3/- for every other under 14, can be described as nothing less than a miserable pittance. That is the big failure of the Act, for it takes away the main point of the Labour Party's proposition, which was to enable a widow with young children to stay at home, and give them the proper attention that they need if they are to be healthy individuals and worthy citizens in the future. But in addition to this, there are innumerable anomalies that would need amending to make the scheme a feasible one, but to consider these here would lead one into too much detail.

Pensions Must Be Non-Contributory.

The main point is, that a scheme which involves weekly payments by the worker—4 1/2d. by a man and 2d. by a woman, is not the pensions scheme which Labour has advocated for the past twelve years, and the Tory Party have merely stolen a popular title for their retrograde step in social legislation in making the worker pay, not only for Widows' Pensions, but for the Old Age Pensions too. Make the worker pay all the time, is the undying motto of the Tory Party. How mean it is, especially when the more we look into the Act, the more we find that numerous people will contribute to the Widows' Pensions scheme for a great part of their lives, and then will be disqualified from drawing anything out. No other country has been so niggardly in its proposals, and yet nearly all the states of America have schemes in operation—the first being introduced in 1913. Denmark followed in 1914, and not very long after Canada, Australia and New Zealand followed suit. It is a scandal that in a country like Great Britain, where the workers are highly organised, and where social legislation is supposed to be comparatively advanced, a lower standard for pensions should be accepted, and the workers should have an additional burden put on their already overtaxed low wages.

No Compromise.

No, we must stand firm, and voice our opposition to this scheme with all our might and will. We must not placidly adopt the attitude that this is the best we can get. And after all it is something! A vital principle is involved, and by letting it appear that Labour accepts this scheme, we should be compromising where compromise is not desirable. We should not be taking a few steps towards our goal, but should be going down a totally different path. Old Age Pensions have not been contributory in the past and wages are much too low to have this additional burden placed on them. The community has made such a sorry mess of the distribution of wealth—the inequalities in the struggle for life are so glaring, that provision for old age and and widowhood must be a social responsibility. Already we have too few social and communal services, and to those who say that the worker ought to contibute his share, we can retort that we do, the difference being that in a social service there is some attempt to make the contribution exacted accord to some extent to the means of the person contributing, whereas, if we are to get everything through some form of insurance the worker is going to be made to pay out of all proportion to his means. No, we must oppose the contributory basis, and no matter how "The Telegraph" or our political opponents may and will misrepresent us, our children and our children's children will at least know that the Labour movement did its utmost to prevent wages being taxed for small benefits which they may, but which quite likely they may not, be entitled to claim.

Book Reviews.

The following books and pamphlets are published by The Anglo-Russian Parliamentary Committee, and can be ordered from the I.L.P. Literature Secretary.

"Present Position of Anglo-Russian Relations," price 2d. (November, 1923).

"Export Credit Schemes and Anglo-Russian Trade," price 1d. by W.P. Coates.

"Why Russia Should be Recognised."

"Russia's Counter Claims " by W.P. Coates, price 6d.

"The Anglo-Russian Treaties," by W.P. Coates, price 6d.

"Anglo-Russian Trade," by A.A. Purcell, M.P., price 2d.

Mr. Coates writes with a directness and virility that makes trade with Russia a simple and comprehensible thing, and a matter of practical politics **now**. He is at present in Russia studying industrial conditions, and many of our Free State readers will remember him as an Irish Transport Union Organiser in 1917-19. These pamphlets are invaluable to the student and Socialist propagandist.

Harry Midgley's Poems.

Harry's little volume, "Thoughts from Flanders" is on sale at all Socialist meetings and can be purchased for one shilling. It deserves a wider publicity than it has so far received, and its value as a plea for peace is evidenced by the fact that the kept press of Belfast ignored its publication, although a review copy was sent to each. The movement should encourage and support its singers, players and writers, and several of Harry's poems could be committed to memory and declaimed at our social gatherings, while "Memories," "Above the Battle," "A Worker's Te Deum, " " and "Shot at Dawn," could easily be set to music by some local Comrade thus gifted, and could be sung by our Choir and our Soloists. When you are making a gift to a friend why should you not give "Thoughts from Flanders," and at Christmas it would be an appropriate message of "Peace on Earth, goodwill to all men." I have never praised a book that was unworthy, or condemned a book unjustly, and I say to you now, that Harry's poems is a good book and is worth the humble shilling. For those who desire a cloth binding the price is two shillings and sixpence.

HUGH GEMMELL.

West Belfast Appeal.

The West Belfast Divisional Labour Party appeals to all readers of THE OPPOSITION for financial assistance. We are contesting **three seats** for the Town Council in January, and we must get £75 for deposit money. We were the first Divisional Labour Party to be formed and in two years we have fought six elections and won an M.P., a Town Councillor and Two Poor Law Guardians. Six tries and four wins. Now we want your help to win Three Councillors in January. We can do it, and to make it easy we have issued a pinhole collecting card. Get your card to-day from the Secretary, 2 Union Street, or send your donation **now** to the same address. Every penny is a pat, every shilling is a shove, and every pound is a punch for Labour.

Give of your best,
And help the West.

Agricultural Wages Regulation Bill.

Mr. Kyle, M.P., North Belfast, is to introduce a bill to regulate the wages and conditions of Agricultural Workers.

Mr. Kyle has the permission of the Labour Party to introduce this measure in the incoming session, and it has been drafted in consultation with the Agricultural Section of the Workers' Union.

The Bill is based on the Agricultural Wages Bill introduced by the Labour Party in Great Britain, and Mr. Kyle is hopeful that the pledges of Lord Londonderry and Mr. J. M. Andrews, that the people of Northern Ireland are to get the same social legislation as the people of Great Britain will be honoured in the case of the Agricultural Workers who are the mainstay of the 6 counties, and provide 60% of the entire working population of the 6 counties.

The Labour Opposition Of Northern Ireland

Vol. 1—No.9   November, 1925   One Penny

Peace Or War?
BY DAVID KIRKWOOD, M.P.

All war is wrong, cruel, barbarous, wasteful and futile, and no real advantage is gained by victor or vanquished. Yet we know that when the crisis comes the public mind is always deluged with the poison of hate, falsehood and bitterness, and the individual seeing his impotence generally resigns himself to his fate and enters into the jingo spirit.

War destroys and maims hundreds of thousands of the finest of the nation's manhood; devastates towns, villages, and huge tracts of country, and causes the death of large numbers of innocent people.

At its close a terrible disillusionment takes place. The new heaven and the new earth, and "a land fit for heroes to live in" never materialises, but unemployment, poverty and misery are rampant throughout the land, while ex-soldiers, their wives and dependants, widows and orphans get little or no consideration from the Government. Of course there are always people who are satisfied that **They Won.**

All wars have proved that differences cannot be settled by the sword.

Peace is not the period between one war and the next. Peace is something different from limitation of armaments. Peace has its own special policy and organisation; its own methods of handling international and national differences, and its own standards of justice of right and wrong. A new spirit must be created in every country, a spirit of security from attack, a spirit of tolerance and of fellowship, and it behoves every one of us to make certain that this new spirit gets every chance of developing.

But, while for the present the imperialist and sectarian war-dogs are apparently sleeping, we have another war raging—a war of international competition in which country is competing against country for the world's markets.

In the middle of the last century owing to Great Britain having obtained a long start over their industrial rivals, British manufactured exports were supreme throughout the world. To-day in many foreign markets, Great Britain is not even the principal supplier and in others she just manages to maintain her place. Before the war this country was said to be the "workshop of the world." The war resulted in us losing that position.

To-day, miners of Britain have to compete with the continental miners on an unprecedented scale with the result that wages paid on the continent are tending to determine wage rates here. This applies equally to the shipbuilding, engineering and textile industries.

In the Far East we have the competition of the coloured races, especially in the textile industries, where the native workers receive about 10/- per month for working 12 hours per day and 7 days per week. The natural tendency of this state of affairs is to force British labour down to the "Coolie level," in order that the British manufactured product will be able to compete in the world's markets with the products of India, China and Japan.

If the workers of Western Europe are to resist this attack on their present standard of life, low as it is, they must be prepared to extend the right hand of fellowship to all nations and races irrespective of colour or religion. **We of the I.L.P. believe, and at the present time are the only Party who believe, in the Brotherhood of Man.**

Why should the human family compete amongst themselves in a relentless and devastating struggle for markets, when there is in the world enough and to spare for everybody? Man has been able to tap the sources of Nature and make Nature do man's work to such an extent that we are now most efficient in production—production being carried on socially and co-operatively. But when we turn to distribution we find that the products of the community's labour are privately owned and controlled, and that goods are only produced in order that a profit can be made for the owners of capital and not because the community requires these goods. Every thinking man and woman must admit that private enterprise has failed to give the workers a comfortable standard of life—a standard which is their right.

This state of affairs must cease. Let the nations of the world call together an economic conference to consider the world resources in staple products such as wheat, cotton, coal, oil, etc., with a view to an equitable distribution being made.

In this way, and in this way only, can the present competitive war be brought to a close with advantage to the workers throughout the world.

If we refuse to take this step against "Capitalism run riot" we shall be drawn sooner or later into other wars more horrible and brutal even than the Great War. The issue is entirely in the workers' hands.

Is it to be a Universal Peace, or a return, in a few years, to another outbreak of hatred and bloodshed?

Hits and Misses.
BY MARKSMAN.

Belfast. Sir James Craig says "The weather may change, trade may change, but Sir James Craig will never change."

Good word **never**, I seem to have heard it before. No Home Rule. Never, never, never. Sir James also said "The people of Belfast need not be in any way discouraged by what was done in Parliament by these Communists or Bolshevists. There was no need to become rattled."

What has rattled Sir James, is it his liver? Or is he tired of being teetotal? You have my sympathy, Jimmy!

* *

Interesting evidence was given by Sir Thomas Neill, London, at the Local Government Commission. He said, "The death rate in this country was higher than in England or Scotland. He recommended the application of medical benefits to all persons insured and uninsured." In fact he made out a splendid case for the Socialisation of Medical Benefits.

* *

Armagh Unionist members left the meeting of the Armagh City Council as a protest against the Council receiving a deputation of Unemployed Workers. No! Don't condemn them too hastily, as the Belfast Poor Law Guardians refused to meet a deputation of unemployed three years ago. But they have learned their lesson.

* *

Aughnacloy Town Council have decided to contract for the lighting of the town by fifteen 80-candle power electric lamps at an annual cost of £41 5s. That will throw more light on the subject.

* *

Omagh Guardians boast of being £1,000 better off than at the corresponding period last year. God help the poor people in Omagh.

* *

Ballymoney Urban Council met recently and made strenuous efforts to conduct business whilst a jazz band discoursed jazzy music in the room above. I am told seven members were making frantic efforts to make themselves heard at one and the same time. When order had been restored, it was proposed that not more than five members should be allowed to speak at once. "Oh, Jazz."

* *

Caledon Woollen Mills, Co. Tyrone, which were closed down for some time, are now reopened with work at full swing. A big contract for R.U.C. clothing materials has been secured by the firm from the Northern Government.

I hope that John Fulton & Co., of Caledon Mills are observing the Fair Wages Clause, as this firm has an unsavoury reputation in Trade Union circles.

* *

Coalisland. Dr. Wilson giving evidence before the Housing inquiry at Dungannon said "The proper course would be to blow up some of the present houses in Coalisland." He told of a family of eight living in a mud-walled cottage, the roof of which was leaking, while in another, seven people were living in one bedroom in a house which was below the level of the river and was always flooded. "Homes for heroes again."

* *

Derry P.L.G. Mr. James Cochrane moved that where possible outdoor relief should be cut down by 25% because farmers were receiving 20% less for their oats than they got last year.

Pity the poor farmers because there has been an abundant crop of oats.

* *

Cushendall fishermen are selling their catches of plaice at 5d. per lb. Belfast fishmongers are charging 1/6d. per lb. for them.

* *

Derry Shipyard will never be opened again. The prophet in this case is Sir John M'Farland, who made the above declaration at a public meeting of the Council.

Meantime shipyard workers must starve, while Capitalism continues to crumple up.

* *

Derry Guardians have accepted the tender of Messrs Eaton & Co., for bread at 7 3/4d. per 4 lb. load. Last year's price was 9¼d.

* *

Dublin Bakers are still charging 10 1/2d. for a 4 lb. loaf delivered at the home, or 10d. at the counter.

Because we have a Co-operative Bakery in Belfast we compelled the Master Bakers to reduce the price of the 4lb. loaf from 10½d. to 9½d.

* *

Cookstown Guardians are dealing with 69 Vaccination defaulters. When are we going to get a conscience clause?

* *

Dungannon Gas Company have reduced the price of gas from 8/4d. per 1,000 cubic feet to 7/11. And nearly time too! I have told you that Lurgan Municipal Gasworks produces gas at 3/5d. per 1,000 feet and sells at 5/6d. per 1,000 feet. Belfast Municipal Gasworks produces at 2/- per 1,000 cubic feet and sells at 2/11 with 20% discount to quarterly customers, and still makes a profit of £84,000. Dungannon people should make their own gas and refuse to be fleeced by a private company any longer.

* *

Enniskillen Guardians have deferred an extensive scheme of painting the Workhouse, because the Chairman, Mr. W. J. Brown, J.P., does not know whether they should paint the walls with the Union Jack or the Tricolour. Certainly there are some funny uses for the Union Jack and the Tricolour.

* *

Fermanagh. According to the "Northern Whig", of 5/10/25, "Fermanagh farmers are **distressed** at the plentiful potato supply. There was never in the history of the country a greater or more prolific crop and those potatoes which were planted in June are a magnificent crop."

God's goodness distresses the Fermanagh farmers.

* *

Free State farmers, speaking of their recent visit to Denmark say—"We saw very few mansions and no cabins; in other words, there were no signs of poverty; everyone was well dressed and well fed, and the cleanliness of the people and their dwellings was remarkable."

Yes! and we will have Co-operation and Socialism here when the people of Northern Ireland will it.

When you've read "The Opposition," please pass it on to a pal.

Tory Sedition!
BY HUGH GEMMELL.

The Tory Party of Ulster have long been notorious for Sedition, Treason and Disloyalty, and many of our present legislators had their unconstitutional activities rewarded by the glittering prizes of office under the Crown. Mr. Hanna, indeed, had the brazen effrontery to quote the "law" on Sedition during the debate on the proclaimed Labour Demonstration, but he, and the other hypocrites, were sharply reminded by the Labour M.P.'s that the Labour Party had always been a constitutional Party, whereas the record of the Government would not stand examination.

Quoth Sir James Craig at Lisburn on the 24th December, 1910. "Let us spend amongst ourselves in the direction of buying arms and ammunition, and say to those who were not with them—'Now you are not going to make us have Home Rule. We are not going to have it at any cost!'"

Here is what he would do with Parliament as outlined at Ballynahinch on the 6th February, 1914—"I say deliberately that the smashing of the whole Parliamentary fabric would be amply justified rather than the situation should be longer protracted. In the face of Civil War, what did it matter if business were made impossible in the House of Commons, what did it matter if the estimates for the forthcoming year were thrown in the waste-paper basket without a single word of discussion." For that he was made Prime Minister and became the upholder of the Constitution.

Said Lord Armaghdale at Belfast on 25th September, 1911—"We will disregard its decrees, we will not pay any taxes it imposes on us. If the Parliament is forced on us we will be prepared to take even stronger measures."

Listen now to the loyalty of Robert Thompson, the Chairman of the Belfast Harbour Board. Belfast, 8th April, 1912—"I learned only a few months ago, Germany has been looking after Ulster developments. She had the drawings all complete of every dock we have in the harbour, including the large new dock recently opened for the Olympic and Titanic. She has also drawings of the approaches of these docks, and, still more, she has an officer named to carry out the necessary campaign." And everybody wondered where the Germans got their accurate information.

Major F. Crawford—who was acclaimed the hero of the Larne Gun Running—was of a similar mind when he said at Bangor on the 29th April, 1912—"If they were put out of the Union... he would infinitely prefer to change his allegiance right over to the Emperor of Germany or anyone else who had got a proper and stable government."

And this is the constitutional habit of Harold Smith, M.P., as reported from his speech at Ballybay, Co. Monaghan, on the 13th July, 1914—"The Minister who gave the order for British troops to advance against Ulster would find there was a convenient lamp-post in Whitehall."

And these are the people who banned a peaceful demonstration of the unemployed that sought to expose the brutality of the Government. What do we think of ourselves at all to allow a bunch of political crooks to restrain the common will of the people? I have reams and reams of their seditious speeches, their disloyal and treasonable utterances and the time may not be far distant when they will be placed in the dock and charged for their crimes against society. On that day I will enjoy myself.

Parliamentary Notes.

The adjourned Session opened with a display of force, seldom if ever, equalled in the city of Belfast, and that is saying something, as Belfast is notorious for displays of various kinds.

S. Kyle had given private notice of the following question; "to ask the Home Secretary by whose authority the Inspector General proclaimed the demonstration that was to be held under the auspices of the Belfast Labour Party (which proposed to demonstrate peacefully) to protest against the Regulations laid down by the Minister of Labour." The Home Secretary replied, accepting full responsibility. The Leader of the Opposition thereupon stated that he would raise the matter on the adjournment, as this was a vital question for the workers. He had not long to wait, as inside ten minutes he was on his feet in a fierce indictment of the Government. A full dress debate followed, which has since been reported in practically every country in the world. **Labour had scored its first tactical victory.**

On the Loans Guarantee Act the Labour Party welcomed the measure because they believe that no Government worthy of the name can be content to allow another government to lay down what taxation etc., the people they are responsible for, will pay.

On the Widows' and Orphans' Pensions measure, Willie M'Mullen made the best speech he has yet made in the Northern House. He riddled the measure and gave us a taste of what he yet may do. The debate was the best sustained since Parliament opened, and was marked by some fine speeches.

In the Old Age Pensions (Thrift Disqualification Clause) Jack Beattie made the truth more plain than ever, that had it not been for the Labour Opposition in the House we would have been waiting for years on this very desirable reform.

The score that will please our women readers most was undoubtedly the question that Mr. Kyle asked the Minister of Commerce, "In view of the fact that the quartern loaf is sold in Belfast at 10½ d., when the Food Council of Britain states there is no justification for a higher price than 9d., is he prepared to take steps to see that this essential commodity is reduced in price?"

It is significant to note that this question was put in on the **7th October,** but the question was not answered until the 14th October, when the Bread Ring announced the reduction of the 4 lb. loaf to 9½ d.

Mr. Grant hastened to claim credit for this, assisted by the Minister of Commerce, but the fact remains that the **Second Score** is with Labour.

Let The Battle Be Joined

The electors of South Belfast are being offered an opportunity of voting against a Government which for sheer brutality and callous indifference to the claims of common humanity, has never been paralleled except in Rome under Mussolini.

The people wanted to vote Labour at the last election but were denied the opportunity, and in sheer disgust at the Tories, they elected a man who had already yielded himself, body and spirit to the Booze interests of Belfast. During the whole course of the present Parliament, South Belfast has been a sealed book, unmentioned and unrepresented. Never once has it figured in the debates, and never once has a Unionist M.P. advanced the claims of the Constituency. One Unionist member, the Right Honourable Thomas Moles, outrages our common humanity by drawing **three salaries and expenses** from the community, and in return he has spurned our interests by studied and contemptuous silence. True enough, he was returned despite the passionate protests and demonstrations of the electors, but on this occasion the Tory Candidate hasn't the advantage of P.R. to protect him, and the fight is a straight one and the issue clear. The rising tide is with Labour, and our power is so great that in the Senate Election we placed our nominee despite the ecstatic and feverish efforts of the Government Benches. The public conscience has revolted against the corruption, jobbery, civic scandals and squandermania that have been paraded before the world as a sample of public virtue in Ulster. And the common people are tired of having their united will for peaceful demonstration opposed by the display of armed force, and the threat of physical violence, that passes for Government.

They carry matters with a high hand, and the Cromwellian example that decorates their parliamentary speeches might well be pressed home to them. Those who rise by the strong hand will assuredly fall by the strong hand, and Cromwell flashed the Northern Government on the screen of History and visualised them in his speech to the Commons on 20th April, 1653. Thus the "Protector":—

"It is high time for me to put an end to your sitting in this place, which you have dishonoured by your contempt of all virtue, and defiled by your practice of every vice. Ye are a factious crew and **enemies to all good Government.** Ye are a pack of mercenary wretches and would, like Esau, sell your country for a mess of pottage! And like Judas betray your God for a few pieces of money! Is there a single virtue now remaining amongst you? Is there one vice you do not posess? Ye have no more religion than my horse! **Gold is your God!** Which of you have not bartered your conscience for bribes? Is there a man amongst you that hath the least care for the good of the Commonwealth? Ye sordid prostitutes, have ye not defiled the sacred place and turned the Lord's temple into a den of thieves by your immoral principles and immoral practices? Ye are grown intolerably odious to the whole nation! You were deputed here to get grievances redressed—**are not yourselves become the greatest grievance?** Your country therefore calls upon me to cleanse this Augean stable—by putting a final period to your iniquitous proceedings in this House—and which by God's help and strength He hath given me. I am now come to do it! I command ye therefore upon the peril of your lives, to depart immediately out of this place! **Go, get out! Make haste, ye venal slaves— begone! So take away that shining bauble there! And lock up the doors!!"**

Vote Labour And Defend The Right.

The Land Question.
BY SOWSEED.

The agricultural industry is one that must have the earnest attention of the Labour Party of Northern Ireland. Shall the land be nationalised and if so, how? At the present time we hear nothing but complaints. The Farmers' Union constantly reiterates that farmers cannot pay their way. Rents are high, local taxation is a terrible burden and the cost of production (labour charges) entirely prohibitive. To meet this, and incidentally to obtain votes, we see the Northern Government passing a Land Purchase Bill. From revenue derived from other industries and sources, grants are made to meet the clamorous cries of the farmers, and still the cry arises "we want more."

Now, one naturally asks, is the position so serious? Are all the sympathetic utterances of public men, and all the reports and articles of the Capitalist press merited?

If so, the case for a change, the need for Nationalisation is imperative.

But is all this indisputable? How is it that the market price of land is so high, almost double the amount paid in pre-war days. Bankrupt concerns generally find a poor market. One would think the stock of other industries such as Linen, shipbuilding, railroads, etc., would not find at the present time, a ready or rising market, but compared with agricultural stock—the land—they would be a poor investment.

In dealing with the land question, there are three interests which call for careful consideration, each one being vital and more or less dependent on the others; the interests of the capitalist, the farmer and the agricultural labourer. The average price of farming land with wuitable buildings would run as follows:- best quality £50 per acre, medium £35, inferior £20. Take the best quality and we find an annual charge of £3 per acre, being the Bank rate of interest at 6% on £50. This remains a permanent charge unless the farmer is not only able to meet it, but also to make a profit to reduce the capital debt. In addition to this amount there is the rent, or land purchase annuity, payable to the Government; average 15/- per acre, also rates to meet local requirements, 8/- per acre. Thus on best quality farms, we have a total annual charge of £4 3s. per acre which must be met before the farmer considers his own needs of the demands of the labourer he employs. Let us for a moment look at this from another angle. On a 50 acre farm the owner pays annually to the Capitalist,

£150 interest

on borrowed money to purchase the farm. Also £37 10s. for rent or Government annuity, repayment of money advanced to buy out the landlord; making a total yearly burden of £187 10s. This represents the interest of the capitalists, and is one which must be considered in any scheme for nationalisation. The other farms of medium and inferior quality can be valued on the same basis. Although the capital value is not so great, the rates and Government annuity are somewhat similar to that on best quality land. The overhead or capital charges would be harder to meet on these farms as the soil is inferior.

In a short article like this, it is hard to give full justice to the various points of interest, but a comparison of the agricultural workers' lot with that of the Capitalist may be of some value. The farm labourer; 25/- average weekly wage. (*Different Counties have different rates*—Ed., L.O.) One man as assistant to the farmer is supposed to be sufficient on a farm as above stated. He gives six and very often seven days of the week for his remuneration £65 per annum; whereas one of his *partners* the capitalist, receives £187 10s. per annum and gives none of his time for his share in the partnership.

The principles of Socialism would

work out badly for somebody if applied to this industry. Would it be the labourer, I wonder? If the Editor wishes the other partner (the farmer) can be dealt with later—on his pathway to nationalisation.

(The LABOUR OPPOSITION exists for Socialism, and articles telling our readers how to socialise the Land and Tools of Industry are always welcome. —Ed.)

The Farm Labourer.
BY OUR PROPAGANDIST.

It is very interesting work organising the rural workers, who think nothing of cycling 5 or 6 miles in order to hear the Labour Gospel. A few days ago I addressed a large open-air meeting of these workers at Cross Roads, Co. Derry, and they are very keen on securing improved conditions of labour for themselves and their dependents. The able bodied men who attended my meeting are being paid an average wage of 22/- per week, no perquisites, no half-holiday and no harvest bonus. They all voted Unionist at the last election, but when asked, they voted unanimously and enthusiastically for a resolution which called upon the Northern Government ot at once set up an Agricultural Wages Board to ensure a guaranteed working week, a half-holiday and a minimum wage.

I think the time is opportune for legislation along these lines, as our farmers have had a splendid harvest and the labourers are not likely to share unless County Committees and a Central Wages Board are called into being at once. In August, 1924, Mr. Noel Buxton, the Labour Minister of Agriculture had the gratification of seeing his Bill become the law of the land with the result that in the best districts of England to-day, farm labourers are receiving a minimum wage of 42/- per week, with a guaranteed working week, a half-holiday and a harvest bonus. In addition to the above, Cattlemen and Horsemen are entitled to 5/- per week extra.

In many of the English districts the working week is fixed at 48 hours.

Our Northern Government have time and again promised to move on parallel lines with Great Britain as far as social legislation is concerned, therefore I see no reason why we should not have an Agricultural Wages Board just as we had from 1917 to 1920, and on which Mr. Archdale, our Minister of Agriculture did good work, and I might point out that Mr. Coyle, who acted as Chairman of the Irish Board, is at present one of Mr. Archdale's permanent secretaries.

Let us have this act of justice done to the men and women who toil in the oldest and most fundamental of all human industries.

"A Worker Looks At Economics".
by Mark Starr.

The Labour Publishing Co., 38 Great Ormonde Street, London, W.C.4.Cloth, 2/6. Paper, 1/-.

We recommend to our readers this interesting little book: it will stimulate interest in Economics, which is very badly needed amongst the new recruits to the movement.

The illustrations of surplus value on pages 36 and 37 might be made clearer without losing cogency, and the author, if he does not agree with Ricardo on differential rent, might at least refrain from using it as the basis of his own opinions.

It is interesting also to notice the value that is placed on Professor Clay's analysis of the savings of the workers on p.29.

It is rather a stunner to be told on the same page that Capitalism is the last of succeeding social systems. One would have thought the author believed that Socialism would provide another social system.

We would suggest if there is a reprint of this stimulating little book that refute would read better than repute on page 18.
—S. Kyle.

Poverty Breeds Consumption.

Dr. Andrew Trimble, Chief Tuberculosis Officer of Belfast County Borough, writes in his report "A consideration of the localities in which patients reside reveals that tuberculosis is higher in the older, poorer, **and more congested wards**, where no expansion is possible, a fact which is at once apparent when we find that Smithfield, Court, Dock, and St. George's stand at the head of the list in deaths from Tuberculosis in the various wards, while Windsor and Cliftonville are at the bottom."

Capitalism destroys Health and Home Life. Vote Labour and abolish poverty.

Notes And News.

The newly-formed Shankill Divisional Labour Party has almost 100 members, and all who wish to join should communicate with Hugh M'Ilwrath, 102 M'Tier Street.

"When the Timber Ring broke, prices fell 50%," said a witness at the Belfast Housing Inquiry.

Comrade Councillor Harry Midgley is again ill, and expects to undergo an operation. The entire Movement will wish him a safe recovery and strength to continue his magnificent work for Socialism.

The I.L.P. Choir is undertaking considerable work this winter and there are vacancies for all parts. They meet Wednesday at 8 p.m. in the York St. Hall.

The Central I.L.P., is running a Bazaar in the Hall in York Street. See page 3.

Outdoor propaganda is being continued during the winter and you will find a list on the back page.

Reports from all the Divisions, both Town and Country, show that the Summer campaign just closed was the greatest ever conducted in Ulster, and the feeling is that a General Election would result in Labour being returned to power.

The "new regulations" are pressing severely on a people already hard pressed, and 203 workers in Lindsay Thompson's were turned down because, on short time, they were **earning more than half** their normal earnings. Complaints are pouring into our office from the Casual Dock Workers in the Northern Ports, that they are being similarly treated. The Shopkeepers are already feeling the difference in their sales and travellers and warehousemen are threatened with the sack. Low wages, or "no wages" do not help unemployment. They make it worse, but the Government does not care. Meanwhile, Sir James Craig gets £65 per week; the Duke of Abercorn gets £150 per week and their cronies are similarly rewarded. When there is work to do, they ignore the Belfast Workers and send the job across the water, and the £9,000 worth of furniture and decorations for Hillsborough Castle were bought from London.

A Tip for Megaw.

Megaw is looking for the robbers, if any. Here they are. Not a shake or a knot but a cool 12/2d. per week on every Parlour house and 9/8d. per week on every Kitchen house built by the Corporation.

Pay attention!

A Parlour house is 16/6d. per week for 40 years and that amounts to £1,716.

It costs £450 to build, or 4/4d. per week for 40 years. That is they steal 12/2d. per week off the rent, or £1,266 on each parlour house.

A Kitchen house is rented at 13/6d. per week for 40 years, and that equals £1,404. It costs £407 to build, or 3/10d. per week for 40 years. That is, they plunder £997 on every Kitchen house, of 9/8d. per week out of your rent.

Who are the robbers?

The land costs 2 1/4d. per week, per house. The Bricklayer gets 3 3/4d. per week, per house. Who are the thieves? The Interest-mongers and the Banks. They steal 12/2d. or 9/8d. per week out of every house *and Megaw is looking for the robbers ! !*

Denis Hope.

Christian Civilization Meetings.

(Customs House Steps East.)

Speakers For November

Sunday, Nov. 1st.—Mr. James Duff, P.L.G.

—*"Poverty And Its Cure."*

Sunday, Nov. 8th.—Councillor Wallace Gillespie.

—*"Labour."*

Sunday, Nov. 15th.—Councillor Bob Getgood.

—*"Unemployment And The Way Out."*

Sunday, November 29th.—Mrs. Margaret M'Coubrey.

—*"Co-operation And Labour."*

Chairman—Robt. Dorman.

All Meetings Commence at 3 p.m.

A Use For The Ulster Parliament.

BY JACK BRAND.

When the "Carson Circus" landed in Ulster with Jimmy Craig as top of the bill, and Dawson Bates and Johnny Gordon taking the part of comedians, most Socialists looked to the "House" for amusement.

But social affairs are operated by dynamic forces other than the antics of Ulster's Comic Opera, and the fact has been overlooked, that a Regional Parliament for Northern Ireland might perform a useful function in the evolution of the social fabric of Ireland.

Socialists accept as a matter of fact that political institutions should reflect the economic structure of their time, if they are to fulfil their proper functions of social adjustment.

May the writer suggest that there is a use for a Northern Assembly, covering a region with a different political history than the rest of Ireland, and which has gone further in economic development.

The Socialist view is, that the structure of a Modern State should allow as much local autonomy as possible, in a form, which will enable the building up of a highly organised international social structure, which could carry out the vast and complicated operations of modern life.

A Regional Assembly in the North is in harmony with these fundamental requirements, and I put forward these points, as an aid to the solution of a problem which has got to be removed, if the workers are to make effective use of their growing unity.

What is wanted in Ulster is a new conception of the work of their Assembly and its problems.

The North of Ireland, an agricultural area, with one large City and a few decent sized towns with an agricultural hinterland, is an ideal unit, if we are going to avoid the turning of Ireland into an industrial nightmare like the Midlands of England.

The solution is in combining the agricultural and industrial operations, so as to develop a stabilised social structure and prevent the growth of Belfast into an industrial hell, like some large English towns which are divorced from the land. This would stop the flow of country workers into an already top-heavy industrial area, with its usual effect of lowering city standards of life, and help the stabilisation of the whole Northern Area.

Certain problems might be taken in hand at once. For example, the drawing up of a regional system of town planning, urban and rural, for the whole Province. The grouping of villages and small towns around a factory or industry either existing or to be started.

The development of co-operative, large scale buying and selling by the farmers' Co-operatives, with the help of the State and workers' organizations.

And as an immediate measure, the development of a state planned system of sewerage, water supply, transport and electric light and power for the whole Province in such a way as to help developments.

The electric light and power supply would solve the Bann drainage and Coalisland coal problems, and prevent the turning of Coalisland into a coal dump.

Socialists will not be under the delusion that the biggest problem before the Ulster workers, namely Unemployment, can be solved by any means other than the assumption of Political Power by the workers so as to carry out measures which will enable them to purchase all that they make in factory or farms, and local problems should be met by local Socialists in a manner suitable to their own area.

The Labour Unionist Association has been officially challenged to a public debate on Socialism on more than one occasion by the I.L.P. but they will not meet us. J.M. Andrews, M.P., is their President.

Book Reviews.

Revolution By Reason:—By Oswald Mosley, Labour Literature Department, 14 Gt. George Street, London, S.W.1. Price Twopence.

If hard hitting and virile thinking will sell a pamphlet, then this one ought to be a "best seller." He says, "We hold that evolutionary Socialism is in itself not enough." Crisis after crisis sends capitalist society staggering ever nearer to abysses of inconceivable catastrophe to suffering millions." "Measures of a drastic and Socialist character must be enforced rapidly over the whole field of industry."

Mr. Mosley argues that banks should be socialised and then conducted for the benefit of the community whose credit they exercise. He urges the expansion of "credit in a novel, scientific and Socialist manner" and "the emission of new money in the shape of consumers' credits" thus securing the availability where it is most required and will be used for the general advantage. The necessary machinery including the establishment of an Economic Council with statutory powers is outlined, and in the short space of thirty pages Mr. Mosley deals also with a number of other points of interest, including, the folly of wage reduction; the Uses of Consumers credits; how to defeat the efforts of Capitalism to sabotage Socialism; Socialist planning to keep down prices; the Banks and the Miners; Gold versus People, and the Fallacies of Mr. Churchill. HUGH GEMMELL

James Keir Hardie—By William Stewart, I.L.P. Publications Department. Price 3/6 net.

15/-, 6/6, 3/6.—Thus runs the price evolution of Willie Stewart's Magnum Opus. The latest edition is identical, word for word, with the others, but the 'make up' of the book is immeasurably superior. One complaint I have, and it is this; the new edition contains only one photo-plate instead of the four in the original edition, and our thousands of recruits would appreciate the photos. Surely the book is not only for those who knew Hardie, but is a monument to his memory for all time. The next edition should contain two pages of small reproductions showing Hardie; his home in Cumnock; Nevill's Court London; going to Parliament; together with the funeral pictures contained in the Reformer's Bookstall Memoir, issued in 1915. And the frontspiece should be the fighting Hardie with the flashing eyes and the head held high, instead of the philosophic Hardie in the present issue. The biography is a clear record of a great fighter who literally gave his life for Socialism, and the development of the class struggle during the last 40 years in Britain is told with singular insight and power. Personal reminiscence, Conference battles, and decisions and the strength and frailty of Leaders are all faithfully recorded, and make the book a necessity to all students and propagandists. Those who knew Hardie, and who know his biographer, will treasure the "Life" for the memory of two great pioneers who fought for human freedom. **Hugh Gemmell.**

The Railways.—1825-1925.—By J.T. Walton Newbold. (Labour Publishing Company—2/6 net.).

Into a small book of 100 odd pages, Walton Newbold has packed an amazing amount of information about the development within the last 100 years of railways, not only in this country, but in Europe, Asia and America.

The main purpose of the book is to show the part they have played in the industrial, commercial, political and social development of the world, and their importance in the transformation of Capitalism from a comparatively narrow parochial affair into an imperialist and international system. Details are given of the construction of railways in this country, and the opposition there was from the landlords. Abroad we trace the large part played by international finance in the construction of some of the main continental lines and the danger to the peace of the world they have been and may become. It is a vast subject which we think could well have been amplified into a larger book, but the information given is nevertheless food for propagandists. **—M.H.K.**

"The Law's a H-ass."
THIS 'BATES' ALL!

"The law is clear and the law must be obeyed and respected, and if hon. members opposite think they will be allowed to continue to hold meetings, even on the street, and preach sedition, they make a big mistake." Mr. Hanna 6/10/25. Hansard p.1168. Bah:—

"The Government are determined to protect the right of free speech in Ulster." Sir Dawson Bates trying to explain why he banned the Labour Demonstration 6/10/25.

The Labour Opposition Of Northern Ireland

Vol. 1—No. 10.   December, 1925.   One Penny

Does Socialism Destroy The Home?
BY HUGH GEMMELL.

A famous Norwegian Philosopher with an unpronounceable name has laid down a model plan for all public debaters. It is this: "Find out what your audience detests the most and then accuse your opponent of it." That sums up the attitude of the employing class towards Socialism. Lies are circulated that Socialism will destroy Religion; that it will drive Capital out of the country; that it will put everyone into a uniform, and that it will destroy the home life of the human family that has been an institution for countless centuries. And the beauty of the lie is enhanced by the fact, that every foul practice alleged against Socialism, is one of the stink-pots that makes Capitalism so offensive.

The truth of the matter is that Capitalism destroys all home life, whether it be their own, or the more humble lives of the toilers. And it is an undeniable fact that the disgusting sex orgies of the rich are paraded in the gutter press to corrupt the morals of our social weaklings, and to inspire all religious people with loathing and abhorrence.

Endowed, as they are, with abundant wealth and countless opportunities, the children of the rich are nevertheless deprived of the natural right to mother love, and from their birth are handed over to the care of a paid nurse. From private tutor, through public school and university, the story of isolation is the same and the unhappy child of the social butterfly learns from birth that Capitalism destroys the home.

Among the working class, the same dread story of misery during childhood manifests itself, except that our wretchedness is washed with the tears and grief of broken motherhood. Thousands of working class mothers are compelled to rise in the raw cold hours of the early morning, and after a scanty meal of bread and tea, drag their baby from the blankets to be deposited for the day in the local baby club, while the mother piles up profits for the plunderers. Capitalism destroys the home! And who among us has not had his soul tortured at the sight of thousands of ragged, barefooted, and often hungry children, yelling with raucous voices on the streets, trying to sell the newspapers that perpetuate their misery and make tainted money from their child slavery. On numerous occasions I have returned home on a wretched night to find a miserable atom of humanity huddled in my doorway, clinging there in sheer despair, in the desperate hope of selling the last paper that realises the profit on the investment made.

Capitalism destroys the home! Private enterprise in Belfast is compelled to admit that it has failed to produce the 10,000 working-class houses that are needed now, and it has earned the unenviable distinction of making two, or more, families live, where only one lived before. A rising death rate from

---

Vote   Labour   <u>Next</u>   Time!

13 per 1,000 to 15 per thousand of the population in Belfast ought to warn the community against the evils of overcrowding and insanitary dwellings, and the warning of Dr. Trimble was a timely one, that consumption was fostered and encouraged by the congested housing conditions in Smithfield, St. George's, Court, and other purely working-class wards. Long spell unemployment completes the misery of the workers, and old men and young men are wrenched from their homes and sent across the water to find the jobs that the captains of industry failed to provide here. That and the emigrant ship are the foul partners in Capitalist home-wrecking and it is time the workers turned from those who have betrayed them so long, and endeavoured to erect and occupy for themselves, the beautiful homes they build for others. Socialism would build up home life, purify public morals, abolish child slavery and free our women from the horrors of the mill and the baby club. The workers have nothing to fear from Socialism.

It is Capitalism that destroys the home !

Hits and Misses.
BY MARKSMAN.

"North Down Herald."—17/10/25, claims that they are unalterably loyal and proceeds—"What is Orangeism? For what does it stand? Is it a mere pawn in the game of political expediency? Is it a mere competition for Commissioners of the Peace and the like? Surely we are primarily and fundamentally a Protestant organisation! If not, let us either throw down our charters and get up our guns—or go to bed!"

* *

I respectfully suggest that the Editor of this "true blue" paper should go to bed and have a good sleep, as thinking along the above lines will turn him out a rank rebel.

* *

Winston Churchill is puttting the wind up his friends by hinting that the reduction of income tax in his last budget was a mistake and the 42 million pounds may have to be re-imposed.

* *

Captain W. Adams, A.L.A.A.—Speaking in Clarence Place Hall, Belfast, said he believed that poverty in the next 50 or 60 years should be eventually eradicated. Why, Captain, a Labour Government in Gt. Britain with a big majority would do the job in 5 or 6 years.

* *

Hairdressers.—Judge Bairstow, in giving judgement at Westminster for £4 5s. 6d. claimed by a hairdresser, said, "No man is always satisfactory. I daresay he sometimes cuts somebody when shaving, or perhaps did not give clients whom he was massaging as much attention as they wanted. That did not justify his dismissal. A hairdresser is entitled to be human." It is good to find a Judge who is so very human.

* *

Bangor U.D.C. have unanimously decided to promote a Bill in Parliament for the erection of Sea Water Baths, a Public Abattoir, and matters relating to Local Government. More power to the Bangorians. There are no flies on the Bangor people.

* *

Ballymoney.—Mr. Best, speaking at a meeting of Antrim Co. Council, objected to the proposal to omit provision of £1,000 for the erection of three wooden huts at Ballymoney Model School, to accommodate 250 pupils. He said the condition of the school was a perfect scandal, as the children had nowhere to sit, one class having to stand while another was at lessons. The Ministry promised to provide accommodation, but the suggested huts were in no way satisfactory.

* *

Coleraine Regional Committee considered a communication from the Ministry of Education. Mr. D. H. Christie said "God knows what the Ministry wants, for I don't." He was of opinion that they had too good a Secretary to have any reflection cast on him by some "hum skum" in Belfast.

* *

Derry.—Mr. W. M'Carter, speaking at a meeting of Rotarians, said "Greed of enhanced profits was the beginning of combinations and trusts, many of which were merciless in dealing with independent competitors, and the final result was that in nearly all civilised countries the main industries were under the control of a few centralised concerns. Fellowship between a trust and its employees was almost an impossibility." Righto, Comrade M'Carter, come and join the I.L.P.

* *

Enniskillen.—Mr. Geo. Whaley, J.P., Chairman of the Urban Council, sanctioned the showing of "The Ten Commandments" on a Sunday recently and was criticised for it. In reply, he said that the Council should have confidence that he would sanction nothing that would lower the dignity of the Council or the moral tone of the town. Good old Dignity and Morality.

* *

Dublin.—21,000 families, comprising 90,000 persons live in one-roomed dwellings in Dublin. Good old Capitalist System.

* *

Glasgow.—132 persons out of every thousand live in a one-roomed dwelling. No wonder Glasgow is going Red.

* *

Belfast.—10,000 Belfast families are clamouring for homes for heroes.

* *

Derry P.L.G., have decided to allow 20/- per week to a widower with 8 helpless children who have no other source of income. Oh my! Such extravagence.

* *

Kilrea, Co. Derry, wants an improved sewerage and water scheme. I visited Kilrea some years ago and found the Mickies and Prods quarrelling about the town pump. On St. Partick's Day, a Green Flag floated over the pump and the Prods got no water that day, and on 12th July, a Union Jack surmounted the pump and if a Mickie looked at the pump he got his head cracked. The trouble was usually settled by foot and horse police cracking all heads in the vicinity of the pump.

* *

Tyrone Co. Council.—There are 49 direct labour schemes being carried out under the supervision of Mr. Leebody, County Surveyor, and Mr. Leebody claims that direct labour schemes are efficient and economical.

* *

Co. Cork labourers cottages are let at 10½d. per week. Oh Lord! soften the hearts of our Northern Councillors, make them like Cork.

* *

Enniskillen P.L.G. have got neither **dignity** nor **morality** in their make up, as they have further reduced the wages of a labouring man from 3/- to 2/- a day. They have also refused an increase of salary to the Head Nurse in Charge of the Fever Hospital. The Nurse has £67 10s. per annum, after 24 years' service.

* *

Strabane U.D.C. are having trouble with building Contractors. At a recent meeting, Mr. Boyle stated that four of the ceilings of the new houses had tumbled down.

* *

Ballymena hiring fair was held on 7/11/25. Ploughmen were hired for six months at £22 to £26. General labourers fetched £18 to £20. Boys £11 to £15. Girls for farm work £16 to £17. Girls for domestic work £9 to £10. Good strong men at Castlederg and Strabane only fetched £15 to £17 for the half-year.

* *

Labour Men Of The North.
BY BOB M'CLUNG.
Councillor Clarke Scott, Belfast.

Clarke Scott spends a great deal of his spare time in looking after the spiritual and bodily welfare of the very poor people of Court Ward. As he says, his Labour views have been deepened and strengthened by seeing "Out" workers sitting from early morning until late at night, with aching back, fingers and eyes working 15 or 16 hours per day for a mere pittance, and living in homes not fit for human habitation. He is particularly interested in securing playgrounds for the children, and is rather proud of the fact that his proposal in the City Council that £1,000 be allocated to secure Municipal playgrounds was agreed to, with the result that we have now six open-air spaces where children can romp to their heart's content without danger of being injured by horse or motor traffic. An active member of the Postal workers' Union, he acted as Committeeman for several years. In August, 1919, he was selected for Municipal honours by his Trade Union and was successful in January, 1920 in being returned as Senior Councillor for Woodvale Ward. He was the official Labour Party nominee, and was one of the team that was officered by D. R. Campbell and Sam. Kyle, and the splendid work done by this team will be forever gratefully remembered by their colleagues in the Labour Movement.

In spite of his loyalty to Labour principles, and in spite of conscientious attention to Municipal duties Clarke Scott was defeated in January, 1923, as the reign of terror was still existing. Standing again as Official Labour Candidate in January, 1924, he won Court Ward in spite of money and influence arrayed against the nominees of Labour. Personally known and loved in Court Ward he is certainly a champion of the poor.

Parliamentary Notes.

Since writing the notes for your last issue many things have happened. Two precedents, at least, have been established by our three Labour members. The first of these was the introduction of a Bill to regulate Agricultural wages by Mr. S. Kyle, who cited the wages paid to Agricultural Labourers as being 25/- in Antrim and Down, and 22/6 in the other counties, and asked for a free vote of the house. Mr. Archdale, Minister of Agriculture, moved the rejection of the Bill, and this was supported by Mr. Rowley Elliott, who was vehement in his statements that agricultural labourers did not want their wages regulated. Mr. Wm. M'Mullen answered the criticism, and the Government refused to take off their whips, and the measure, despite the assurances given of parallel legislation, was defeated by 18 votes to 8.

On the Unemployment Insurance Act, Mr. J. Beattie gave the Government some home truths in his own way. Mr. S. Kyle stuck to his original point that "Extended" benefit was as much a right as was "Standard" benefit, on the grounds that the contribution from the Worker and Employer was based on the fact that "Extended" Benefit was being paid. Mr. Wm. M'Mullen, speaking to a Labour amendment to abolish the waiting period altogether, said the extension of the gap from 3 days to 6 was indefensible.

On the Widows and Orphans "Insurance" measure, amendment after amendment to increase the amount, to make the scope of the measure wider, to get pensions for the unfortunate illegitimate children, was voted down by the Government.

The other precedent was established, when Mr. S. Kyle gave notice of a vote of 'No Confidence' in the government owing to their ineptitude in dealing with the Unemployment Problem. A very heated debate took place on the new Regulations on Standard of Family Income. Mr J. Beattie denounced the Government right, left and centre, for their infamous proposals reducing the standard from 46/- to 40/- for a family.

Mr. Wm. M'Mullen held that the Government was responsible for murder in consequence of the death of an ex-Navy man, who had been denied his Unemployment Insurance Benefit.

On the adjournment of the House till the 8th December, an interesting debate took place in which Mr. S. Kyle succeeded in drawing the Prime Minister to deny that he had been called to London to meet representatives of the Free State, though they were in London at the same time, and that as the Prime Minister only met the first Commissioner of Works on the Wednesday, he could have stayed over for the Unemployment Debate on the Tuesday. The fact is slowly but surely being driven home to the admirers of the Government that Sir James has no policy, never had any policy, except to scare the timid electors with bogey cries of "Not an Inch," "Save the Boundary," etc., etc.

The New Bogey.

Sir Robert Lynn, Editor of the "Northern Whig," was speaking in the Y.M.C.A. the other night, and someone asked him what the Northern Government would do for a "bogey" now that the Boundary Bogey was dead. "Oh," said Robbie John lightly, "we will always have a 'bogey,' so long as there is a single Socialist left in Belfast." Sir Robert is the local anti-sosh Goliath, but don't judge him too harshly, because he was perfectly willing to go to America with Mr. Saklatvala, the Communist, and who does not remember him at the Irish Banquet in London, standing up to honour the toast of "God Save Ireland," while lusty voices sang the once "Rebel" song. A man is known by the company he keeps, and Sir Robert would make a wonderful "Eloquent Dempsey."

Sam Kyle, M.P.—A baby boy has been born to Mrs. and Mr. Sam Kyle— Parliamentary Leader, and the healthy youngster secures its own way by well sustained obstructionist tactics. The "Home Government" always capitulates.

Is It War?

When the Socialist Movement in Northern Ireland challenges the ascendancy of Toryism, and seeks to educate Democracy towards control in industry and of the political institutions that link up the economic activities of the community, it need not hope to escape embarrassment, or to find its progress unhampered by the Capitalist enemy. As a matter of fact, every weapon in the armoury of the "Boss", from foul lies in the kept Press, to arrest and imprisonment without trial will be used to perpetuate the outworn system of wage-slavery. And the natural right of all men to speak their minds freely in public on questions affecting the common-weal, will be suppressed by King Kapital and conveniently termed "sedition". The imprisonment of Comrade Sam Patterson is a case in point. **Sam Patterson was not arrested ! The Socialist Movement was arrested !** And if you doubt the logic of that, you can turn up the Hansard record of the Northern Parliament for the 6th October last, and there you will find speech after speech by responsible Ministers of the Government, crowing aloud in their jubilation that organised Labour had abandoned its Unemployed Procession merely because the Home Secretary raised his little finger. On that occasion, Mr. Hanna, Parliamentary hack to Sir Dawson Bates said, "If hon. members opposite think that they will be allowed to **continue** to hold meetings, even on the street, and preach sedition, they make a big mistake." That was the signal for war against free speech in Ulster, and so soon as public indignation at the Patterson injustice has been mellowed by time, another and more deadly blow will be aimed at Labour. Organised Labour should be ready to meet the onslaught and should accept it, eagerly and willingly, as a trial of strength between Individualism and Socialism. We have nothing to fear. Right is on our side, and we are the only political force in Ulster that has unswervingly upheld constitutional practices and retained the faith of Democracy in the Ballot Box. And why should we fear, when in Belfast alone, out of a total electorate of 200,000, we are assured of the allegiance of 50,000 Socialist voters? The truth is, that at the last General Election in the Six Counties, more votes were cast against the Tory Government, than were cast in its favor, and the recent harsh and repressive measures were inspired by the knowledge of their waning power. Capitalism is a dying institution in Ulster and the hand of decay is on every public board that it administers. Our privately-owned industries are bankrupt or stagnant, our credit is shattered and our public bodies have become the object of suspicion and distrust. In one instance, a searching public enquiry had to be ordered to still the wrath of the citizens. Labour is next for industrial and political power in Ulster, and the whole Movement should press forward to the goal with inspired energy and renewed zeal. Let January be the testing time and let us send a strong team of Labour Men to the Corporation to redress the manifold wrongs of our people.

Let no man say to himself, "Oh I won't be missed if I don't help with the work." That way disaster lies. Remember that the strength of a chain is its weakest link; the speed of an army is its slowest unit, and the measure of social prosperity is the degree of comfort, or rather misery, of the most destitute citizen. On with the fight!

Letters To The Editor.

15 Tudor Place,
Belfast.

Dear Comrade,

I was delighted to read in the *Forward,* a lengthy quotation from Robert Blatchford's "Merrie England." I think it is such a pity that those Masterpieces, are allowed to go out of print. The reading of his three great books, for they are great, made more Socialists than all the lectures and sermons put together, and would again; they are an education and an inspiration. If the younger Comrades could only get a chance to study "Britain for the British," "Merrie England," and "God and my Neighbour." It was the latter cleared my orthodox mind from superstition for which I can never be grateful enough. His kink and sympathetic, and delightfully Socratic manner of writing, also his fine logic, is very impressive. I think he should be crowned with glory and honour while he is still with us; when he tells us what he sees through his telescope, it is fascinating. I have a few of his books, and I would be pleased to lend them to any young Comrade who would desire to read them.

Wishing you great success in your noble efforts for the glorious cause of Socialism and Education,

I remain, Ever truly,
Mary Jackson.

Broughshane,
To the Editor of the **Opposition**

Now that the Government has adopted the Contributory Pensions Scheme, would it not be possible for our three Northern M.P.'s to arrange with the Ministry of Labour for those Members of Trade Unions who would be prepared to pay, say, 3d. or 4d. more per week on their Health Insurance card, and have a Pension of 25/- or 30/- at 65 (as 10/- is no good).

Hoping you will invite your readers to consider this, and have our three members' opinion on it.

Yours sincerely,
Frank Gulbraith.

(It should be remembered that the Labour Party is opposed to "Contributory" Pensions, and insists on Pensions being Non-contributory. —ED.)

Dear Mr. Editor,

On behalf of 200 tenants and their families, in all about 1,400 people, who occupy Labourers' Cottages in the Antrim Rural and Urban District, I am asked to use your columns to convey to Mr. Sam. Kyle, M.P. their sincere thanks for his generous act in appearing at the Rent Inquiry held at Antrim on Saturday, 7th November last. It was only another proof, if one were required, of the Labour M.P.'s interest in the cause of the workers, the class to which the Labour M.P.s belong. It is worthy of notice that when about 900 electors were in trouble about the rent of their cottages, out of all the M.P.s, County Councillors and Rural District Councillors who are supposed to represent us in this area, Mr. Kyle was the only public representative who turned up at the hearing to defend us, all the others were conspicuous by their absence. But I presume they were, in their own estimation, better employed in playing bridge or whist than in seeing that justice was done to the tenants, whom they despise when there is no election on. They may call our Labour representatives "Red" or whatever name they like, but when the workers' grievances call for redress, it's Mr. Kyle and his colleagues who come to the rescue, and believe me, Mr. Editor, we will remember with gratitude the Labour Champion's attitude on the seventh day of November, in the year of our Lord, One Thousand Nine Hundred and Twenty-five. With very best wishes for the success of the great Labour movement in general, and for the success of your wee paper in particular.

Signed on behalf of the Antrim
Cottage Tenants.
"Cranfield."

(The best thanks you could give us would be to get those 900 Tenants to send 900 P.O.'s for 2/- and we will send the **Opposition** to them, post free, for a year.—Ed.)

Book Reviews.

The I.L.P. Publications Department is very active and a lengthy list of books and pamphlets is to hand. Among the more recent and important are "How to End War," by A. Fenner Brockway. The causes of war (economic) are examined and explained, and the logical development of Capitalist Production, viz., Imperialism, is outlined in masterly fashion. Dependent Nations and the colour question receive consideration and a constructive policy of total disarmament is boldly advocated.

"Socialism for Business Men." by J. Ramsay MacDonald, M.P. This was a speech delivered to the Liverpool Rotarians and is a re-statement of the Socialist conception of society. The language is remarkably fine and reminiscent of Wilde's 'Soul of Man under Socialism.'

"Make the Workers Free" by Fenner Brockway, is the industrial policy of the I.L.P. and should be studied by every

member and supporter. This pamphlet in particular, should be possessed by our speakers. All these are twopence each, and can be obtained at the I.L.P. Hall, 48 York Street.

"The Socialist Review," for December, price Sixpence, contains informative and challenging articles on Eugene V. Debs; the Japanese anti-Socialist Law; the Fallacy of "Compensation," and Capitalist Policy in Australia.

"Songs from the Shipyards," by Thomas Carnduff. 1/- nett from all booksellers. Carnduff sings with a strong, clear note, full of the rugged vigour of those who toil in the great productive centres of industry. Here are no fainting females imploring a lover to be true, but timber and steel and the mechanical forces that make puny man the master of the world. Other poems tell of the sweet beauty of the night, and the glory of the dawn, and the mystic glamour that enshrouds our City at the midnight hour. But I shouldn't have read "The Hungry Folk." The picture of human misery is so very terrible that I want to go out and take the town to pieces. I have been watching the work of T. C. for some years now, and it is good and still improving. The present songs are a sure foundation for a noble building.

—HUGH GEMMELL.

The Christian View-Point.
The Challenge of Poverty.
BY J. M'A.

The existence of poverty constitutes a challenge to the common Christianity of all who so designate themselves, to the reality of the Faith, Hope and Love, which on the authority of the apostle, are the trinity of essentials.

For poverty denies our faith in man's potentialities, our hope for his destiny, and all-embracing love within us, the greatest of the three.

It asserts a callous materialism destitute of all sense of spiritual values, proclaiming that soulless and anti-christian philosophy the basis of the social structure.

For such insistent reasons the abolition of poverty becomes our task.

When you've read "The Opposition," please pass it on to a pal.

John Bull Out In The Cold.

BY JAMES MAC.

An old English farmer's wife, on a very cold day in winter, went into the rick-yard, where a man was thatching the ricks, and said to him, "John, it is a very bitter day, you must be starving; I will go inside and make you up a mug of warm ale with ginger in it. That will comfort you." John thanked her very kindly and waited. He is still waiting. The old woman forgot—or was careless about keeping her promise; so thought John. The truth was that on arriving in the kitchen, where a big fire was blazing, the old wife turned herself two or three times before the fire, and then said: "really the climate seems quite altered. I think John will do." Let us apply this short story to modern politics in so far as they affect Labour. Stanley Baldwin and his supporters represent the old farmer's wife, John represents the workers of Britain. Twelve months ago, the "old woman" of Westminster promised if he was sent back to the House by a substantial majority, employment would be increased, and John would be comfortable. He was sent back, but on reaching the cheerful blaze of the Government kitchen, he turned round, thought the "climate had altered, and that John would do." So John is still waiting out in the cold.

Even if the Government had been honest and made conscientious efforts to solve the problem, they would not have succeeded. No Government can create employment. It is an econ-omic problem beyond their control, so long as the system of Production for Profit *is tolerated by the people*. Unemployment is one of the evil concomitants of the present iniquitous, capitalist system. In normal times, it comes in ever-recurring cycles. With the advent of these cycles, the workers, who produce all the wealth, suffer extreme hardships; whilst the other

The New Ireland.

We record history's triumph or its loss,
   And mould the future from its past effects,
And thus equipped, we separate the dross—
   From ancient glamour and delete defects.
And so emerges Ireland from the ages,
   In stern virility resolved to change;
Ignoring all those patriotic sages,
   An economic structure to arrange.

Emotional impulsiveness has gone
   To be replaced by sentiments more pure;
The kindred claims fraternal have outshone
   Those baser things our social trend endure.
A rebirth springing not from governing power,
   Nor yet the product of a certain plan,
But with necessity's creative hour—
   Evolves a revolution in the man.

Divison leaves no progress in its wake;
   Hence North and South must link in common aim;
One Ireland is the weapon which shall break
   This system and usurp for nobler claim.
Fiery passion yields to reasoning quest,
   And hope gives way to moral surety;
Yes, this is Ireland at her very best—
   Her natural basis for security.

Mutual comprehension of those laws
   Which operate against the working-class
Effects a combination for the cause
   Of freedom in transition for the mass.
Corrupt tradition teaches us abhor
   Our Northern or our Southern fellowman,
And nurtured by the poets' metaphor
   Has hindrered merging in a solid "clan."

Let history of our class cement our force;
   United action justify demand;
Nor Boundary myth the workers let divorce
That Ireland may become at last our land.

—C.J.M'C.

section of the unemployed, the aristocracy, are revelling in luxury and voluptuousness.

During a sitting of the French Chamber, in 1845, General Foy in a speech before that assembly made use of the word "Aristocracy". A voice from the Ministerial side asked for a definition. The General replied: "Aristocracy is the league; the coalition of those who wish to consume without producing, live without working, occupy all public places without becoming competent to fill them— that is the Aristocracy." Yet it is from the ranks of this class that the Upper House is selected for the purpose of putting a veto upon popular legislation. One great lesson to be learned from English history is: that the workers must act for themselves, and depend not upon Liberal or Tory politicians. Look on this picture of England a hundred years ago. Mackenzie in his "Nineteenth Century" says: "during the first seven years of the Nineteenth Century, English ships conveyed annually across the Atlantic 40,000 Africans for the slave trade. The British Parliament had expressed its approval of the slave traffic in twenty-six acts, and was not roused to its suppression until after twenty years of agitation... The colliers were slaves, bound to their service for life, bought and sold with the works at which they laboured. Women and children worked in the coal-pits. They dragged about little waggons by a chain fastened round the waist, crawling like brutes on hands and feet in the darkness of the mines. Children of six were habitually employed. Their hours of labour were fourteen to sixteen daily. There was no machinery to drag the coal to the surface and women climbed the wooden stairs with baskets of coal upon their back." You may ask why did the people not revolt? But it must be remembered that associations of workers were illegal in Britain previous to the Repeal of the Combination Acts of 1824. At a celebrated popular meeting held in St. Peter's Square, Manchester in 1819, to advocate simple Parliamentary reform, an unsuccessful attempt was made by the authorities to arrest the chief speakers. An order was then given to the military to charge, and many people thereby were seriously injured. This event has been recorded in history as the "Peterloo Massacre."

Recently we had an example of the power of organised labour in securing simple justice. Baldwin's Government only granted a subsidy to the mining industry, when it was found the other powerful Unions of the country were prepared to actively co-operate with the miners in the event of a strike. When the "old women" of Westminster went into the Government kitchen last winter, poor John was forgotten about in the cold outside, until the threatened coal strike. John will be suddenly remembered again at the next General Election and after it.

Men or Horses?

My desk is littered with reports and leaflets issued by the Northern Government, and it was while I was idly browsing through them that my pulse was quickened by leaflet No. 25, issued by the Ministry of Agriculture. It deals with the rearing of horses, and among other suggestions, it says: "In the rearing of young horses, whether thoroughbred or otherwise, particular attention must be paid *from the start* to every *detail* affecting the life of the animal, if the best results are to be obtained. The feeding and care of the dam have very important effects on the well-being of the foal, and every care should be taken to see that she receives proper treatment during that period... *Heavy work and long hours* should be avoided... a liberal diet is necessary... for a week or so before foaling the mare should be released from work... nothing is gained by starving the mother and stinting the foal. Such a course is false economy and will result in stunted development and want of endurance in the animal afterwards... on no account should cruelty or harshness be permitted."

No right thinking individual will object to the foregoing, but we have a right to ask why the Government values horse-flesh more than it values human beings. We Socialists have repeatedly urged that a Ministry of Health should be established to protect the child life and the mother life of the community. We know scores of instances of mothers working in our Northern Mills until within a few hours of childbirth, instead of being released on full keep like the horses. We know hundreds and hundreds of cases of stunted growth and arrested development in our children, simply through starvation and malnutrition and bad housing, and we have said repeatedly that this was false economy no matter how it was viewed. Every evil that Mr. Archdale wants to avoid in the horses, has been endured by the working-class under the Tory administration. Long hours, overwork, mal-nutrition, harshness and cruelty. We know them all and have suffered them all, and when we died under the ordeal, a new wage-slave was ready for the yoke. Wage-slaves are cheap and plentiful, but when a horse dies it costs the "Boss" money to replace it. That is why the Ulster Capitalist Government is so tender hearted. The sooner we get "horse sense" the better.

HOTSPUR.

What is Capital?
BY MARK STARR.

If you give a Scotchman a drink, that is "capital"; to get him to give you one, that is "labour." Thus the comedian on the difference. But according to Lord Leverhulme, "Adam's spade was his capital." Sir Hugh Bell, the coal and iron master, has a similar notion, for he insists that the man who practised abstinence from immediate satisfaction, and shaped the first flint was the first capitalist. The little "Pay Day Talks" distributed by employers urge that "Capital is money usefully employed." Lady Astor has burbled nonsense about the capitalist saving us from the "dark, wild road." Lord Birkenhead has repeated the assertion that capital is savings. Obviously these definitions are defenses of the right of the capitalist to continue his rule, and they try to rally the shortsighted thrifty workers, blind to any larger good, because of their endangered capital, "their little all."

Capital, is, however, essentially different from savings and means of production. Both can become capital, as a sewing needle can become a death dealing instrument. But it is not a matter of argument—it is a matter of arithmetic—to prove that a man cannot become rich by his own efforts. Adam, if he had *saved* £3 a week for 50 weeks a year during 6,000 years would still have £100,000 to collect, before he owned one solitary million. One orthodox professor, Hadley, is frank enough about the start of capital, for he says that "capital originated in robbery" which is unkind to those thrifty and brainy ones of the Leverhulme-Bell fancy. Even if granted an initial honest acquirement, there is a vital difference between money put away in a stocking, and money used to buy shares which yield an interest year by year and still remains undiminished to the end of capitalist time!

Capital implies demand over labour and its exploitation. The would-be capitalist who shipped his means of production and workpeople to a virgin country found that out when they deserted him to start on their own. Just as a stick cannot exist without two ends, so capital is impossible without a working-class, forced to sell its labour-power in order to live.

In the sense that the dead hand of past accumulated wealth will be lifted from the shoulders of living labour, we hope to destroy capital, and its integral exploitation. As for destroying it in the alleged sense—well, in Germany they destroyed the relation of monarch and subject without hurting a Hohenzollern hair. The present relation of capital and labour can also be removed without hurting one spindle or one locomotive. Money will not be able to become capital any longer. Out of the product will be set aside the funds needed to rebuild and extend the means of production no longer used for exploitation. Social needs will rule instead of profit considerations.

Notes And News.

The inmates of Co. Antrim Asylum cost £1 per head per week.

The cost of administering the Northern Government is £138 per hour.

The witnesses—Viscount Bangor, Senator Hill Dickson and Dr. Nolan—stated that attached to the Asylum—Down District —they had a farm of 176 acres which showed a *yearly profit of about £1,000.* Some of our Belfast Capitalists, who can neither pay decent wages, make a profit or get orders, should go there and learn lessons from the loonies.

Said Lady Londonderry, "The great issue all over the world today was the struggle between the forces of ordered progress and the forces of revolution and disorder."—10/11/25. Said Lord Londonderry, "Whatever it may cost in blood and treasure, we shall find that the Trade Unions will be smashed from top to bottom."—13/8/25. Now, gentlemen, what is the verdict? Is it D—— and disorderly?

The **Opposition** is nosing its way

steadily into the out-of-the-way corners of Northern Ireland, and our post bag reveals that its outspoken exposure of public perfidy is much appreciated. We need now to follow this up with propaganda meetings.

Coleraine I.L.P. is steadily adding to its membership, and the Branch Secretary J.F. is to be congratulated on his pluck and perseverance.

The Shankill Divisional Labour Party has settled down to work. The Branch meets every Wednesday at 8 p.m. in number 2 Luke Street and new members are invited. The officials are: President, Sam Geddis, Secretary, Thos. M'Dowell, 90 Northumberland Street, and Treasurer, John Martin.

A Divisional Labour Party has been established in Duncairn Ward and some remarkable work is being put in to win the Ward for Labour.

The January elections promise to be exciting, and Labour is fighting on a wide front. We expect to contest 14 or 15 seats, and with a fine body of workers and carefully laid plans, we are fully confident of victory. If you are not working in your "division" you should report at once. People who swear "they are always on the side of the workers" and give mealy mouthed lip service to the class struggle without helping the Movement one little bit, ought to go home. They are a danger to the Movement.

West Belfast Divisional Labour Party now has a Pipe Band, with drums and pipes all complete. This is a most welcome asset to the Movement and there is tons of work for them, including piping in the haggis on Burns' Night.

At the urgent and repeated request of numerous Comrades, Hugh Gemmell has consented to organise and conduct a *Speaker's Class.* Many names are already enrolled and if you wish to join, just call or send to Comrade Gemmell at 41 Albertbridge Road. Our job is propaganda: last year when the I.L.P. ran five classes per week, we turned out chairmen and speakers for the Movement. The Tutor gave his services for love of the Cause. This year we handed over our students to a man with £4 per week; £68 per year of expenses, and dozens of guineas of affiliation fees from Local Trade Unions, plus rent free class rooms and . . . we have got no speakers. There is certainly something wrong. The I.L.P. should do its own work.

The Labour Opposition Of Northern Ireland

Vol. 2—No. 11.   January, 1926.   One Penny

Sugar Beet Factories For N. Ireland.

By THE LABOUR OPPOSITION SPECIAL INVESTIGATOR.

Work for Farmers:
Work for Engineers:

Work for Builders:
Work for All Sections:

Answering a question by Mr. Sam Kyle, M.P., Mr. Archdale, Minister of Agriculture for Northern Ireland, said that the "Government of Northern Ireland had no intention of establishing a Sugar Beet Factory." This is one industry that our Government could undertake with credit to themselves and with beneficial results to the people that they are at present misgoverning. Mr. Philip Snowden, Chancellor of the Exchequer in the Imperial Government, announced in March, 1924, that the Labour Government had decided to pay a subsidy for a period of ten years, in order that this young industry would be placed on its feet. However, this Socialist also laid it down that farmers must be guaranteed for at least four years 44/- per ton for topped and washed beet of 15 1/2 per cent. sugar content, and that **75 per cent. of the machinery required must be manufactured in Great Britain.**

Some of my readers may disagree with subsidies being paid, but if a subsidy is to be justified, surely it is justified in helping to create an entirely new industry. Why should we depend upon other countries to supply us with a necessary food which we are well able to manufacture for ourselves. Our soil is very suitable for growing the Beet, and the experience of farmers, not only on the continent, but in Canada

and Great Britain goes to prove that where farmers have grown Sugar Beet as a commercial venture they have continued to grow it as a rotation crop. Owing to the necessity for deep cultivation and the action of the roots during growth, **the crop enriches the soil** and has a very beneficial effect on the corn crops following it. The factories undertake to supply the seed at 6d. per lb., 12 1/2 lbs. of seed being required to the acre. The farmer is guaranteed a cetrain price before he sows the seed. English farmers are to-day receiving 54/- for Beet, which contain 15 1/2 per cent. sugar content. The Beets are the colour and shape of parsnips and when the sugar is extracted by powerful machinery the pulp is sold as feeding stuff for cattle, and dried pulp will fetch up to £8 per ton in the open market.

With all the prospects which I have enumerated, still our Mr. Archdale, like the shy young maid of Victorian days, says—"Oh, I don't know." There are four different groups of capitalists operating in Great Britain to-day. The Anglo-Dutch Group, The Anglo-Scotch Group, Messrs. Tate & Lyle, Ltd., and a Private Company.

Our old friend Lord Weir of "Steak" house fame is head and tail of the Anglo-Scottish Group, and he will be anxious and willing to build the factory,

Vote   Labour   This   Time!

make the machinery, pay 54/- to the farmer and 50/- per week to the Labourer. Yes! he is a philanthropist provided our Government pays the subsidy. All he wants is the profit. And it is only fair to state that the subsidy, spread over a period of ten years, will amount to about three quarters of a million pounds in the case of a factory capable of dealing with 1,000 tons of Beet per day. Such a factory will cost £150,000 for buildings and site. Machinery £160,000. 50 per cent of this money could be paid in wages locally, as we in Belfast could manufacture from drawings by experts, all the machinery required.

A factory erected in Coleraine, Comber or Downpatrick would provide work and wages for a people who are suffering from 26 per cent. unemployment as against 11 per cent. in Great Britain. Previous to Snowden's subsidy there were three factories operating in Great Britain, next season there will be 20 factories in full swing. The Free State are getting a factory erected in Carlow. Contracts for over 5,000 acres of Sugar Beet have been entered into between the Factory owners and the farmers, and still Northern Ireland lags behind.

Hits and Misses.
BY MARKSMAN.

Armagh citizens are supplied with gas by a private company at a cost of 6/3 per 1,000 cubic feet, but Lurgan gas manager can produce 1,000 cubic feet of municipal gas at 1/8½d per 1,000 cubic feet. Public ownership and control, or in other words Socialism, is the only hope.

* *

Armagh has now got a Catholic Labour Party. These are the people who in the past have condemned the Unionist Labour Association. What we want is a Labour Party without suffix or prefix, we neither want orange labels or green labels. "Up Labour."

* *

Armagh Synod some time ago discussed the position of the Clergy. Mr. W. S. Green said it cost £2,000 to educate a man at Trinity College, and then he was offered a miserable pittance of £200 per year. He also said the Episcopal Church of Ireland has £9,000,000 stored up. We wonder is this more of this Bolshie gold.

* *

Belfast's Lord Mayor says—"Belfast has the cheapest gas in the United Kingdom except for one small town near to the coalfields. The Chemical Department connected with the undertaking made a profit of £60,000 last year. The electricity undertaking was better than ever and it was hoped to reduce the cost of production." At a time when private enterprise is squealing about bad times, Sir Wm. G. Turner is able to boast of the success of Municipal ownership and direct labour. It is also worthy of note that our municipal chemical works made a clear profit of £60,000 last year and that after paying a minimum wage of 62/6 per week to labourers. "Nuff sed."

* *

Belfast.—Mr. Wm. Grant, M.P., says—"300 of the best shipwrights in Britain are walking the streets of Belfast unable to get work and bricklayers are not responsible for dear houses in Belfast." Really! Mr. Grant, you must be more careful about what you say. Why! The above remarks are seditious. Rank sedition in fact.

* *

Belfast. Mrs. Annie Power, 269 Crumlin Road, has been fined in £10 for selling sweetmilk which was below the standard. Mr. Toppin, R.M., said—"This was the worst milk of which he had ever seen a sample."

* *

Ballycastle. —James M'Kinley was fined in £4 and costs for selling milk which contained 23.5 of added water. The usual defence of "Sold as it came from the cow," was unsuccessful.

* *

Ballymena. Rural District Council unanimously decided to arrange for the erection of 160 double cottages and 15 single houses at an estimated cost of £60,033. This is a splendid effort for a Rural Council.

* *

Ballyclare. Messrs. Finlay & Agnew (Fleshers), were fined in 40/- and costs for exposing for sale meat which had not been passed by the Council's Inspector.

* *

Coleraine and other Regional Committees are very much concerned about the regulation requiring parents to pay 2/6 for a Doctor's certificate when a child is one day absent from school.

* *

Coleraine Branch of the Ulster Farmer's Union have considered the new Land Purchase Act. The Rev. R. Moore, B.A., said "The Landlords were pulling the wires in every conceivable fashion and men whom the farmers knew would be antagonistic to their interests were being appointed to administer the Act." More sedition and from a clergyman too!

* *

Co. Derry farmers are annoyed because they are only receiving 3d. per stone for splendid Skerry potatoes, whereas the Belfast consumer pays 8d. per stone for first pick and 7d. per stone for second pick Skerry potatoes.

* *

Co. Derry farmers are also annoyed at only receiving 8/6 per stone for average quality flax, whereas they used to receive up to 40/- per stone in 1918-19.

* *

Derry Petty Sessions. Wm. Ramsey was fined in £10 and £1 costs for selling buttermilk containing 233 parts of water to each 100 parts of milk. Its wonderful how Private enterprise encourages adulteration in the food of the people. Profits! Profits!! Profits!!!

* *

Dungannon Flute Band met Sam Kyle, M.P., the other night at Dungannon Railway Station with the result that he had a splendid audience and spoke for an hour or more. He has also addressed labour meetings in Derry and Bushmills recently.

* *

Dervock Petty Sessions. Mr. James M'Henry, farmer and publican summoned a servant man named Pat M'Collum for larceny of a bicycle wheel and a watch valued at 5/-. Informations were refused. Mr. R. D. Oinkerton, J.P., declaring that "a man who brings a case like this should get six months."

* *

Kilrush District Court. Justice Gleeson in giving a decree for 19/- and no costs or expenses, said—'The butcher had arranged with the farmer that a rotten old sheep should be sold to the public at a price that would have meant a profit to the butcher of 500 per cent. The farmer would have to return the 19/- as the sheep had died of "staggers" before there was time to kill it.

* *

Derry Poor Law Guardians have instructed the night nurses in the Infirmary not to allow any patients to smoke at night.

* *

Strabane Urban District Council heard complaints from two tenants, Messrs. Harbinson and M'Clean, who claimed compensation for loss, damage and medical attention due to the falling off of the plaster of ceilings. The claim is in respect of new houses recently erected and the Ministry of Home Affairs still refuse sanction of payment to the contractor until the houses are put in proper order.

* *

Strabane Poor Law Guardians decided to grant outdoor relief to two old women who live in a stable without furniture. It's tragic, but cases of people who live in barns and stables are all too common.

* *

Derry.—Mr. Frank Gilliland, J.P., Co. Councillor of Derry believes that trade unions should impress upon the workers the necessity of longer hours and harder work. Frank is comfortable and well-fed and I have noticed him dining and wineing in a well known Tory Club near Castle Junction. Well, Frank I suggest that you start preaching to your clubmates and try and impress upon the Linenlords that they made a big mistake in 1924, when they advanced the price of yarn by 40 per cent. and cloth 20 per cent., once again losing the overseas market.

* *

Denmark. Brains and efficiency have built up in Denmark a system, which, while enabling the farmer to obtain a much higher price per pig, than is obtained in Gt. Britain or Ireland, does allow higher wages to be paid and yet permits bacon prices to be far lower than our own. We advise our own farmers to educate themselves and to co-operate with each other, as our brains are as good as the average brains elsewhere. It is deplorable but our Irish farmers do not use their brains collectively.

* *

Maghera, Co. Derry.—A correspondent informs me that Colonel Clarke, a gallant loyal landlord farmer is at present paying 22/6 per week for general farm labourers. There are no perquisites of any kind. No free rent, milk, turf, not even a half-holiday. The gallant Colonel usually employs six labourers and at seed time and harvest time he employs extra men. Never mind, we have still our freedom, religion and laws.

* *

"The Farmers' Gazette," 26/12/25, says—"A Banquet is to be held early in the New Year at Belfast, to celebrate the wonderful yields of Mr. J. A. Caldwell's two well-known cows. It is intended to have the two cows present, boxed in the centre, in a roped enclosure. From each cow a glass of milk will be given to every person present." That is a Capital idea and we would not be surprised to learn that Sir Sam Kelly will have a Banquet to celebrate the wonderful yield of coal at Coalisland. A ton of coal will be stacked in the centre of the hall. Each guest present will receive a bucket of coal, provided they bring their own buckets.

* *

Court Ward Labour Party are moving to the Left very rapidly. Rumour says they have left the people of Court Ward without a candidate. We hope Dame Rumour lies and that they will right this at once.

Labour Men Of The North.
BY BOB M'CLUNG.
The Editor, Hugh Gemmell, Belfast.

Hugh Gemmell is the stormy petrel of Northern politics, and his career has been punctuated by a series of rests—or arrests—when he was the guest of His Majesty. Like the Salvation Army collector, he requires only two more "cops" to make the dozen. His father, and all his people before him, were born and reared in Conlig, Co. Down, and there is no doubt that much of the stubborn fighting qualities of our Northern people have been infused into the blood of our Editor. His writing is plain, direct and forceful and has a kick like an army mule, but it is on the propaganda platform that his gift of virile expression and vivid description get full play, and have earned him the nickname of "hot-stuff." His pen name is "Hotspur," and he has contributed to all the well known Labour and Socialist Weeklies. He is an ardent I.L.P. member and has been connected with the Party over a period of 18 years. He is also a member of the West Belfast Divisional Labour Party, and is the Official Labour Candidate, nominated by them to contest the Councillorship of Smithfield Ward. He believes in Trade Union organisation and was formerly President of the Glasgow and

Hugh Gemmell

District Council of the Shop Assistants Union. When the "Shop Assistants" withdrew from Ireland, our Comrade threw in his lot with the National Union of Distributive and Allied Workers and endeavours to extend their influence. He is Lecture Secretary to the Joint Committee of the I.L.P., and was responsible for the series of Ulster Hall Demonstrations that inspired the

Movement during the past year. During the past seven years he has conducted classes in Belfast for the study of Economics, General Industrial History, Irish Industrial History, and Public Speaking, and has trained all the young men and women who have recently become speakers for Socialism. He was one of the small group of Educationalists who established the N.C.L.C. in Belfast, and is extremely popular in the class-room.

His services to the Movement are all voluntary, and he earns his own living outside its scope. Young and active, swift and merciless, I trust he will be long spared to serve the great cause of Socialism.

The School For Scandal!

"For the buildings, viewed as a whole, are bad—bad in numerous cases with the obvious defects common to other human structures, built of bad material, low and sometimes leaky roofs, inadequate lighting, insufficient ventilation. They are in nearly all cases bad in respect of those features which constitute excellence in a school, such as the supply of properly-sized classrooms, central halls and corridors, sanitary conveniences for teaching staffs, special rooms for medical inspection, suitable apartments for woodwork, drawing and domestic economy, and spacious playgrounds. Judged by these standards, Irish school-buildings are notably behind the times, and, with the best will in the world, it will be a herculean task to bring the Province abreast of modern requirements."

That illuminating paragraph is taken from the Times Education Supplement of the 26th December, 1925, and is just as sweeping an indictment of Capitalism as any Socialist could urge.

These schools (sic) were built by Private Enterprise to impart a scanty instruction to the children of the Working Class, and the Boss took jolly good care to send his own children to decently built and well-equipped establishments. Socialists have always insisted that the best is not too good for the children of the workers, and the recent improvement in school-buildings and

To bottom of next column

One Year in Hell ! !
BY HUGH GEMMELL.

The year has closed on one of the most disastrous periods ever encountered by the Working Class of Northern Ireland. It was formerly our constant pride and boast that we had five of the largest industries the World had ever seen, and to these we have added the doubtful privilege of possessing the highest death-rate in the group of British Islands, and of possessing a swollen unemployed register two and a half times greater than that of Gt. Britain. The five largest industries were never an asset to the Workers of the Province, because we neither owned them nor received an adequate share of the goods we produced in them. But the highest death-rate and the largest unemployed army are exclusively ours, and no one can deny that we merited the comments of the Minister of Labour in his Christmas message, and his caustic congratulation on our patience.

In Belfast, we commenced the year with a report from Sir Crawford M'Cullagh that we were short of 10,000 working class houses. We finish the year with a report that we are still short of 10,000 houses, and the institution of an enquiry that revealed a state of corruption unparalleled in the history of Capitalism.

Persistent questioning by the Labour M.P.'s wrung from the Minister of Labour the reluctant admission that many thousands had been "struck off benefit," and it is estimated that 20,000 of our people have been turned adrift

---

equipment in Belfast, is the result of many years of persistent effort. We want now to "speed up" the educational programme and as the best way to get anything done is to do it yourself, the workers should send representatives from their own class— Labour Representatives—to conduct the affairs of the community, and to make sure that the children are properly looked after.

without any means of support. The Minister had reason to congratulate us on our patience. During March, the Labour Party indicted the Northern Parliament as being the most costly and the most wasteful in the World, and in April the revolt against squandermania spread to the Government supporters, who voted against them in a debate that was disastrous to the prestige of the Tory ascendancy. Loyalty at £138 per hour was felt to be too expensive. May and June witnessed a steady increase in our misery, and when the Prime Minister was being pressed to redeem his promise to "solve the unemployment problem in Ulster himself," the Government suddenly rose and announced its intention of having a four months' holiday on full pay. The Labour Party protested. It was in vain! They fought the adjournment. They were voted down! The Opposition warned the Government that provision would have to be made for the unemployed. The warning was dismissed with contempt. But when September came it was found that an Order in Council had empowered the Minister of Labour to "strike off benefit" some thousands more of our people, and then our patience burst and a Demonstration of protest was organised. It was proclaimed by the Home Secretary's Order. From henceforth we are free to starve, but we must starve in silence. One Comrade, indeed, did protest too vigorously, and for his temerity was given free quarters in the Crumlin Road Gaol. With the approach of Armistice Day it was felt that some recognition ought to be given to those who had fought for the Capitalist Class. The Bible and Literature were searched for an appropriate text, but the honour was finally given to Shakespeare, where Coriolanus says, "The mob? oh, give them bread and circuses" and on the eve of the 11th November, Belfast witnessed the revolting spectacle of its ex-service men struggling on the street for loaves of bread flung from an upstairs window in Garfield Street.

Yet the Province is rich in potential and actual wealth. The soil of Ulster covers mineral wealth of great value, and it could be developed with comparative ease and safety. Our warehouses are glutted with goods, and our artizans are as capable as any in the World. Why, then, do we starve? It is because we permit the Capitalists to take the wealth that we produce. Let us, in the incoming year, make a stern resolve to change all that and give the wealth to those who produce it. Organise your industrial forces, extend your political influence and replace every Capitalist public representative by a chosen member of the Working Class. **Let Class Loyalty Be Your Motto For 1926.**

World Controlled By U.S. Capital.

With 200 billion dollars now invested abroad, the United States is playing a thrilling, tragically melodramatic game around the world. United States capital peacefully penetrating Canada controls a third of Canada's industries; a third of her producing mines; a third of her provincial bonds and municipal debentures and an increasing amount of dominion bonds. In Bolivia peaceful penetration is turning into political domination by American bankers. The United States is a power in the far east, where for 30 years Americans have worked for concessions in China. In the near east America's Standard Oil is participating in the division of oil spoils of war.

In Mexico and Hawaii American business men have entered into local politics even to the extent of encouraging and subsidizing revolutions. The Hawaiian revolt was put over by American sugar planters. United States armed forces intervene in countries where American investors do not receive satisfaction demanded from local authorities: ask Haiti, Santo Domingo, and Nicaragua. When a territory accepts U.S. control, military occupation is supplanted by an American financial commission or civil domination. Armed conquest of territory has taken place by the United States in the Philipines and purchase without consulting the population's wish in the Virgin Islands. The U.S. settlement of European war debts by mortgaging directly or indirectly European industry to American bankers is setting a new precedent in imperial practice.—From "The Industrial Worker," Seattle.

Correspondence.

Dear Comrade,

Lisburn, 24/12/25.

Received your copy of **Opposition** and letter, for which I thank you. And please allow me to state that it is absolutely the best since your first issue. The article on "Does Socialism Destroy the Home," is the complete statement. Not a single weak sentence, it is like a boxing champion who is victor of a twenty round championship without putting his hands wrong once. Also the article on "Is it War," **top hole, 'nuf sed.** Carry on the good work, it is better than bombs, bayonets, or police batons, and after all, the pen is mightier than the sword.

Yours in Comradeship,
Alex. Crawford.

A New Year's Resolution—

"I PROMISE myself to work harder than ever for Socialism, and to buy an extra copy of The Labour Opposition for a friend."

Parliamentary Notes.

The adjourned session resumed on December 8th, when Mr. S. Kyle moved the following motion: "That this House has no confidence in the Government owing to its failure to deal with the unemployment problem or to recognise the urgency and importance of a menace which has been getting more and more out of hand owing to the ineptitude, dilatoriness and incapacity of the Government to institute large and well considered schemes of employment and to take steps to restore the economical and commercial prosperity of Northern Ireland." Mr. Kyle in speaking to this motion mentioned the facts that the Royal Commission had placed before the Government and denounced them for not taking these proposals up. Sir James Craig spoke for the Government, and as Mr. M'Mullen subsequently said, pointed out that this Right Hon. gentleman had done his best and that Right Hon. gentleman had done his best, but as Mr. M'Mullen said, the trouble is, that their best is not good enough. A very interesting fact was revealed during the Debate on the agreement arrived at between the British Government, The Free State Government and the Northern Government that an arrangement had been arrived at regarding the Unemployment Fund of Northern Ireland, which as everybody knows is hopelessly insolvent, but despite pointed queries from Mr. M'Mullen and Mr. Kyle, the Government have kept the particulars of the Secret locked up, so that we have to in the words of Mr. Kyle "Shut our eyes and open our mouths and see what the British Government is going to give us." How responsible ministers can be content with such a position of affairs they alone know. I suppose it was to give a semblance of reality to the Northern Parliament that the agreement mentioned above was brought before the

House. The Northern Government has not done so well out of it as the Free State apparently has, unless of course the Imperial Government takes over our entire liability in connection with the Unemployment Fund. In the course of the debate Mr. M'Mullen said, Parnell's name would live in history far beyond Sir James Craig's or Lord Carson's as he had stood for a United Ireland and further he studied what must be borne in on any thinking person that this country can not afford two Parliaments. Nevertheless it does seem that an advance to this end has been made as it is fairly obvious that when the two Governments meet it will be difficult for the Northern to be in an inferior position to the Southern. It is interesting also to note the stress that Sir J. Craig has put on the point raised by Mr. Kyle, of the necessity of a Customs Union; all this goes to show that some advance has been made. Mr. M'Mullen raised the question of the prisoners arrested and interned without trial and pointed out that the general amnesty of political prisoners might be extended to include the recent arrests and though the Home Secretary did not give any assurance that they would be set free, it is unthinkable that they should be further detained when men who have been tried and convicted are to be released. Mr. Kyle on the same day had asked a question re the release of Mr. Sam Patterson, and on the adjournment debate mentioned above raised the question again. The Parliamentary Secretary of Home Affairs gave him an assurance that Mr. Sam Patterson would be released at an early date; everybody hopes that before these notes are in print the freedom of Mr. S. Patterson will be an accomplished fact. Mr. Beattie did very useful work in getting the facts as to the numbers of workers turned down by the Ministry of Labour for Unemployment Benefit. The number of claims stated by the Minister in reply to Mr. Beattie's question as being turned down from the 1st December, 1924, and the 30th September, 1925, as not being "making every reasonable effort to obtain Employment suited to his capacities," as being 7,179.

The senior member for East Belfast, led the attack on the Finance Bill which sought to impose fresh and additional taxes on Motor Vehicles. The Government were forced to give way on the 12 cwt. and the 1 ton vehicles largely due to the pressure of their own supporters, but it is safe to say that had there been no Labour Party in the House the owners of these vehicles would have to pay the increased taxation. The House has been all agog about the Specials and their demand. If Sir James Craig and his Government were not talking with their tongues in their cheek and if the Specials really had been determined to get just treatment and not merely the tools of a few superior people there is no doubt they could have done ever so much better than they have done; however, they no doubt realise that all the talk of the Government about their heroic services, etc., etc., was just the usual talk of Governments when they want men to do their dirty work and is exactly the same treatment as all Governments have meted out to the men who have fought their battles and won their wars. Did not Kipling the jingo poet say:—

"Its Tommy this, and Tommy that, and Tommy go away. But its always Mr. Atkins when the band begins to play."

The three Labour men have put up a good fight and have laid the foundations of the Party in the House, have earned the respect of their enemies and the hearty good wishes of every Labour man in Northern Ireland. That they may do even better in their second session is the sincere wish of the "Labour Opposition of Northern Ireland."

Clifton for Labour.

MRS IDA BOYD.

Mrs. Ida Boyd has been nominated by North Belfast I.L.P., and approved of by the Labour Party as Official Labour Candidate for Clifton Ward. She has lived for the greater part of her life on Crumlin Road and is well fitted to voice the opinions of the democracy in the Council Chamber. Of a pleasing personality, and a capable speaker, she has been identified with the I.L.P., since she was 16 years of age and is at present Vice-President of North Belfast I.L.P. For many years she acted as Lecture Secretary and her work brought her into contact with very many of the well-known Labour men and women of Great Britain. She was a personal friend of the late Keir Hardie and Willie Walker, and to-day enjoys the friendship of James Maxton, Tom Johnston, Davie Kirkwood, James Walsh (the Miner poet), and many other M.P.'s who are prominent at Westminster. She has played a prominent part in organising the Women's Sections of the Labour Party and acted as Honorary Secretary. Her husband is Mr. Wm. Boyd the well-known Secretary of the Labour Party of Northern Ireland. In Clifton Ward we have a good candidate, and a good cause. Her victory will be your victory **so enrol as a worker** and make sure of the return of Mrs Boyd for Clifton and Mrs. M'Coubrey for Ormeau and so speed the day when poverty and want shall be abolished from our land.

Look Out for our
Special Election Number!!
On Sale Next Week.

Price,   One Penny.

The Farmer's Paradise.

BY SOWSEED.

"With potatoes at pre-war level, grain about 20 per cent., cattle 30 per cent. and costs of production 75 per cent. over pre-war standard, we have to look back for a great many seasons to as bad a result at the close of the year, and it will be a difficult matter to close accounts on the right side for the average tillage farmer." "Belfast News-Letter," 23/12/25.

Rent, Rates, Interest to meet as usual, costs of production 75 per cent. over pre-war standard. With the price of agricultural products about 20 per cent. above what was current in the same period, how can accounts square? Let us assume that the foregoing states the case correctly. I believe it is a fair summary, and if so, what must be the result to the farming industry? If in pre-war days the industry was only marking time, at the present rate how long will it be till bankruptcy ensues? However, the farmers of the North of Ireland are hard-headed and shrewd like their Scottish ancestors, and once they realise the import of the situation they can be relied on to utilise all their energy to avert disaster. Rates must be paid; the money goes for good roads, and other essential public utilities. No chance of cutting down there. The rent is based on Land Purchase Agreements; every payment brings complete ownership a step nearer, therefore the rent or rather the purchase annuity must be met. Interest, ay! there's the rub. Farmers buy the land themselves, just as city people buy houses or business premises. They think it will pay. They put the chain of interest round their own necks, it galls, but it's no use rebelling. In bygone days landlords assessed high rents, they were absolute and often cruel, but landlordism is a thing of the past. Rebellion, fighting and strife altered the system of Irish Land tenure. Capitalism has taken the place of landlordism. Where-

133

as landlordism by the impositions of its iron will and strength incurred the hatred and resentment of the Irish farmers, capitalism is embraced. The farmer willingly subjugates himself to this new power and not only determines to pay the interest charges, but hopes one day to be a capitalist himself.

The "News-Letter" speaks of the costs of production, what does the phrase mean? It is not used solely by farmers nor in regard to farm production only. The capitalist press writes brilliantly and unconvincingly on this subject, trying to set forth how these costs can be lowered without hurt to anyone or to any interest. The farmer has a more direct and simple way of expressing his meaning, he is not a politician trying to please nor a capitalist hack obscuring the issue. Rent and Interest will be paid, but **the hired labourer must go.** He (the farmer) his wife and family will work harder and it maybe without hope of payment (costs of production could not be any lower). His children may suffer; his own and his wife's spirit and health may be broken, the agricultural workers may drift into the towns and cities to swell the numbers of the unemployed. They cannot claim the dole; for some reason or another, they are excluded from unemployment insurance, but they can accept low wages and break the power of Trade Unions. All these things may happen, but the industry will be saved and rent and interest paid as usual.

The portrayal is not bright, but when the Spring comes and the sunshine dispels the gloom of winter our spirits will revive and brighten. When land nationalisation is accomplished and when Socialism has broken down the evil grip of Capitalism, then our farms will be smiling and productive and our land workers busy and happy.

Parallel Legislation.
BY HOTSPUR.

Gt. Britain has a population of 45 millions. Ulster has a population of one million and a quarter. The number of workers unemployed in Gt. Britain is 11 per cent. of the population. The number unemployed in Ulster is 26 per cent. of the population. The unemployed workers in Gt. Britain are assisted by the Poor Law Guardians; rents are paid and an adequate scale of outdoor relief is granted. In Ulster, and in Belfast particularly, that relief has been refused. Taxation in Gt. Britain is higher than in other European countries. But taxation in Ulster is over £10 per head, per annum, and is said to be the highest in the World.

The death rate per 1,000 of the population in London is 18.9. The death rate per 1,000 for seven of the principal towns in Northern Ireland is 22.2. You can think what you like, but my opinion is that when you sent a member of the employing class to do your work on public bodies, you did the worst possible thing for yourselves and for the whole community. Personally, I am going to try and change all that and I am going to **VOTE LABOUR** at the January Elections.

Notes And News.

Our next issue will be a special election number and will contain Labour's Municipal Programme, with photos and biographies of our Candidates. It will be on sale next week and as the number will be limited, you should make sure of your copy . . . . early.

Councillor Harry Midgley is the delegate from the Central Branch of the I.L.P. to the Scottish Divisional Conference at Edinburgh on the 11th January.

The North Branch decided not to send a delegate.

Sam Kyle, M.P. has accepted two engagements to speak in Glasgow during January.

He is to speak for the I.L.P. in the Hall, 48 York Street, on Sunday the 17th January, 1926.

And Willie M'Mullan, M.P., speaks in the same hall on Sunday the 14th of February.

There is a meeting there every Sunday at 7 p.m., and if you go there you will find good fellowship and an explanation of what Socialism stands for.

Every Friday night is Fellowship Night, at the Hall, and there is singing and dancing from 7-30. The fun is really good, and members of the I.L.P. can bring a friend. The admission is sixpence. If you are not a member of the I.L.P. you ought to join. You pay 1/- entrance fee, and 9d. per month. The women pay 4d. per month.

The class for the study of Irish Industrial History conducted by Comrade Hugh Gemmell at the East Belfast Labour Party Hall, 5 Mountpottinger Road, has just finished. It was voted a great success and 56 students were enrolled. This was the more remarkable since we receive no publicity of any kind. A new class for the study of Economics, in the same Hall, and under the same Tutor, will commence on Wednesday, the 20th January, 1926, at 8 p.m.

If your Trade Union or your Political party is Affiliated to the N.C.L.C. you are entitled to attend free of charge. Otherwise the fee for the course is 2/6. Fees, if any, go to the funds of the Belfast Labour College. The services of the Tutor are voluntary. We are waiting until after the elections before starting the class because the students say that it is the duty of every organised worker to assist in the return of the Labour Candidates.

Last month we published a statement that the I.L.P. had handed over its students to a man with £4 per week, etc. We are informed that the statement is not correct, and we take this opportunity of dispelling any misunderstanding that may have arisen.

Labour's Municipal Programme
**Together with Photos and Biographies
of all the Candidates will be contained
in the Special Election Number of
The Labour Opposition.
Secure your copy early.**

The Dole, The Poorhouse And The Jail.

The Government expect an unemployed man on the dole to live on

18/- a week.

But each inmate in the Poorhouse last year, cost the authorities

£65—10/-, or £1—5/- a week.

Prisoners sentenced to Hard Labour cost the authorities

£84—10/-, or £1—12/- a week.

Convicts cost the authorities

£100—7/-, or £1—18/- a week.

We expect the Unemployed man to live on half the money that it costs the Government to keep a Convict.

"The Forward"
Glasgow.

The Labour Opposition Of Northern Ireland

Vol. 2—No. 12   January, 1926   One Penny

LABOUR'S MUNICIPAL PROGRAMME.

Holding that those who produce the wealth of the Community should direct the affairs of the Community, Labour therefore believes in an extension of Municipal Trading and Municipal Ownership, with its higher standard of living, and its cheap and efficient services to the public.

Housing.—Owing to the acute shortage of houses and the consequent overcrowding in Working Class Districts, Labour pledges itself to speed up the building of Working Class Houses **to be let** at rents which the workers can pay.

Education.—Labour stands for the finest education that the Community can offer to its children, and believes that it should be free to all from the Public Elementary School to the University. We are firmly pledged to the provision of meals for school children, to the provision of free books and, where necessary, the provision of clothing.

Milk.—We stand for the establishment of a Municipal Milk Depot, in order to safeguard the child-life of the City.

Coal.—And for a Coal Depot to supply cheap coal. If the Corporation can buy coal at 1/11 per 10 stone bag in order to make Gas, it can do the same for the household needs.

Vacant Houses.—We demand the compulsory letting of all houses that are now vacant.

Playgrounds.—It was Labour Members in the Council who secured the Children's Playgrounds and Open Spaces. We want these in every Ward so that the children may play in safety and happiness.

Ante-Natal Clinics.—Labour believes that healthy child-life and mother-life should be the City's first care, and has succeeded in getting two Clinics established in Belfast. We want now to extend their benefits so that all mothers will be well provided for.

Municipal Banks.—Labour stands for a Municipal Bank so that the City may obtain money at a low rate of interest for the development of public services. This would provide money for the erection of houses that the workers could afford **to rent.**

We believe in cheaper gas and cheaper trams, and we believe that the Workers should "mind their own business" by sending their own representatives to replace those who maladministration of the City's affairs is costing **you** £100 per day in Lawyers fees at the Housing Inquiry. We are confident of victory, and we ask you to turn out early on Friday, morning the 15th January, and **Vote Labour**.

Leave home **EARLY,** take your neighbour,
Bring your husband, vote for **LABOUR.**

Hits And Misses.
BY MARKSMAN.

Lisnaskea Poor Law Guardians. Mr. Coffey at a recent meeting said, it had been calculated that the cost of food and fuel for an inmate of the Workhouse was 4 4 1/2 per week, and the establishment charges in respect of each inmate was £1 3s. 6d. per week.

* *

Tipperary Co. Council have passed a resolution informing all owners of labourers' cottages whose sons are employed on the county roads that unless their rents are paid their services will be dispensed with.

* *

When a Lord Chancellor of Great Britain loses his job (£10,000), he falls back upon his unemployment pay of £5,000 per year for life. No questions are asked. He does not stand in a Bureau Queue. He is not summoned to the Labour Exchange and asked can he use a fourteen pound hammer. He gets his money sent every quarter in an envelope. No Court of Referees. No Rota Committee. No where are you looking for work? How much does your father earn? Yet we are told there is no class war.

* *

Mr. John Wheatley, Minister of Health in the last Government said:—The 9/9 which you pay as rent for the house in which you live is distributed as follow:-

Materials and Profits	£0	1	10 1/2
Labour	0	1	3
Land	0	0	1 1/2
To Moneylenders	0	6	6
Total	£0	9	9

* *

Labour Candidates declare that child life is sacred and all the chief necessaries of sustenance must have easy access to the home. **Milk** particularly, must be Municipalised from its production until it reaches the consumer.

* *

Housing.—Belfast requires ten thousand working class houses to meet the needs of those at present homeless or badly housed.

* *

The King of Norway is trying to eke out a royal existence on a miserable pittance of £48, 000 per year.

Shame ! ! ! Other Kings are paid as follows:-

King of Siam	£700,000
King of Italy	640,000
King of England	580,000
King of Japan	450,000
King of Spain	355,000
King of the Belgians	215,000

I understand it is not desirable that Kings should be paid on a piece-work basis.

* *

Coleraine Rural Council have decided to hold up Castlerock Water Supply Scheme pending the Council's Solicitor being satisfied that those who are offering land for sale are in possession of the Title Deeds. If the land were to be Nationalized to-morrow, many land-"owners" would have to do what the ancestor of the Duke of Abercorn did, viz., resort to forgery.

* *

Lurgan ex-servicemen are to contest seats for the Urban Council in January. "Peace hath her victories, no less renowned than war."

* *

Newry Poor Law Guardians have learned that the recent outbreak of Scarlatina will cost the ratepayers £2,000. Prevention is better than cure, and decent houses with proper sanitation would be a less costly experiment in public health.

* *

Armagh Nationalists have stood down in favour of eight Trade Union Candidates, nominated for Armagh Town Council. These eight seats were formerly Nationalist seats. Having achieved Nationalism, the fight is now clear between Capital and Labour.

* *

Mr. W. P. Nicholson the well known preacher, is being accused by certain church elders of adopting a style of oratory intended to appeal to the vulgar by gross personal abuse of others, and glorification of himself. Oh! my dear friends, how those Christians love one another.

* *

Ulster Bank Limited have declared a dividend of 21 1/4 per cent. and they still have a reserve fund of one million pounds. We notice that Lt. Col. J. Jackson Clark,

H.M.L., is a member of the Committee. Is this the gent who pays 22/6 per week to his farm labourers? 22/6 to pay rent and maintain a family in decency and comfort. 22/6 with no perquisites and "no nothing" as the Yankees say.

* *

Belfast Education Committee. The Chairman, Alderman Duff, who was a defeated Unionist Candidate at the last Parliamentary Election, said:- "I had prepared a careful statement on the estimates in connection with the Education Scheme for the current year, but the interest of members is shown in their attitude towards me." We understand that Alderman Duff was very indignant at his colleagues for marching into the luncheon room to partake of the free lunch, at the time when he was justifying the expenditure of over £200,000, and refused to make his carefully prepared speech on the matter because of the attitude of his friends, who showed contempt and indifference on this most important question.

* *

Lisnafillan, Co. Antrim, is to have an artificial silk industry. A new company has been formed, and six directors, three local linen lords and three Englishmen, will **control** the works.

* *

Lurgan Urban District Council have instructed their Sanitary Committee to report on the house occupied by S. M'Nulty, who alleges that there is no door to his home, and he might as well be living outside.

* *

Lurgan. The Ministry of Home Affairs are still delaying the fixing of rent of the labourers' cottages recently erected in Lurgan district. The houses were ready for occupation two months ago, and the prospective tenants are at present living in hovels quite unfit for human habitation.

* *

Londonderry Poor Law Guardians considered a letter from Dr. Cunningham in which he complained of the dispensary premises in William Street. Mr. Finlay said there was a beard as long as a goat's on the walls because of the damp.

Labour's Women Standard Bearers.

MRS. IDA BOYD.
The Official Labour Candidate.

Mrs. Ida Boyd has been nominated by North Belfast I.L.P., and approved of by the Labour Party as Official Labour Candidate for Clifton Ward. She has lived for the greater part of her life on Crumlin Road and is well fitted to voice the opinions of the democracy in the Council Chamber. Oi a pleasing personality, and a capable speaker, she has been identified with the I.L.P., since she was 16 years of age and is at present Vice-President of North Belfast I.L.P. For many years she acted as Lecture Secretary and her work brought her into contact with very many of the well-known Labour men and women of Great Britain. She was a personal friend of the late Keir Hardie and Willie Walker, and to-day enjoys the friendship of James Maxton, Tom Johnston, Davie Kirkwood, James Walsh (the

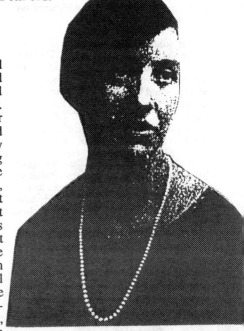

MRS. IDA BOYD.

Miner poet), and many other M.P.'s who are prominent at Westminster. She has played a prominent part in organising the Women's Sections of the Labour Party and acted as Honorary Secretary. Her husband is Mr. Wm. Boyd the well-known Secretary of the Labour Party of Northern Ireland. In Clifton Ward we have a good candidate, and a good cause. Her victory will be your victory **so enrol as a worker** and make sure of the return of Mrs Boyd for Clifton and Mrs. M'Coubrey for Ormeau and so speed the day when poverty and want shall be abolished from our land.

MRS. MARGARET T. M'COUBREY.
The Official Labour Candidate.

Mrs. Margaret T. M'Coubrey, who is contesting Ormeau Ward in the forthcoming Municipal Elections as the nominee of the Central Branch of the Independent Labour Party, has for many years been closely identified with the Labour Movement. She came prominently before the public of Belfast in the days of the Suffrage Campaign and during the war was a fearless exponent of the anti-war policy of the I.L.P.

Mrs. M'Coubrey, is also actively associated with the Co-operative Movement at home and abroad and an enthusiastic worker for International Co-operation. She is on the Board of Management of the local Co-operative Society, the Editor of the Belfast issue of "The Wheatsheaf." and a well-known contributor in the cross-channel Co-operative press.

Mrs. M'Coubrey has held several offices in the I.L.P., and at the present time is Vice-President of the Central Branch. An able speaker, a clear thinker, a valiant fighter for freedom, and as described in her Election Address, "an Active Practical Woman."

Gemmell For Smithfield.
MR. HUGH GEMMELL.
The Official Labour Candidate,
Editor, Labour Opposition

Hugh Gemmell is the stormy petrel of Northern Politics, and his career has been punctuated by a series of rests— or arrests—when he was the guest of His Majesty. Like the Salvation Army collector, he requires only two more "cops" to make the dozen. His father, and all his people before him, were born and reared in Conlig, Co. Down, and there is no doubt that much of the stubborn fighting qualities of our Northern people have been infused into the blood of our Editor. His writing is plain, direct and forceful and has a kick like an army mule, but it is on the propaganda platform that his gift of virile expression and vivid description get full play, and have earned him the nickname of "hot-stuff." His pen name is "Hotspur," and he has contributed to all the well known Labour and Socialist Weeklies. He is an ardent I.L.P. member and has been connected with the Party over a period of 18 years. He is also a member of the West Belfast Divisional Labour Party, and is the Official Labour Candidate, nominated by them to contest the Councillorship of Smithfield Ward.

Smithfield is the most congested district in Belfast, and the death rate per thousand of the population is higher than in any other Ward. Other Wards, with more room to live than Smithfield has, are provided with Children's Playgrounds. Smithfield has none! Other Wards have Public Parks within their confines. Smithfield has none! The great urgent need is for houses but not a single house has been built to replace those that have been condemned. Ninety per cent. of the householders are users of the penny in the slot meter. They pay more for their gas than quarterly consumers, and they pay in advance, yet they recieve only a paltry discount of sixpence in the pound, whereas the quarterly consumers get four shillings discount for every pound, and get five months clear credit as well. Glaring inequalities like these cannot pass unchallenged, and the people say that only Labour will fight their battles. Foul lies and vile slanders will not deter them and they are determined to send Hugh Gemmell to voice their demands in the Council Hall of Belfast. Smithfield is a sure win for Labour.

It is better to place a cross opposite the name of the person and the principle you stand for, than to erect a cross in the graveyard to the memory of an innocent child slaughtered by Capitalism.

"Tis not in mortals to command success, but we'll do more. ⸻ deserve it."

---

* *

Derry.—Hats off to the Labour Party of Derry! they are being cursed and damned by the Orange and Green factions, and tell it not in Gath, also by the Republican Party. Derry Labour men and women are out to oppose all comers. That's the stuff, Up Derry!

We don't want praise from our political enemies. It is like a Boa-Constrictor which covers its victim with its filthy saliva before swallowing it, in order to make it go down easier.

Gimley For Falls.
MR. JAMES GRIMLEY.
The Official Labour Candidate.

Mr. James Grimley entered the Labour Movement before he was twenty years of age. As a member of The Socialist Party of Ireland he became associated with the late James Connolly and actively assisted him in his trade union work. He played a prominent part in the Dock Ward election of 1913, where James Connolly was the Labour Candidate. He rendered considerable assistance to the Dublin workers in the big strike of 1913, by holding meetings and taking up collections which were sent to strike headquarters.

Grimley is convinced that the Labour Movement in Ireland should derive all its inspiration from within its own

MR. JAMES GRIMLEY.

shores. A strong opponent of conscription during the European War, he was a friend of conscientious objectors who sought the hospitality of our shores. Worked for the Labour Candidates in 1918, and again contributed to the remarkable victories of Belfast Labour men in the Municipal Election of 1920. Assisted Harry Midgley against Sir Robert Lynn in 1923, and again in 1924. In one week's time Grimley organised the Monster Demonstration held at Corrigan Park to voice Labour's protest against the continued detention of men in prison and convict ship without charge or trial. If Falls Ward is true to itself, it will return Grimley this time with a big majority.

Gordon For Dock.

DAWSON GORDON,
The Official Labour Candidate.

For 25 years, Dawson Gordon has been a Trade Union Leader in Belfast, and his nomination for Dock Ward gave the keenest pleasure to his hosts of friends and well-wishers.

He was little more than a boy when he gained the confidence of his fellow-workers and was appointed Secretary of the Flax Roughers Trade Union which later became the Flax and other Textile Workers Trade Union. He is a well known figure at all the Annual Conferences of Irish Trade Unions and other Labour gatherings and he acted as Secretary of North Belfast I.L.P. from 1907 to 1910. Dawson was Official Labour Candidate for Shankill Ward in January, 1908, and again in 1920. He was defeated in 1908, but secured election in 1920, and did splendid work on behalf of the needy and distressed. In 1923 the Belfast Labour Party decided not to contest the Corporation elections as Belfast was being controlled by mob law, and anarchy held the City in its grip.

As a champion of the unemployed workers, Dawson Gordon is entitled to

DAWSON GORDON,

the support of every unemployed man and woman. His wide knowledge of public affairs, and his previous experience on the Corporation, make him an ideal candidate for Municipal Honours, and that this fact has not been lost sight of by the Electors of Dock is evidenced by the enthusiastic meetings and the support that is given to him wherever he goes. He will win!

Newcastle, Co. Down is also in the field. Sorry we can't afford to send speakers to Newcastle, but you have had Sam Geddis with you recently and all our speakers are needed in Belfast at the moment.

Castledawson.—For probably the first time in its history the town had a socialist as visitor on Wednesday evening in the person of Mr. Robert Pickering from Largs, who spoke for some time on "Politics for the Working People."

141

Geddis For Woodvale.

MR. SAM GEDDIS,
The Official Labour Candidate
For Alderman.

Mr. Sam Geddis served an apprenticeship to the Ironmoulding and has always taken a prominent part in the Ironmoulders' Trade Union, having acted as Chairman and Committeeman for years. He has always realised the necessity of organising the lower paid workers, and became a member of The Workers' Union in 1906. He actively assisted to win Barrow-in-Furness for labour in 1906, when Charlie Duncan defeated the wealthy Tory shipowner, Sir Charles Cazer.

An ex-soldier he has served in India and Burmah and has been identified with the trade union and labour movement in America. Claims to have been Chairman of Belfast's First Divisional Labour Party and is at present Chairman of the Shankill Labour Party. He is employed at present as a full time official of The Workers' Union and is taking a keen interest in Housing and in improving the condition of building trade workers. If he is successful in winning Woodvale Ward for Labour his voice will be heard to good purpose in the Council Chamber.

Keady. Just as we go to press we have received report of a most enthusiastic labour rally. Councillor Bob Getgood's telling speech in Keady Town Hall, with the five chosen Labour Candidates seated on the platform is something to be remembered in Keady for ever. Catholics and Protestants vieing with each other for who will be selected to carry the Labour standard to victory. We hope for a labour majority in Keady.

"The Opposition" is steadily growing in Power, Circulation and Influence. What we need now is a Weekly, and every new reader and every fresh subscriber is a definite step towards that goal.

Corcoran For Pottinger.

MR. GEORGE CORCORAN,
The Official Labour Candidate.

George Corcoran, Organising Delegate of the Painters' Trade Union, Candidate for the Aldermanship of Pottinger Ward, is a very pleasing personality and has very great ability. That has been recognised by the Commissioner at the Building Inquiry, at which Mr. Corcoran represents the building trade workers, and has been the sole representative building trade official who has stated the workers' point of view in the Inquiry. It was Mr. Corcoran who organised the unemployed demonstrations to the Poor Law Guardians and made a very good impression with his clear statement of their claims, demanding equal treatment for the Unemployed of Belfast with the Unemployment of Gt. Britain.

He was elected by his fellow Trade Unionists to the Trade Union Congress for the years 1923, 24, 25, representing all his members in this country. He was elected delegate for the Painters in 1925, and since his election has fully justified the confidence reposed in him by his fellow-members. He is a member of various Public Committees, including the Belfast Employment Committee, Committee of the Kings' National Roll, member of the Rota Sub-Committee and a member of the Building Trades Federation. He is one of five brothers who served with distinction in the Army during the Great War, and at one period of the war he had a brother along with himself on every one of the far flung battle fronts. He is a man of shrewd, practical sense, endowed with the gift of easy speech, and a man who never rests until his words are translated into deeds. Pottinger has reason to be proud of its choice for Alderman, and as he lives in the Ward, he can speak with some authority and with personal knowledge of its needs. The unemployed men and women of Pottinger have cause to regard him with respect and affection, for his personal advocacy of their claims on many courts of referees has been the means of brightening hundreds of homes and driving the wolf from the door for a little while longer.

The prospective Alderman was one of the founders of the East Belfast Labour Party, and was the first Secretary of that very active body of workers. Of George it might be said "'Tis not in mortals to command success, but we'll do more . . . deserve it."

Duff For Pottinger.
MR. JAMES DUFF, P.L.G.
The Official Labour Candidate.

James Duff, P.L.G., is the nominee of East Belfast Labour Party for the Councillorship of Pottinger Ward. He claims that he is well fitted to voice the claims of the workers in our Council Chamber as he has resided on Newtownards Road for the past 35 years and knows every street. He started to earn his living when only 8 years of age, and the tragic struggle of his early years made him realise the need of every child to have a sound elementary education in order to fit it for the battle of life. Without a well nourished and well educated child population, no people can hope to prosper or leave their imprint on the sands of time. We must build from the bottom up. Since he was returned as a Guardian of the Poor he has tried to live up to the title and hundreds of homes in East Belfast can testify to his untiring devotion and service to the community.

James Duff was one of the very first Irishmen to become a member of the Workers' Union, of which Charles Duncan, M.P., is General Secretary, and to-day he sits on the governing body, and has been elected time and again without opposition to that responsible position. He is a familiar figure at all Labour Party Conferences and Trade Union Congresses and his intimate knowledge of men and affairs enables him to reach decisions that make him a valued member of Committees, and a formidable opponent in the debates. He has always stood by the workers, and we trust the workers will now stand by him.

Johnston For Victoria.
MR. JAMES JOHNSTON.
The Official Labour Candidate.

James Johnston, an old N.A.U.L. Trade Union Official, is contesting Victoria Ward for the Councillorship. Jimmie has done his bit for his class, and is an old Tramway worker, who became so prominent in ventilating the grievances of his fellow-workers that he was soon appointed Branch Secretary. Later on he became their full time official and planned the campaign that has made the present fighting front such an effective force in maintaining wage standards.

If Belfast Tramway workers enjoy good conditions of labour to-day, the credit is due to Jimmie Johnston, who has stood up to their bosses and fought the workers' battles in season and out of season. He received his early train-

MR. JAMES JOHNSTON

ing in the I.L.P. and used to be called "The Champion Literature Seller."

Our Candidate is a man of high character and stern determination, and all the buffetings of public life have not made him swerve an inch from his allegiance to the cause of Labour. His zeal, his experience as a Trade Union Secretary, and the fact that he has lived in the Ward for countless years make him a Candidate worthy of the people, and the electors would bestow an honour on themselves if they returned as the Councillor for Victoria, James Johnston.

From Shankill in the North, to Ormeau in the South, Labour in Belfast is fighting on a wide-flung battle front. We fight no rear-guard action but carry the attack against the fortified position of King Kapital with his entrenched masses of Civic Corruption, adulterated milk, rotten houses and high rents. Capital is crumbling at every point of attack, and Labour is sweeping forward to final victory supported by the determined will of an awakened democracy. One more advance, another "great push" and the ten champions of Labour will be carried triumphantly to the City Hall to clear up the mess the Bosses left behind in their retreat.

*　　*

"The great only appear great because we are on our knees. Let us rise!" Remember that all the good things of life are produced by Labour, and he who enjoys the fruits thereof without working for them, is stealing the bread of the Workers. He who will not work, neither shall he eat.

Malcolm For Cromac.

MR. JOHN MALCOLM,
The Official Labour Candidate.

To contest a seat on three occasions inside a period of five years establishes somewhat of a record even for Belfast. Certainly if pluck and determination deserves success then we may say that John Malcolm is already the Councillor for Cromac. Formerly a Corporation wage-earner, John has done splendid work on behalf of all Corporation employees. He seems always to haunt the precincts of our Marble Hall, and he is so persistent in his demands that he is looked upon with terror by some of our political bosses in the Corporation. Formerly the representative of the Municipal Employees' Union, his union has now linked up with two bigger unions and we look for a bigger field for his activities in the future.

Victory in Cromac has only eluded us by a small margin, and now that changed economic conditions have compelled the Workers to change their political opinions, it looks as if victory were already assured. When employers demand reductions in Corporation employees' wages it is time to send the Union Organiser to the Council to keep the wages up.

MR. JOHN MALCOLM

144

"Out Of Evil Cometh Good."

The mysterious disappearance of a thousand Austro-Hungarian soldiers nine years ago, was cleared up by the unexpected return of a Hungarian who had long been regarded as dead.

This man is one of the thousand soldiers known to have been captured by the Russian Army in the Carpathians in 1916. They were reported to have been sent to Siberia, but as all the men vanished years ago they were thought to have perished.

By the return of this soldier it is known that the 1,000 have settled in the bleak territory to which they were sent, founded five villages and are well on the way to the development of 400,000 acres of land allotted to them by the Soviet Government.

They have married Tartar, Mongol, and Chinese wives, and are so well content with their lot that they will remain permanently in their new homes.

The prisoners were exiled to the side of the Amur River, near the Chinese-Mongolian border, by the old **Russian Government,** says the Budapest correspondent of the Central News. They appeared to be forgotten, and as time went on they turned their attention to agriculture and various other trades. Most of them were former Hungarian army officers, and nearly all university graduates. Among them are a university professor, three doctors, an architect, two Catholic priests and a rabbi, while others are masters of useful trades.

At the time of the Russian revolution the prisoners had two choices—one was not to recognise the Red Government and suffer punishment as prisoners; the other was to join the Red Army. Although all of them were against the Soviet idea they felt that the second choice was in their best interests. When they joined the army they were placed in the same battalion. The **Reds** gave them about 400,000 acres of land, agricultural machinery and everything farmers need. Their duty was to guard the border from Mongolian and Chinese attacks.

In this way the villages began. The men built houses, agricultural buildings, brick factories and a flour mill. Within a short time they had formed a small industrial centre in a territory where only wild tribes had existed.

They all married Chinese, Mongolian, Korean and Russian girls, but they did not forget their mother tongue, and they created a new European civilisation. They built churches and schools where the Hungarian language is spoken, and their wives are now adopting this language. There is no money in the villages, business being done by the ancient methods of exchange. Most of their output is sold in Vladivostock, where their business also is transacted by the exchange of their produce for articles they need.

We hear that Mr. L. M'Curdy, Organiser of the Amalgamated Transport and General Workers' Union, signed the nomination paper of that well-known enemy of the workers, Mr. Martin Hopkins, the opponent of Mr. James Grimley the duly selected candidate of the West Belfast Labour Party, and who is the official Labour Candidate adopted by the Labour Party (N.I.), for the Falls Ward.

If this is true, and we hope it is not, the delegates of the Amalgamated Transport and General Workers' Union will have trouble explaining the action of a member of an affiliated organisation, in addition to the action of Mr. Ryan of the same organisation standing down at the last moment after being adopted by the Labour Party as the official Labour Candidate for Dock Ward.

Correspondence.

Moose Jaw,
Sask., Canada.

The Editor, Opposition Of Northern Ireland.

Dear Sir,

Your little paper has found its way here and I hope that every comrade will push the sale of it just as if his or her future happiness and well-being depended upon its success. I see that you had Kirkwood in the Ulster Hall and gave him a rousing reception. "More power to ye!" I hope that the cause is growing and increasing in numbers. I hope that you are having fine propaganda meetings where the aim and object of each comrade is to show a united front to the common enemy and the concern of all is to obtain converts to the cause of Socialism. There are no ideals here I am sorry to say. Their only ideal is 100 cents, 1 dollar. Every phase of the American's or Canadian's life is tested by that standard. I see that the wise Tories at Westminister have arranged for assisted fares to this country as low as £3. Please warn your people to act cautiously as they will find it very hard to obtain work except on farms at poor pay and only in the summer months at that. It seems to me that your Government is anxious to get a lot of people anywhere at all as long as they are out of their sight. With all good wishes.

Yours sincerely,
Langley Hall.

THE WORKERS' UNION.

District Office :
13 SKIPPER STREET,
BELFAST.

Divisional Organiser :
ROBERT M'CLUNG

POLITICAL ACTION Is alright, but what about INDUSTRIAL· ACTION ?

JOIN THE UNION THAT IS CONSISTENTLY WORKING FOR A LIVING WAGE FOR YOU !

When you are WORKING we fight your battles.
When you are SICK we pay you 'Sickness' Benefit.

The First Socialist Pipe Band.

The West Belfast Divisional Labour Party has again upheld the proud traditions of the pioneer branch by giving to the Movement the "first Socialist Pipe Band." Formed less than four months ago, they have to-day six pipers, four side drummers and one bass drummer to play such stirring music as makes the blood tingle and the step grow lighter. 'Fathered' by Peter Connor and John Mullan, and trained in the subtle art of pipe music by the skill and patience of their Pipe-Major, Michael Magee, they made such rapid progress that they were able to make their first public appearance at the Ulster Hall, Newbold Demonstration.

Lungs expanded, bodies swinging, red streamers flying in the air; no one who witnessed that eventful march will ever forget the inspiring sight as they approached the Ulster Hall and entered its portals. Down the aisles and on to the platform, drums vibrating, pipes skirling, marched the pioneers, and as the red pole of the leader was raised aloft and then spun like a wheel by dexterous fingers, the drums gave their last beat and the pipes trailed away on a falling note. And while yet the dulcet strains of music hung quivering in the silent air, the great audience showed its appreciation of their worth by round after round of generous and sustained applause. It was a triumph for the first Socialist Band, and I salute the pioneers. The Branches should support them and engage the band for all their processions and public meetings, thereby bringing inspiration to a Movement fighting for power.

HUGH GEMMELL.

When you are UNEMPLOYED we pay you Out-of-Work Benefit.
And FIGHT YOUR CASE AT THE LABOUR EXCHANGE.
BEST BENEFITS. BEST ATTENTION.

DON'T DELAY ! ——— **JOIN TO-DAY !**

The Red Flag, p.7   *The Fellowship Of Socialism*, p.4.

The Labour Opposition Of Northern Ireland.

Vol. 2—No. 13   February, 1926.   One Penny

A HAPPY-GO-LUCKY SOCIALIST.
BY SLUMDOM JACK.

I pity the poor Socialists who are for ever engaged in an economic imbroglio, and I rather envy the man, who, psychologically speaking, is so intellectually dead as to be entirely incapable of recognising the fact that he is existing in a state of economic bondage. It requires no small amount of philosophic fortitude to enable a man under any set of mental-disturbing conditions to keep the right end up and to remain as cool as a cucumber and as snug as a bug in a rug.

Long before my dad, who was a blissfully ignorant biped, had any intention of "kicking the bucket," he slipped me the following piece of philosophic advice in a dirty little boozer in a soul-destroying street, in this generous and hyper loyal city: Said the pater, "Jack, my lad, when you have rubbed your back against as many corners as this chicken, you will wake up to the discovery that there is something fudamentally out of order in this system of Society; but after viewing things from the corner of most streets my sincere advice to you is: no matter where you go keep up your heart, should your belly trail the ground. We have but a short time to live, and no mathematician can figure out how long we are likely to be dead. So, Jack, my lad, if owing to depressing economic and soul-disturbing conditions, you feel disposed to grow melancholy, try to remember that the grave is the proper place in which to grow fat on the marrow-bones of misery and melancholy." And that advice has been my guiding star ever since, and I can assure you I just know as much about the miseries and social degradations of the Capitalist system of society as the bloke next door.

As a Socialist propagandist, I believe I know how to go about my job. My job in this super-sensitive city is to bore a hole into the rock of super-stition, bigotry and class ignorance, and get in the dynamite of Socialism, and blow up the rougher elements of industrial democracy and free them from all dope-manufactured influences; and to pass along the rough elements to the smoothers and refiners of our Movement. The intellectuals. You get that? Right! The card that slits you in twain and calls one part the physical man and the other part the spiritual man is a rather stiff proposition, as he is all out for your spiritual

WANTED, A LABOUR J.P.

The list of Justices of the Peace in Belfast now totals 262. Promotions to the Magisterial bench are of weekly occurrence. It can be stated without fear that these magistrates are Nationalist and Unionist in politics. They belong to the Employing Class. They are opposed to Labour. When Labour wants a hundred or more Personation Agents sworn in at elections, they are compelled to go to their political opponents for the service. Labour in Belfast voted 24,000 strong on January 15th. At the Parliamentary Elections they command a following of 50,000. That is a very substantial portion of the community, and we are entitled to representation on the City's administrative boards. But.....we have not one single Labour J.P. What are we thinking about, and how long are we going to tolerate it?

— HUGH GEMMELL.

salvation and refuses point blank to have anything to do in reference to the methods to be adopted in working out the salvation of the physical man. These coons tell me I must be born again, and when I say I hope so, and when I also express the lively desire that when that second birth affair pulls off I shall be born without a stomach you should see their dials. I was born once, and, needless to say, I didn't come into this world "skipping up the golden stairs." "Jack," says one would-be-spiritual-window-cleaner, "where will you spend eternity?" I am prepared to tell any man where I shall spend eternity if he will inform me where I spent my time before I came here.

Listen, boys, when I was born into this world fifty-two years ago, it took very little ground to hold my baby body, but before I was allowed to rest my little body in the land of my birth, my poor mother, who was a wage-slave, had to fork out the kudos to a Landlord for permission to allow my cradle to remain on what he had the audacity to call his ground. Suffering poker! how long shall we go on tolerating such humanity wrecking humbug?

Hits And Misses.
BY MARKSMAN.

Mr. Hall Caine, Unionist M.P. for East Dorset, says; "The present cabinet from a business point of view has up to now been a dismal failure." Right you are! H. C. I have said the same thing many a time. Of course, great minds, think great thinks.

* *

Sydney.—The 44 hour working week is now an accomplished fact in all industries in Sydney, Australia.

* *

Mr. Woolworth's daughter has lost jewels valued at one million dollars. So you see the idle rich have their own troubles. However, sweated wages and mass production will enable her Da to replace them for her. (I don't mean her troubles, but her jewels).

* *

Northern Ireland can boast of 38,440 motor vehicles or one for each 48 people.

* *

The Free State has 25,000 motor vehicles or one for each 85 people.

* *

Strabane tenants residing at eight dwellings in Derry Road are in clover. They are paying neither rent nor rates as the landlord cannot be traced.

* *

Enniskillen live register shows 134 unemployed men, etc., Mr. W. J. Brown, J.P., P.L.G., says—"There is plenty of work for men if they would work for the wages that farmers and employers are able to pay them." Of course, we have only 26 per cent. unemployed. Gt. Britain suffers from 11 per cent. and at Trafford Park, Manchester, it was advertised that employment would be provided for six men and next morning 3,000 men applied and were told that the vacancies had been filled overnight. The police were phoned for, to disperse the 3,000 men who were genuinely seeking work. What do you think of that Mr. Brown, J. Pee, Pee, Pee.

* *

Newry U.D.C. are to spend £17,500 on a Municipal electricity scheme. More converts to Socialism. Eh! What?

* *

Limavady boys were charged some time ago with stealing a turkey. They stated that they sold the turkey for 8/- as they needed the money in order to go to the Cinema and see "The Ten Commandments." I learned the ten Commandments at the Sunday School. They are easily learnt, but the job is to keep them.

* *

Derry P.L.G. are spending 8d. in the £ on outdoor relief.

* *

Drumbo ploughing competitions were held on Saturday, 2nd. January. The Rev. Dr. Duff who distributed the prizes, said— "Farmers were never so prosperous as they are to-day." Well, Drumbo labourers, what about it; how prosperous are you? Are you organised in your trade union? Don't delay.

Join to-day.

* *

Castlederg P.L.G. have considered correspondence relative to Widows' and Orphans Pensions. The Chairman (Mr. Gamble) stated that they have plenty of paper at the Ministry of Home Affairs, and more time to write than he has.

* *

Larne P.L.G. have decided to remove from their outdoor relief list, the names of all widows and orphans receiving State pensions.

* *

Fermanagh.—This is a boundary problem. There is a schoolhouse situate in Fermanagh, Northern Ireland. The teacher is being paid by the Northern Government, yet all the scholars come from Donegal in the Free State. The explanation is that all the roads leading to the school are in the Free State. Notaninch!

* *

Cookstown. Kate Nugent was fined in £3 and £1 costs at Cookstown Petty Session for exposing for sale a number of rotten eggs in the market place. It is a fact that many of our public boards are captured by dishonest merchants who refuse to allow prosecutions of a similar nature to take place.

* *

Mr. Lloyd Campbell, M.P., says— "Communism has eaten its way among the employers as well as among the workers. There were employers to-day who were out to ruin the Empire." This is a shocking state of affairs, and Tony Babington should be told about it.

* *

Derry.—Frank Gilliland J.P. Co. C. wants to send deputations to Belfast to put the fear of God in Ministers' who introduced measures which heavily burdened the ratepayers. Some humourist, is Frank.

* *

The Free State is not a state of freedom, as it is unlawful to sell, expose for sale, or keep for sale any salmon or trout.

* *

Workman, Clark and Co., Ltd.— Debenture holders have decided to take action in the Ulster High Court, relative to the issue of the prospectus.

* *

Sir John Foster Fraser contributes a remarkable article to the Illustrated Sunday Herald, 24/1/26. Talking about winter holidays in Switzerland, he says "Tens of thousands of **English** folk get a fine tonic every winter, playing for a few weeks among the snows of Switzerland." He does not say how many of these English holiday makers are shipyard labourers, spinners or miners. Again, he says -"There are 113 Swiss hotels filled with the English."

"The wealthy travel in stuffy sleeping-cars and loll about luxurious hotels. This is the seventeenth unconsecutive winter I have come to the Alps to wallow in snow and sunshine." These facts are worth bearing in mind when the bosses tell us that they are losing money and that we must agree to lower wages and longer hours.

Clifton Ward For Labour !

Do you labour by hand or brain?

Do you reside on Crumlin, Oldpark, Antrim Road or Cliftonville?

If so, you are eligible to join Clifton Divisional Labour Party. Further particulars from—

Wm. Clark, 48 York Street, Belfast.

Labour Unites "Mickey" And "Prod" At Keady.

Keady is an old world Irish Town, situated in Co. Armagh, on the Border. The principal industry being linen textiles. The Workers' Union decided to contest five seats in the Labour interest and were successful in winning four. The fifth candidate being defeated by an Independent who polled 2 votes over Labour. The new Council will consist of four Labour, four Nationalist , and an Independent, who is pledged to vote for a Labour Chairman and to give general support to the Labour policy. Lady Craig says Socialism is creeping forward. In Keady, we are advancing by leaps and bounds. Up Labour!

Observations On The Municipal Elections.

"Defeat! who is it speaks of defeat,
I tell you a cause like ours
Is greater than defeat can know.
It is the Power of Powers."

Once more the defending hosts of Conservatism have held at bay the attacking forces of the Socialist Army. A breach was made at Dock Ward where our good Comrade Dawson Gordon was returned by the somewhat narrow majority of 42.

It is difficult to pick out the best fight, they were all so good. Mrs. M'Coubrey had perhaps the most difficult Ward, but she gave a very good account of her Stewardship. Much useful and necessary propaganda work being done in that "backward area." It is reported that the opposition to Mrs. M'Coubrey was not spontaneous, but was carefully arranged by a one time prominent member of the Co-op., but who, thanks to the good work of Mrs M'Coubrey is now a back number. Its funny how spleen and ill-breeding shows.

In Clifton, Mrs. Ida Boyd put up a splendid fight, held magnificent meetings, and the meetings at Henderson Avenue, Marsden Gardens, and Atlantic Avenue prove that there is an interest being taken in the "cause" by people who formerly evinced no desire to hear the Gospel. Dock Ward, by returning that earnest worker for Socialism, Dawson Gordon, has done a good day's work for the City. Dawson, as he is popularly known, is one of the very best, and with his experience gained in 1920-23, will be a valuable asset to the little group of devoted workers in the City Council. The fight in Woodvale will live in history for the remarkable success attending the meetings of Sam Geddis, which were held in all sorts of places, where, a few short years ago, meetings would have been impossible. More will be heard of the Shankill Labour Party, who certainly showed by their spirit and determination that they are in the true line of the traditions of the party. George Corcoran and James Duff have nothing to be ashamed of in the results in Pottinger, as never before had such a stir been created in the east. James Johnston in Victoria put up a good fight against tremendous odds. The result in Cromac where Mr. Malcolm has fought on five occasions, proves the need for a divisional or Ward Labour Party in that Area and much propaganda remains to be carried on.

West Belfast Labour Party fought Smithfield and Falls Wards. In Falls, James Grimley improved on his vote of last year, and in Smithfield, Hugh Gemmell, whom we all thought would be returned was beaten by a narrow margin of votes. The Electors of Smithfield and Falls, who heard Gemmell speak, will agree that it is a tragedy that a young man of such eloquence and energy should not have had the opportunity of serving his fellow-citizens. Booze has triumphed in Smithfield and the triumph of the cause has been delayed, that is all.

The ground has been ploughed, now for the harrowing and the sowing of the seed and some day, may it be soon, we or our sons and daughters will reap the harvest.

Labour will Govern this Country.

Labour will administer the affairs of Belfast, and every Council in Ireland in the interest of the poor, needy and oppressed.

These are the ideals, aims and aspirations of the Labour Party of Northern Ireland.

MANY THOUSANDS who have followed the political fortunes of Lord Carson and Sir James Craig, will be glad to learn that their work for Ulster is to be suitably rewarded, and that they are to be 'hung' together in the Belfast City Hall.

The Rising Generation— And The Bosses.

(An enlightened teacher set his pupils an essay on the Municipal Elections, and the following is the effort of a 12 year old Scholar. Keir Hardie was right when he said that the Midwife and the Gravedigger were on our side - Ed.)

The Belfast Corporation is composed of 60 members (15 Aldermen and 45 Councillors). An Alderman is elected to sit in the Council for 6 years and a Councillor for 3 years.

The Election campaign in Clifton Ward was keenly contested, the candidates being Mrs Ida Boyd (Labour) and Mr. D. Lyle Hall (Unionist).

Mrs. Boyd was well received by the workers who are slowly awaking from their apathy. They are now recognising that waving a Union Jack and singing "God Save the King" and "Dolly's Brae" will not fill their stomachs.

Mr. Hall relied on the "Old, old story" of your bosses are your true friends. We may rob you of your wages, refuse you work and squander your money on fourth quality timber, but nevertheless we will do our best. This is perfectly true as they always so their best for their own friends and the needs of the workers don't matter. Mr. Hall being well supplied with every assistance because of the fact that he is Vice-President of Belfast Chamber of Trade. The Chamber of Trade is composed of Shopkeepers and Capitalists.

After a day of spiritless polling the result was declared at 10-15 p.m., on Friday, 15th January. It was expected that Mr. Lyle Hall would win, as the Labour gospel has never been well received in this ward. Nevertheless , Labour supporters are not at all dismayed as they have gained a great many more votes than on previous occasions, so

"Let tyrants rage and traitors fear,
We'll keep the Red Flag flying
here."

The Fellowship Of Socialism.

BY HUGH GEMMELL.

John Ruskin left a phrase to the Socialist Movement as part of his heritage, and that phrase was "Fellowship is life, lack of Fellowship is death."

Now the meaning of Socialism is simply Fellowship or Companionship, and the word Socialism is taken from the Greek Socious, a companion. The "Movement" as we always affectionately call it, aims at pleasure and joy and happiness, and endeavours always in its literature and oratory, to promote the material happiness of the people. Thus we incorporated into our phraseology the great phrase of Colonel Ingersoll, "the time to be happy is now, the place to be happy is here, and the way to be happy is by making other people happy."

Colonel Ingersoll was no Socialist; indeed he was an anti-Socialist, but Socialists believe in using the best from all sources, no matter whether it be sympathetic or antagonistic.

The common proverbs of the common people have an unerring instinct for truth, and a hoary old proverb that is as true now as on the day it was coined is " there is a little bit of bad in the best of us, and a little bit of good in the worst of us."

During the past few years, I am sorry to say, a spirit of antagonism has manifested itself in our Movement among some Comrades, and instead of looking for the best in our character, and using that best to condone minor faults and failings, they have magnified slender errors into crimes of malice, and erected a barrier against Fellowship. These Comrades have failed to absorb the spirit of the Movement. They have missed the cultural beauty and spiritual exaltation that made Socialism a living flame of Purity and Truth in the days before the War.

Unemployment has not helped to sweeten our temper, for once again the unerring truth of ancient proverbs asserts itself and says that "Satan will find mischief still for idle hands to do."

When the struggle for existence is narrowed down to the border line of actual physical starvation, and when one day is long enough to decide between a roof and the starry canopy of Heaven; when a careless phrase from the lips of a pampered clerk in the Labour Exchange is sufficient to send a man home to his wife and children with the terrible news that there is no money for food, clothing or shelter, and the grim spectacle of the Workhouse rises before his eyes, then in that man's mind there can be no thoughts of Fellowship, or Comradeship, or even the ordinary courtesies and etiquette of life. Life for him has been stripped of all its embellishments, culture has become a sham and a mockery, and his soul is dead to beautiful music or inspiring words. He has become Ishmael, a social outcast, and his hand is raised against all mankind. He is not to blame, and once again we find the truth in an ancient proverb and we know that "he is more sinned against than sinning."

He is the product of Capitalism, an outcast of Capitalism, and a living testimony of the utter failure of Capitalism to ensure the happiness of the individual. He is a danger to himself, a menace to society, and the spirit of ill-will and mental viciousness that radiates from him affects all society, and even the armour of Socialist good will is not proof against the acid bitterness of his ill-will. The malady attacks our Comrades who are least prepared to resist it, those who have not yet had time to absorb all the cultural beauty and Comradeship of our Movement. They become soured and disaffected, and when they encounter any expression of our spiritual appeal, they spurn it with contumely, and dismiss it with contempt. It is in order to regain the "Soul of Socialism" that nights of Fellowship are held. Let us speak no evil; let no smouldering suspicion warp our judgment of each other and let us seek for the best that is in all of us. Let our songs and stories be free from vulgarity and let them be "the simple annals of the poor."

Whatever hatred we have, let it be a hatred of falsehood, of trickery and deceit; of oppression and corruption; of shoddy clothes and slum houses; of adulterated food and slum mentality. If we hate, let us hate Capitalism, and disease and destitution, and let us hate War with such terrible intensity that when the Master Class blazons forth the call to human slaughter, the Workers of all lands will say with one united voice, "No! a thousand times no! Not a man, not a penny, not a gun!"

For religion lies in doing good, and this is our battle-cry. "Workers of all lands unite, you have nothing to lose but your chains; you have a world to win!"

Election And Flags.

During the Municipal Election, quite a lot of party capital was made out of the National Flag, the "Union Jack," the British Flag, particularly by the conservative party nominees. They waved it, flaunted it in the faces of all and sundry and generally trailed it in the mud, and that is how they cheapened and abused the National Emblem, as they have always done before. As I watched the dismal, half-hearted Tory entourage with its Band, flag-waggers and joy-riders, pass by, I wondered how many of those Tory touts and paid hacks knew the history and significance of the flag which they so ostentatiously waved and sullied, and treated as *their* particular emblem. Alas! it is typical of their narrow outlook generally. A filibustering jingoism, down with all and up with me sort of style, so typical of Tories everywhere.

They came to the place of meeting and the oration began. Such an oration; it told of the fine work done by the Tory cum Capitalist big Biz representatives, carefully omitting the particulars as to their voting in the Corporation. Then came the inevitable slander of opponents. The dirty dogs, their stock had run out, so they talked about nailing flags to the mast, and so forth, little dreaming how they lowered the prestige of the British flag by making it an Election rag on which to wipe their dirty feet. Not one item of constructive value for Municipal Management did they expound. They leave that until they get there, and then it is done for *vested interests*. They raved about the "Red Flag." As a citizen of this British Empire I respect the National Flag, knowing as I do its history good and bad. But I realise that beside a love of home country, we as Socialists, and I in particular, believe that we must have an International love for other countries and their peoples, in order to have a full measure of happiness and comfort, nationally and internationally. What could be, and is a better symbol of that, than the Red Flag. I say, let other peoples have their National Flag, but let the Red Flag be the symbol of Internationalism and revered as such. **O.S.C.**

Lady Anderson, C.B.E., a short time ago said—"They could not blind themselves to the danger which presented itself in a form of Socialism, which was really allied to Bolshevism." No! my dear lady, we are not Bolshies really, and the Capitalism which you dear ladies are trying to bolster up is born of the Devil and condemns the majority of our people to live in dread of the Workhouse, and thousands to be housed like swine. Dear Lady Craig says Socialism is creeping onward. No! Dear Lady. Socialism is marching steadily forward to ultimate victory.

Lady Craig speaking to Ulster women Unionists, said—"Socialism was the thing that they had to fight now. **It was creeping in steadily,** not only in the towns but in the small country places."

Ill Fares The Land.
BY SOWSEED.

"Ill fares the land
To hastening ills a prey—
Where wealth accumulates
And men decay." —*Goldsmith.*

"The hired labourer must go." To save the Agricultural industry from ruin, I pointed out in my last contribution to the **Labour Opposition**, the farmer has decided to lower the costs of production by working harder himself; by compelling his wife and family to do the same, and by dismissing the hired labourer. Our Editor sets the latter part out in block type! Now the question arises, where shall the agricultural worker go, and what shall he do? He cannot go on the "dole" for he is not in an insurable occupation; therefore he is compelled to adopt one of the following alternatives: stay where he is and starve, emigrate and by hard work at low wages, send home more produce at a price which still further depresses the agricultural industry, or migrate to the towns and cities, and by competing with his fellow-workers, again bring wages to the subsistence level.

Why does our Capitalist government refuse the right of the "dole" to the agricultural labourer? Is it not because they know it is the best weapon they can forge to break the resisting power of organised labour? Men from the country districts know little or nothing of the power or principles of Trade Unionism; they flock into the towns and are ready to accept work on any conditions and on any terms. They are ready to wrangle with their fellow workers like a dog for a bone. This is exactly what our employing and governing classes want and for which they are continually planning. After the war, fear of the results of demobilisation was the cause of the introduction of the "Allowance" system—men fresh from the battlefield well fed and full of fight would have proved a menace if they had been thrown out on the country to starve. But now, through prolonged economic suffering, their resisting power is almost gone, they cease to be a danger, they are quietly pushed out without an "Allowance," without the "dole" and join the agricultural workers in their unconscious struggle for work at the lowest rate of remuneration, which the employers will offer.

What are our Labour Parties doing to meet and to resist this capitalist onslaught? In "Revolution by Reason," written by Mr. John Strachey, page 85, on this subject, viz., the right of the workers to claim work or maintenance, he says, "here large and glaring as an electric sign on Piccadilly Circus is the writing on the wall for Capitalism." The introduction of the "dole" is the doom of the Capitalistic system. Labour and Socialistic workers, here is the slogan that frightens Capitalism, "Work or Maintenance." Full maintenance. What is the use of wasting time clearing up the messes created by unscrupulous Capitalists. Let them clean up their own dirty creations; if you take the time to do this for them they will have another ready when you have the first one finished. Instead, go out to the lanes and streets of our towns, to the hills and dales of our countrymen and proclaim this great message of emancipation; "Work or Maintenance!" Let us blazon it on our banners, and let our hearts be filled with this inspiring thought: it is the end of capitalism. The right to live, the "dole," the "allowance," call it what you will, the enemy—Capitalism is afraid of it. His knees tremble, his hand sags to his side, soon he will be like the giant, prone before the whirling attack of his agile and determined opponent.

Why should the agricultural worker go? He likes to work on the land, his home is there, all his associations are there. He would rather stay. Is he to be denied the privileges of the town workers because it suits the schemes of Capitalism! When land nationalisation becomes an accomplished fact, the land will require more workers, not less. The agricultural worker must be insured against unemployment. It is a standing disgrace against the whole community that he and his should be allowed to starve during periods of depression or through seasonal changes which occur in his occupation. If granted, it would be like a two-edged weapon, it would cut down the terror of starvation—it would hew to pieces the bonds of serfdom.

I had begun to write on the Nationalisation of land, but it can wait till next month. It came into my mind that if the rural workers are all to leave the land, what would be the good of Nationalisation to graze sheep on a few ranches owned by wealthy landowners. The proposition seemed ridiculous. My vision of busy farms and happy workers had vanished. Perhaps my mind had become bitter; but Mr. Editor, **the hired labourer must not go.**

A Night Wi' Burns.

The Independent Labour Party in Belfast has always cherished the memory of those who have fought for human freedom, and on the night of January the 25th, a crowded hall testified to the esteem and love in which Robert Burns was held by his fellow men. Margaret T. M'Coubrey presided, and as each choral or solo item came forward on the programme, she introduced it with a vivid little vignette of its history and significance. She also delivered "The Oration" and touched all our hearts and sweetened our minds in traversing the life and fortunes of Scotland's National Poet. The I.L.P. Choir was voted a great success, and Colin C. Caldwell, the Choirmaster, is to be heartily congratulated on his achievement. The choir certainly sings with a great deal of artistry and 'understanding,' while in the bolder pieces they sweep forward with a commanding spirit that carries the audience upward to a spontaneous ecstacy of applause. The solos, duets and trios were taken by Magsie McAlister, William Bookless, Lily Davison and Sandy Smylie, and the ovation accorded to each and all of them was a more eloquent tribute to their merit than my pen could record. The art of accompaniment is a gift, and too often, fine singing is 'drowned' by an aggressive personality at the piano. That charge could never be levelled against Mrs. Davison, and she accompanied the singing with a restrained harmony that enriched the vocal score. She was assisted at the piano by a lady whose name I failed to secure.

Piping in the Haggis was great sport, and when pipe-Major Magee swung up the centre aisle followed by "The Haggis".s.s" — assisted and under control — there was a great shout of acclamation and merriment. The red robes with the mystic symbols that clothed the 'officiator' were a daring departure from convention, as also was the "Haggis Dance" to the skirl of the pipes.

With 'Auld Lang Syne' and the 'Red Flag' we concluded a happy, fraternal and inspiring night that will help us all along the road to Socialism. **HOTSPUR.**

War ! What For ?

War is hell, of hell begotten,
And in issue, hellish too;
Some would cast a glamour round it—
Draw reality from view.
Deck it with the tinsel trappings
Of a chivalrous crusade
Call, on war, God's benediction,
Claiming His almighty aid.

Drag the vampire into daylight,
Stripped of every false array;
Blaster of the time that has been;
Menace to the coming day
For its blood-lust is unsated
By the holocaust of years,
Death and anguish, plague and hunger,
Broken lives and women's tears.

But into the future peering,
See fresh victims come along;
Children now, with winsome graces
Happy hearts and blythesome song:
Children now, within them ripening,
Lofty thought, its deed and word,
At the threshold of fruition—
New-found offering to the sword.

Shall it be? The cry goes upward:
Heaven above, to earth replies:
We have left mankind unfettered,
In your choice the answer lies.
—**J. G. M'ALONAN.**

Suffer Little Children!

At the meeting of the Departmental Commission on Local Government Administration held in Parliament Buildings, Dr. T. F. S. Fulton, School Medical Officer to the Belfast Education Authority, appeared before the Commission and gave evidence. He stated that in his opinion *no hard and fast line* could be drawn between Public Health Services and School Medical Services, and that in the interests of economy and efficiency the two services should be co-ordinated under one control. For instance, he considered that in a County Borough there should be a Medical Officer of Health with a Deputy, the latter to be in charge of school work as head of a sub-department. This system gives the School Medical Officer wider general experience, very close co-operation in the control of notifiable and infectious diseases, and permits the staff to be available for emergency work. The School Medical Officer should be in charge of Child Welfare work, as that would enable a complete supervision to be held over children from birth, until they attained the age for leaving school, unless they ceased to come under Child Welfare schemes before they attained school age. This system made it harder for the authorities to lose sight of delicate children, and also enabled them to compile a more accurate history of the child from a medical point of view.

Regarding work in the county, the witness was of the opinion that there should be a Medical Officer of Health in charge of the county, with assistant officers appointed to deal with each district, these officers to act as Tuberculosis Officers, School Medical Officers, Child Welfare Officers and Public Health Officers for their district. He recommended this system as being more economic, because officers could arrange their work in such a way that they could be employed with less loss of time, and there would be a tremendous saving in travelling expenses, etc., which would become a very heavy charge if one officer were appointed for a specific job in the country. It would also lessen the number of officers who might be called upon to inspect any one house.

Dr. Fulton was very strongly against the appointment of part-time medical officers to do School Medical work, on the ground that such part-time officers might be called away urgently on their own private work after having made arrangements to carry out school inspection in the presence of the parents. In the case of medical inspection, it was essential that an officer could arrange his programme weeks beforehand, so as to enable him to carry out his work punctually and methodically, and with the least possible inconvenience to the childrens' parents.

The witness then dealt with the nursing staffs, and gave suggestions as to how such staffs could be combined with economy and efficiency.

He then proceeded to deal with afflicted children and stated that totally deaf and blind children should be educated in a residential school, while those who were only partially deaf or blind might be treated in special day schools.

Regarding mentally defective children, Dr. Fulton stated that a central institution should be established for the whole of Northern Ireland in which these children could be dealt with. It might also be possible in this institution to arrange for the care of children otherwise afflicted, but he recommended that each class should be segregated.

If an institution for sane epileptics for the whole of Northern Ireland were set up, he did not see why provision should not be made for children in this institution who would be specially dealt with there.

Notes And News

The Coalisland Branch of the Labour Party of Northern Ireland held a public meeting in the local picture house to protest against the administration (mal-administration) of the Unemployment Insurance Act. The principal speaker was Senator Robert Dorman from Belfast, and the Chairman presided over an enthusiastic audience that crowded the building. This meeting is one of a series that has carried the torch of revolt through the length and breadth of the Six Counties.

Sir James Craig boasted in 1924 that *he* would solve unemployment in Ulster himself. But in January, 1926, unemployment in Belfast increased by 894 persons. If the P.M. were in private employment he would get sacked for a result like that. He is not fit for his job, and the people ought to get their Prime Minister from the ranks of the Workers.

Every Sunday night at 7 o'clock, a propaganda meeting is held in the I.L.P. Hall at 48 York Street. Admission is free, and there is always a good lecture on political or educational matters, followed by discussion. You should come.

The Nationalist Party and the Unionist Party in Ulster have now definitely united against the advancing forces of Socialism. The old parties are in full retreat and eloquent proof of that was furnished at the last general election when more votes were cast against the Government than for it. The evacuation of the Belfast Old Town Hall by the Unionist Party, and their retreat to Glengall Street is a signal victory for Labour. Hurrah!! Although Labour only secured one extra seat at the Belfast Municipal Elections, our vote rose enormously, and a Belfast Labour Town Council is not far distant. A report has reached us that Castledawson wants to establish a branch of the Independent Labour Party, and if the local Comrades will write to this office we will make the necessary arrangements.

On Sunday the 7th February, Frank Nolan will lecture on Anti-Vivisection in the I.L.P. Hall in York Street. On Sunday the 14th February, the lecturer will be Councillor Wm. M'Mullen, M.P., and his theme will be one of historical interest to the Irish Working-Class.

The Joint Committee and the I.L.P. Choir are running a real Irish Night on the 17th March and the tickets will soon be available. Those who crowded the Hall on Burns' Night know how good these "nights" are, and they always come back again.

On Sunday the 14th March, Hugh Gemmell will deliver an address on "The Paris Commune of 1871," to commemorate its anniversary.

The Lecture Secretary has something up his sleeve for the month of May that will make your eyes pop out of your head. Three new divisional Labour Parties have been established in Belfast, and the work of organising the town is proceeding rapidly. Encouraging reports are to hand from all the divisions, and the work of unification is well advanced.

Town And Country.

Limavady R. D. C. decided to postpone payments to road contractors until an investigation was made by the County Surveyor. The Chairman said an enquiry would be held in regard to cetrtain allegations. Oh, those Contracts!

* *

Lloyd George says—"We were spending £400,000,000 of money in order to buy from abroad, produce which could be raised in this country."

* *

Belfast Harbour returns show that we exported 95 asses and 3 goats, all four legged, I understand. We also imported 3 goats and **no** four-legged asses.

* *

James A. Turkington of Belfast Old Town Hall Gang, says that—"Names like Saklatvala and Pollitt stink in the nostrils of real trade unionists." What does James know about real trade unionism? He has been repudiated by Belfast trade unionists time and again.

* *

Fermanagh Co. Council want a loan of £4,000 for the purchase of road making machinery. Naturally this was opposed by the Farmers' Union. At the inquiry held recently, it was alleged by representatives of the Farmers' Union that the direct labour system was robbery and that any old road will do the farmers. Mr. J. P. Burkitt, Co. Surveyor, put up a spirited defence of direct labour which so impressed the Inspector (Mr. John Bates) who declared "That he would have to report upon the necessity for the machinery."

* *

Mr. Smith Gordon says—"Ireland which is a poor country, has £150,000,000 invested abroad." Can we not have a list of the Irish Patriots who have this money invested abroad?

* *

Derry Education Committee report that "In all but three of the elementary schools, cod liver oil emulsion is being provided, under medical direction, for delicate and under nourished children." This is the sort of thing that Labour men and women have been fighting for, for thirty years past, and the Unionists, and the churches have called us Bolshies and Communists for doing so.

* *

Antrim Petty Sessions. William French, Fountain Street, Antrim, was fined 30/- and costs for selling buttermilk containing 32.9% more water than the quantity usually allowed for churning. The defence put up was that it was being sold as it came from the farm. Of course, blame the other fellows.

* *

Fermanagh Co. Council. Mr. W. J. Brown, J. P., gave notice of motion that all farmers with land valued at over £40 per year be given a free motor licence. To him that hath, shall be given, etc.

* *

Mr. Mitchell-Hedges, the well known traveller says—"It is astounding to discover upon analysis, how far we are behind the United States of America, Canada, and many other up-to-date countries in business methods and ideas." He never mentions wages and hours of labour, in which we are also very much behind.

The Red Flag.
Words by JIM CONNELL.
Air—"Maryland."

The people's flag is deepest red;
It shrouded oft our martyred dead,
And ere their limbs grew stiff or cold
Their hearts' blood dyed its every fold.
CHORUS
Then raise the scarlet standard high!
Within its shade we'll live and die
Tho' cowards flinch and traitors sneer,
We'll keep the red flag flying here.

Look round, the Frenchman loves its blaze;
The sturdy German chants its praise;
In Moscow's streets its hymns are sung;
Chicago swells the surging throng.

It waved above our infant might
When all ahead seemed dark as night;
It witnessed many a deed and vow—
We must not change its colour now.

It well recalls the triumphs past;
It gives the hope of peace at last.
The banner bright, the symbol plain
Of human right and human gain.

It suits to-day the weak and base
Whose minds are fixed on pelf and place,
To cringe before the rich man's frown
And haul the sacred emblem down.

With heads uncovered, swear we all
To bear it onward till we fall.
Come dungeon dark, or gallows grim,
This song shall be our parting hymn.

The Labour Opposition Of Northern Ireland

Vol. 2—No. 14   March. 1926   One Penny

[The front page of this issue carried the picture which appears on the cover of this book, together with the note which follows.]

(This eloquent Cartoon was specially drawn for **The Labour Opposition**, by Comrade Willie Gordon, of the Shankill Ward Labour Party. It is a further proof that in the Socialist Movement we have artists, poets, musicians and writers superior to anything produced by the master class.)

Hits And Misses.
BY MARKSMAN.

Alderman "Ossie" Jamison, Nationalist Member of Belfast Corporation, speaking at a meeting of Electrical Engineers, said—"Belfast could claim a measure of prosperity at least equal to, if not greater, than that existing in any other city of its size in the United Kingdom."

Such Tosh! Such Bunkum! Why! "Ossie" doesn't seem to know that we suffer from 26 per cent. unemployment as compared with 11 per cent. in Great Britain. And again, every City across the water pays an adequate sum of outdoor relief to destitute citizens, which is denied to Belfast citizens. Now that "Ossie" has been made High Sheriff, he seems anxious to prove that there are no slums or poverty stricken people in Belfast. I hope that some of his friends will show him this paragraph . . . and also the next one.

*   *

Belfast P.L.G. recommended Infirmary treatment in the case of a married couple with one child. They were destitute and found living in one room with seven other persons—men, women and children. The man was a shipyard worker and the wife a textile worker. Both man and wife were turned down at the Labour Exchange, in spite of their good industrial records— This is how Sir James Craig keeps his promise! *He solves the unemployment problem by cutting off the "Buroo money" from a shipyard worker who tramped 45 miles to the Silent Valley and 45 miles home again in a vain endeavour to secure work.*

*   *

Belfast Labour Exchanges turned down 1,842 claims for benefit during the month of January. They hope to beat this record in February. 510 of these people were refused benefit, on the grounds of family income, and yet these people are all insured persons. Some Insurance, eh?

*   *

Northern Ireland. There are 6,073 unemployed Building Trade Workers in Northern Ireland.

*   *

"Belfast Telegraph," 9/4/26, Says: "Arnott & Co.—The usual 4/- per share on Ordinary Shares with £10,000 to premises and £5,000 to employees' fund," not bad for Arnott's. Same

paper, same date, says, "Selfridge & Co. The net profit for the past year is £504,160." The poor shareholders in this sheltered trade will receive 15 per cent. Selfridge's profits for the year 1925 are the largest in the history of the Company. "Nuff Sed."

* *

Greyabbey Petty Sessions. George Paton was fined £5 7s. 0d., with 17/6 costs in each of two cases for selling milk which contained 93.44 per cent. water. It was stated in court that "Paton" supplies a Belfast firm with milk. I think it is more correct to say that he supplies a Belfast firm with water coloured with 61/2 per cent. of milk and the poor of Belfast are paying milk prices for dirty water.

* *

Monaghan Town Council has 12 members, 8 of them were returned as Nationalists, and 4 as Unionists. At their first meeting after the election, Mr. Wm. Martin, who is the Deputy Grand Master of County Monaghan Orangemen, was **unanimously** elected as Chairman. Mr. Martin, in returning thanks, said—"Questions of religion and politics were gone, and they were going to work together for the general welfare of their common country." We hope so, says I. But we doubt it, says we.

* *

Pomeroy Petty Sessions. Robert Hodge, Grocer, Cabra, Dungannon, was mulcted in £5 9s. 6d. costs, with a fine of 10/- per egg for exposing for sale six unsound eggs. There is, however, no confirmation of the rumour that Mr. William Grant, M.P. was expected to address a meeting in the neighbourhood.

* *

Clydebank. Bailie Miss Rea says that — "Some unemployed workers betted and danced, and refused to pay rates." Other members of society bet and dance but refuse to work after leaving college.

* *

Mussolini. The special correspondent of "Belfast Telegraph," writing, 13/2/26, says—"This winter, the eastern Alps are swarming with Italian soldiery, Caribineri, and Secret Police. The local newspapers have been suppressed. Outgoing and incoming mails are liable to secret censorship at all times. Promises by the Italian Authorities to the Tyrolese are being broken repeatedly." So you see even the "Tele." sometimes tells the truth about the "Castor Oil King."

* *

Mr. John F. Gordon, M.P., had tea at "Westbrook," the residence of the dear lady who is President of Cromac Women's Unionist Association, and the tea was served in the drawing-room. After which "J'honnie" told the dear old ladies some ghost stories about Socialism, and dear me! but Mr. Gordon is a nice man.

Johnny Gordon.
Elected 1920—Still Going St(rong.)

Mr. John F. Gordon, Unionist M.P., was present in the Willowfield Unionist Hall, when a paper on Compulsory Voting was read. During discussion "Johnny" advanced the view that we had too much compulsion already and stated that "when you are born you have to be registered, when you get married you again have to register yourself, and when you die, you are compelled to go and register your death." This sally was greeted with convulsive laughter in which Mr. Gordon did not join. He just stood there as the saying is, like a pea on a mountain. As he was still unable to see his blunder, the Chairman, amid renewed laughter, had to tell the M.P. that he could not register his own death. The incident created great merriment on the Woodstock Road, where people say that, speaking in the political sense, Mr. Gordon is long since dead, if he only had the wit to stiffen.

HOTSPUR.

On The Appointed Day.

BY SOWSEED.

"On the appointed day, the 1st of May, 19—? all private ownership of land shall cease." Let us take another glance at this pronouncement. On a stated day in a stated month of a stated year all private ownership of land shall cease. The nationalisation of land has become an accomplished fact. Many times has the question been put to me how would you set about land nationalisation? Well, the foregoing is the answer — a short clause in an act of Parliament, endorsed by our legislative assembly and the change is effected. What could be more simple? One might be pardoned for trying to imagine the effects of such a change on the minds of the present owners of land if this short clause were adopted without preliminary discussion. Consternation would be a mild word to use in trying to depict the feelings of men who to-day feel themselves as owners, as dictators over something where they thought they held absolute sway and tomorrow saw that old-time idea, that relic of barbarism, the feeling of possessorship broken and crumbling to pieces before the onward march of progress.

I feel certain, and many will think with me, that nothing could be worse than the present system, but how are the interested parties, the landholders, the farmers to be converted to the same attitude of mind. There are only two ways in which this can be done. Force or persuasion. To use force by a Labour Government without an educated public opinion as the motive power is to me unthinkable. Industrial workers, town dwellers, give little or no thought to a problem of this kind. If there be an abundance of food at a moderate cost their minds are little troubled as to how or where it has been produced. The world is wide and if home products are unobtainable then other places will provide the necessary supplies. Isn't

Denmark there, America too, the Colonies have always an abundant surplus, a Labour Government trying to force nationalisation on farmers and landholders such as we have in this country with no better support than the careless thought of a heterogeneous crowd of urban and city electors, would be broken to pieces on the edifice it was trying to erect. To my mind persuasion through educative methods is the only way by which the pernicious land system of our country can be altered. The farmer must be shown that it would be a greater advantage to pay a small sum to the State as rent than to pay a heavy interest charge to Capitalism for the doubtful boon of private ownership. Those who think carelessly or not at all on the subject, must be taught how substantial their gain would be if instead of an annual capitalistic charge of three pounds an acre that amount could be reduced by half and in a short time utterly abolished by the adoption of the socialistic principle of land nationalisation. They must be led to see that by lessening the burden of Capitalism, costs of production will be lower, consequently lower prices can be accepted. The retention on the land of such a vast sum of money which has now to go to the Capitalist would create a demand for farming implements and equipment. New and more up-to-date buildings, more and better supplies of manufactured articles of every kind. On the one hand, farm produce for the towns, on the other, industrial products for the country.

Again look at the benefits which would accrue to the rural workers if this terrible burden—self imposed though it may be—of perpetual interest were removed. Not only would the industry revive to requisition more labour, it would revive with new power and newer and better ideas. Just as the old saying is true that "love begets love" so the farmer finding his pathway easier and his outlook brighter would be more inclined to generous thought and action regarding the lot of his helpmate - the agricultural labourer.

Some friendly critics are exercised in their minds as to why under State ownership there should be any charge on land. This opens up the argument - Confiscation versus Compensation. But sufficient unto the day is the evil thereof. Next Month.

Labour Conditions In Mexico.

Mr. A. A. Purcell writing in the "Monthly Report" of the National Amalgamated Furnishing Trade Association says -

"From 1918 onwards, the Trade Union movement has developed into a substantial body of over a million organised workers, with signs of increase every day. This is of the highest importance to the Mexican worker, because, although the constitution fixes a six-hour day for below-ground workers, and an eight hour day for all other adults, it needs the force of Trade Union organisation to make it effective.

Night work for women and children is barred, and where night work for men is needed, it is limited to seven hours. The wage clause is rather original, and makes it incumbent upon the employer to pay a minimum wage which shall be sufficient to satisfy the normal necessities of the life of the workman, his education and recreation.

The proprietors of all undertakings must provide the workers with comfortable and hygenic dwellings. In addition, schools, hospitals and other institutions necessary to the community must also be established.

The industry is also responsible for all compensation to workers for injury, illness or death, sustained through their work.

The wages must be free from all embargoes, compensations or discounts. The firm dismissing a worker without a substantial reason or because a worker has joined a Trade Union, or having taken part in an authorised strike must either indemnify him with three months' wages, or fulfil the contract. Quite naturally these conditions are being bitterly opposed by the National and International Capitalists, and it is the latter interests that predominate and are consequently a tremendous menace to the workers of Mexico. Even during the last few weeks, the British and U.S.A. Governments have protested against provisions of the Mexican Constitution which involve the conditions here referred to.

The Trade Union Federation proceeds with its work, and whilst it may be slow, it has always the help of the Mexican Government in its many attempts to see that the spirit and intention of the Constitution is carried out. The visitor can see the business of the Union in operation. If a strike is in progress at any undertaking it will be indicated to all and sundry by a huge red and black flag being planted prominently outside the premises. This flag is the official banner of the Trade Union Federation, and remains on the spot until the dispute is satisfactorily settled. All this is a great change of front compared with the position a few short years ago, when the mere fact of a strike would have been the signal for the proprietors to have the military at their disposal to "disperse the strikers with the necessary shootings."

The Independent Labour Party Lectures attract crowded houses every Sunday night in their hall, 48 York Street. Among the outstanding addresses delivered there recently was one on "Socialism," by Senator Dorman, in which he traversed the subject from A to Z. A very special feature of these meetings is the solo item, and some of the finest singers in Belfast come there to assist in making life worth living. Every Friday at 8 p.m. is Fellowship Night, and for the humble sixpence, you can command Songs, Dances, Games and Fellowship. You should come.

On Sunday, the 28th February, Willie M'Mullen, M.P. speaks on 'The Irish Worker, Past, Present and Future'. On March the 7th Councillor Harry Midgley will deliver an address on "Fear." On March 14th, Hugh Gemmell speaks on "The Paris Commune." March the 21st is a special 'Woman's Night,' with a lady speaker, a lady presiding, and Magsie M'Alister as the soloist. March 28th is booked for Mr. J. H. Harris. He is Secretary of the Anti-Slavery and Aborigines Protection Society, is a member of the League of Nations Union Executive, is a constant writer on these subjects and has attended all League meetings at Geneva.

The Illusion of Workers' Prosperity.

BY OUR FINANCIAL EDITOR.

Take the cash in hand, and waive the rest,
Oh! the brave music of a distant drum. — *Omar*.

We have been asked on several occasions to offer some explanation for the extraordinary increase during recent years in the funds of the Belfast Savings Bank. We use the term "extraordinary," in view of the trade depression, unprecedented in severity—with its concomitant of low wages, irregular employment, and unparalleled unemployment—through which we are still passing. There is a wide-spread impression, fostered by the speeches annually delivered by the business men who are benevolently interested in the welfare of this Bank, that the sum due to depositors (£3,216,000 for 1925), represents money saved by the workers of Belfast.

Sir William Coates, at the last Annual General Meeting, referred to the "abundant evidence of the important position which the Bank occupied in the life of the working-class community, for whose benefit it was originally established." Now, we dissent from this view and its implications, and we are inclined to the opinion, that an analysis of the depositors' occupations and respective accounts would reveal a *marked decline* in working class savings. Whence, then, the increase in the funds?

From our observations of the depositors and our knowledge of the local trade situation, we believe that it is mainly due to the growth of small trading in Belfast. Grocers, Tobacconists, Confectioners and others, can confirm this last statement in reference to trade. Consequently, there are more people now in small trading with money to deposit, who instead of utilising the ordinary banks, have taken advantage of the better terms obtained at the Savings Bank. A comparison will make this clear.

In the ordinary banks no interest is paid on current accounts; withdrawals are made by cheques bearing a tax of 2d. each; and a bank fee of one guinea per year is charged for each account kept. On the other hand, the Savings Bank pays $2_{1/2}$ per cent. interest on its balances; no cheque books are required; and no banking fee is payable. For the many small traders in our city, most of whom pay their accounts by cash, the Savings Bank is more attractive. One does not need to be a financial expert to appreciate the reasons given.

Let us compare the returns of the Belfast Savings Bank with those of the Post Office and Trustee Savings Bank issued by the British Government.

BELFAST SAVINGS BANK.	
1920, amount due to depositors	£2,072,000
1925, amount due to depositors	£3,216,000
POST OFFICE SAVINGS BANK.	
1920, amount due to depositors	£266,508,000
1925, amount due to depositors	£285,400,000
TRUSTEE SAVINGS BANK.	
1921, amount due to depositors	£99,304,000
1925, amount due to depositors	£83,570,000

It will be noticed that, whilst the funds of the Belfast Savings Bank have increased by over 50 per cent., those of the Post Office have increased by only 7 per cent. approximately. The Trustee Savings Bank return (which includes the local one), actually shows a decrease, since 1921, of 16 per cent. or over £16 millions. These figures are surely striking enough.

We regard the P.O. Savings Bank as more representative of working class savings, though the figures are not necessarily, in our view, an indication of prosperity among the workers generally, when taken alone, and without qualifications. It should be acknowledged however, that no cognisance is here taken of holdings of Government Stocks, Savings Certificates, Co-operative Societies, House Purchases, etc., because these have not been introduced by those whom we are now criticising, though we realise the importance of such factors in any broad survey of the question. We shall be satisfied if we succeed in dispelling the illusion of "working-class prosperity" as far as Belfast is concerned at the present time, and we submit this explanation as a reasonable one of the increase in the funds of the local Savings Bank.

Clifton Ward Labour Party have secured a home at 45A Louisa Street, Oldpark Road. The rooms will be open each night from 7 o'clock and new members will be made welcome. The Secretary, Wm. Clarke, 45A Louisa Street, is anxious to get in touch with all Labour sympathisers residing in the district. The Parliamentary representative, Mr. Sam Kyle, M.P., for North Belfast, will be in attendance each Thursday from 10 to 12 noon, and will give advice to his constituents on Soldiers', Widows' and Orphans', and Old Age Pensions, Labour Exchange Problems, etc, etc.

Labour's Fighting Forces.

The **Workers of Comber** have revolted against the Unionist Party of the Boss, and have turned to the Labour Party —their own Party— to save what has been left by the robbers, and to secure that the wealth they produce in the future shall be enjoyed by those who produce it. A strong and growing branch of the Labour Party has been established and a public meeting is to be held in Thomson's Hall, on Friday the 12th March at 8 p.m. Councillor Harry Midgley, of Belfast, will be the chief speaker, and the chair will be occupied by a

---

A Really Helpful Poem.

If you have had no job for donkey's years,
That's not so bad as it at first appears,
    It should not make you fret.
For there are some at Monte Carlo who
Have never in their lives had work to do,
    Yet *they* don't get upset.
And as for money it's a source of woe,
Just ask some millionaire if that's not so;
    He'll soon to you explain—
How day and night it troubles him, that he
Can't quickly give away his cash, and be
    Just nice and poor again !

If rain comes splashing through your roof that's not
A reason why you should "rear up" a lot,
    And utter rank sedition.
Pure water is a boon we all desire,
For it, you know, removes the dirt and mire,
    With ease and expedition.
If in your house the temperature's at zero,
Don't make a fuss, just prove yourself a hero
    In sticking things like that.
Or, if you think how our good British Bosses,
Through foreign Reds sustained enormous losses,
    You'll very soon feel hot !

If you have got no food don't be annoyed;
Are you aware that poisons are employed
    In food adulteration ?
The fact that you to-day have not had much
Boracic Acid, Arsenic or such,
    Should cause you much elation.
But don't because your hunger's unappeased,
Become so foolish as to be displeased;
    Don't speak above your breath,
Or wave your arms or get into a passion,
But in a peaceful, law-abiding fashion—
    Go home and starve to death.
                W. G.

Comber man.

* *

The **West Belfast Labour Party** are giving up their rooms in Union Street, because they are unsuitable. Premises on the front of the Falls Road are being negotiated and it is expected they will be ready for the members at an early date. The popular propaganda meeting in Barrack Street, is, of course, continued on Sundays at 8 p.m.

* *

The **West Belfast Pipe Band** is a flourishing institution, and the side drums - presented by Jim Connolly to the Belfast Dockers - look as if their proud owners sat up all night to polish them. A big effort is being made to obtain a suitable uniform for the first Socialist Pipe Band and Funds are urgently needed. Comrade Councillor Willie M'Mullen, M.P., P.L.G., has been elected first President of the Band and Comrades Hugh Gemmell and Councillor Midgely have been elected Vice-Presidents.

* *

Clifton Ward Labour Party is making steady progress, and without any fuss or flourish is proceeding with the task of organising the ward for Labour. A public meeting under their auspices was addressed by Mr. Sam Kyle, M.P., and also by Jack M'Mullan. The hall was crowded, the audience enthusiastic, and the membership roll turned over to a fresh page.

* *

South Belfast Labour Party has been formed. The president is Mr. Cleland, the Vice-president is Mrs. M'Leod, the Treasurer is Mrs. Getgood, and the Secretary is Edmund Gordon, 50 Fernwood Street. A strong Ward Committee has been set up and thus the latest Labour advance has been consolidated. The South is the final division in Belfast to fall to Labour's assault, and the Northern Capital is now encircled by Labour's fighting forces. The details of registration and organisation should now be studied and developed so that when election day comes round, Labour may reap the reward of its sowing.

* *

Dock Ward Labour Party, after Council Dawson Gordon's spectacular victory over Mr. Gray, is enjoying a well deserved "breather." Not that they have slacked off in the work. By no means. It is just that all work and no play makes Jack a dull boy, and they have promoted a Social Evening, that will inspire them to fresh efforts and, we hope, fresh victories.

* *

Shankill Ward Labour Party is touching the 200 mark, and their premises in Luke Street are a veritable hive of industry. The Shankill men are noted for their shrewd practical methods and, if they have been hard to win for Labour, there is also not the slightest doubt that they will yield to the Labour Party an allegiance and a sterling fighting quality that will tell in the battles that are to come. With a political foresight that might well be copied by other Divisions they have inaugurated a Speaker's Class at 2 Luke Street on Thursdays at 8 p.m. and the services of Hugh Gemmell have been secured as their voluntary Tutor.

* *

Court Ward Labour Party has always displayed energy and initiative, and their Tom Mann meeting in the Ulster Hall was the crowning triumph of a winter full of propaganda work. It takes confidence to conduct a meeting like that, but Willie Houston, in the Chair, carried the proceedings without a hitch. Tom Mann has lost none of his ardour or his logic, and he built up his indictment of Capitalism with masterly skill. The enthusiasm was positively volcanic and when Tom Mann called for three cheers for Socialism you could almost feel the building shaking. The spirited singing of the Red Flag, led by Tom Mann himself, is something to be remembered, and should serve as a salutory lesson to those who sneer and say that it does not matter.

"Let cowards flinch, or traitors sneer,
We'll keep the Red Flag flying here."

* *

East Belfast Labour Party keeps pegging away with their propaganda on Sunday nights at the Bridge End, corner of Mountpottinger Road, and there also, on Wednesday, Hugh Gemmell conducts their studies in Economics. The Branch boasts a very fine group of young men, imbued with the finest spirit of Socialism, and in the incoming summer they will be put to the practical tests of propaganda for the Cause. The rooms are open every night for indoor games and fellowship and new members are made to feel so very much "at home" that there is never any awkwardness or restraint. They believe in education, for propaganda, for emancipation; fellowship to lighten the burdens of life, and . . . .Socialism for all.

* *

The Left Wing.
BY "PLEBIAN."

"It is rather unfair to those of us who have grown grey in the cause of Socialism to see the new young men advancing the thoughtless doctrine of their peculiar ultraism."

The above is typical of the opinion to some, or rather, the majority of those Comrades in the working-class movement, who, with a childish selfishness to retain their recognition as pioneers, endeavour to pour scorn (sometimes they give fatherly advice) on the idea of a Left Wing Movement. One hears much of impulsive youth—of hot-headed products of stormy debates, of irresponsible men, who, with no special object in life, are determined to create in the Labour Movement a chaotic state of affairs.

Let us examine this sinister organisation which exerts such an unholy influence over young men. In the first place, this demon ideology of Left Wingism seems to have produced—or captured—all the students of economics, etc., in the Socialist Movement. These Comrades have not swung to the Left, because that particular wing affords a splendid opportunity to air their Marxian views in relation to Modern Society, or espouse this oft-snubbed doctrine to accelerate the questionable progress of the Labour Movement; but simply because they feel and know that the Socialist (?) outlook of those grey-headed monuments of the Class Struggle, are merely following, or wallowing in the wake of Capitalist destruction. Utopian perhaps, they are, yet if romantic visions of the "Day that is coming" obscures the class-struggle—then it is time a more practical spirit was introduced. That is why this militant body—this minority group are aware of the fact that the only way to fight Capitalism—is to shatter, first of all these illusions of our Right Wing Comrades, who think that Capitalism only needs sufficient encouragement to co-operate with the Working-Class; at least their attitude suggests this inference.

Furthermore, the Left Wingers are not content to be an Extreme Section of the Socialist Movement. They won't rest until they have purged the Party of adulterated Socialists, in order that a class-conscious organization of militant pioneers may get on with their task of destroying Capitalism. We have tasted the bitterness of Capitalism, therefore is it any wonder, we desire to spit it out at them?

Ireland has added her terrible quota to the world's woes, and, *as the particular conditions of a Country justifies a particular form of action*, it is perfectly natural that a Country, the working class of which have suffered economic hardship for years, should give birth to a movement which is only the expression of a tortured community, and who are compelled to react (in a form suitable to the conditions existing) against Capitalism, or any other obstacle in the way of economic emancipation.

* *

"It is rather unfair to those of us who have grown grey..." Good Lord! Is this the outcome of centuries of strife, of corruption, degradation, slavery, murder, immorality and destrution..." *They Starve who don't deserve to live.*

Socialism And Human Nature.

BY DAVID A. M'LEAN.

We who are engaged in propounding the Socialist message are often met with the retort that, "you cannot change human nature," and this reply allows our opponents to hop about considerably before facing the issue.

Many of the mean and cowardly acts that we see committed from day to day are a direct result of the present "system" or chaotic scramble if you like. People who live in constant dread of losing their means of livelihood are often compelled to resort to shady acts, that they would shrink for doing, were they assured that opportunity would always be given them to support themselves and their dependants.

As I stood outside the Belfast Hippodrome last week, my attention was drawn to a number of lads engaged in a skirmish, endeavouring to dispose of some programmes at a "wing" each. These programmes had been rescued from the gutter and the race to every new arrival in the queue was a striking example of the "struggle for existence."

"You cannot democratise human nature," says Mr. J. F. Gordon in a recent speech. Well, this is all right in a speech, but when it comes to a serious argument, one wonders why Mr. Gordon receives £20 per week.

When these opponents of ours assume that human nature is something bad, they immediately condemn the system they are endeavouring to defend, because the human nature of the people who own and control all our means of life is just the same human nature, and it often manifests itself in ways extremely detrimental to the bulk of the community.

If all the production of the world was carried on for use, each and all of us would be democratically responsible, whereas if our captains of industry make a greater profit out of bullets, bombs, bayonets, etc., they will not cause bread to be produced.

The argument that the workers engaged on a Government job or other communal undertaking will not do a fair day's work, and say "it is coming off a broad board" is perhaps true of some workers, but when the people know that the harder they work the shorter the hours of human toil will be, quite the opposite will be the result. The position to-day leads the workers to believe that the harder they work the sooner they will be lined up outside the Labour Exchange.

With the coming of Socialism there will be a public consciousness aroused against the slacker who will be looked upon as a parasite. The interests of one will become the interests of all. This can only come about along educational lines.

If we all realised that we were producing goods for use instead of producing rent, interest and profit, we would then enter into our work with joy, and accept the proverb coined by Sir Thomas Lipton, that "there is no fun like work."

As I said at the outset, many of the shady acts committed around us have their root in an outworn system of society, and I would add that human nature cannot be defined because it is largely the product of environment, and given a chance is capable of rising to heights of glory and splendour hitherto unrecorded in the records of man.

————

The "Right" Wing ! !
BY HUGH GEMMELL.

(To which is attached the "head," for clear, correct thinking so that the Movement may be guided on the "right" path. And the "tail," to act as a rudder, and steady the Movement when it is buffeted by political storms or in danger of being carried out of its course by treacherous cross-currents engendered by the gulf-stream (the engulfing stream) and the monsoons (or hot-air currents).)

THE HIGHER PRAGMATISM.

"Where to go for wisdom has become a question of serious import. The ancients are discredited; Plato is boiler-plate; Aristotle is tottering; Marcus Aurelius is reeling; Aesop has been copyrighted by Indiana; Solomon is too solemn; you couldn't get anything out of Epictetus with a pick. The ant, which for many years served as a model of intelligence and industry in the school books, has been proven to be a doddering idiot and a waster of time and effort. The owl to-day is hooted at. Greybeards give glowing testimonials to the vendors of patent hair-restorers. There are typographical errors in the almanacs published by the daily newpapers.

"College professors have become... But there shall be no personalities.

"To sit in classes, to delve into the encyclopedia or the past-performance page, will not make us wise. As the poet says, 'Knowledge comes, but wisdom lingers.' Wisdom is dew, which, while we know it not, soaks into us, refreshes us, and makes us grow. Knowledge is a strong stream of water turned on us through a hose. It disturbs our roots. Then, let us rather gather wisdom. But how to do so requires knowledge. If we know a thing, we know it; but very often we are not wise to it that we are wise, and... But let's get on with the story."

—O' HENRY, IN "OPTIONS."

To save time and space I will not quote "Plebian," but deal, in their order, with the points he makes. The "greybeards" don't deplore your 'ultraism,' because there is neither ultraism, altruism, doctrine, policy, organisation, consistency, logic, or construction among those who chalk "up Moscow" on the back of a taxi-cab, and shout "excelsior" with the pervervid enthusiasm of some ecstatic young pulpiteer weeping over his spiritual salvation. The fact that the Labour Movement is not in chaos, is due to the good sense and sound judgment of those who prevented you.

Disruption was certainly attempted. The 'young men' have neither a monopoly of Economics nor of Marxism. And in Marxism they have completely missed the basic importance of the Materialist Conception of History. Bob Dorman is a Marxist, so am I. But Bob Dorman is an old man, and I am a young man, so where is your logic. The I.L.P. classes were Marxian. We gave birth to the Left Wing. Like begets like.

We admit that this "minority group" is engaged in fighting us, instead of fighting the "Boss." We are painfully conscious of that fact, and we want you to stop it. Battles are never won by defeating your allies, and then fighting your enemies. It's bad logic and worse sense. What we want you to do is to organise a 'united front' - a right, left and centre - and get on with the job of fighting the boss. "Plebian" need not talk of purging the Party of adulterated Socialists. Fancy a minority purging a majority! Could you complain, after that outburst, if the majority voted you out of the Party. Then you would not be an "extreme section." You would be an extreme outside, compelled to form a Party of your own, and a policy of your own, and that is more than the 'young men' have courage or knowledge to do now. Of course, you prefer to "bore from within" and whether to bore from within or bore

167

from outwith, has been a debateable point in minority tactics ever since the Socialist Movement was born. The deplorable ignorance of Socialist History displayed by the 'new young men' is enough to make Karl Marx and Daniel De Leon turn in their graves. "Plebian" makes his worst blunder in his second-last paragraph because it is there that he misses the clear teaching of Marx's Materialist Conception of History. Instead of studying Ireland's historical foundation and endeavouring to shape a policy and build a party that will agree with those needs, he and the other 'new young men' embrace every imported organisation and do not stop to examine whether it is applicable to Irish Working Class historical needs. Don't misunderstand me; if it is good, let us adopt it; if it is not suitable, let us reject it, but "Plebian" has allowed himself to be caught by the centuries old trick of the "Shoneen" who drives a foreign wedge into our Movement and forces us apart. Here is what the Independent Labour Party stands for:—

"OBJECT

The I.L.P. is a Socialist Organisation, and has for its object the establishment of the Socialist Commonwealth. The Socialist Commonwealth is that state of Society in which Land and Capital are communally owned, and the processes of production distribution and exchange, are social functions. The Independent Labour Party believes in democracy organised both in its political and industrial aspects, for communal ends. The basis of political democracy must be the whole body of citizens exercising authority through a national representative assembly, directly elected by the people, with a decentralised and extended system of local government.

The basis of Industrial democracy must be:

(1) The organisation of the wage and salary earners, and

(2) the organisation of consumers.

A central body, representative of the people both as producers and consumers, must decide the amount and character of communal production and service necessary. The internal management of each industry must be in the hands of the workers, administrative, technical and manual, engaged therein, operating in conjunction with the representatives or the organised consumers. Experience will determine the methods of co-operation and the detailed form of organisation, as step by step is taken towards the attainment of the Socialist Commonwealth."

That is the I.L.P. position.

Now "Plebian" and the 'new young men' where do you stand?

A statement has reached us from a reputable source that two members of the Labour Group who are on the Relief Committee of the Poor Law Guardians, do not attend these meetings. In consequence, many genuine cases are turned down by the Unionist-Nationalist combination, and the work of the remaining Labour men is greatly handicapped. If this is true, some satisfactory explanation ought to be given, and failing that, a change ought to be made.

This is a Poster displayed in the window of a house in a principal street of the loyal town of Newtownards.

**Turned Off The Dole !
Then Turned Out Of My Home! !**
With a wife and three children.
Is It Justice?
After a man shedding his blood in the
Fields of Flanders, for such as
The Members of the Ulster Parliament.
Loyalists, Beware of Your Leaders !
The Claimants to extended Benefit are being disallowed at the rate of 50 per cent. or more. Poverty and Destitution are rampant in our midst. The Bowels of Compassion of the Guardians are closed against Claimants for relief.

As we go to Press we learn that Magsie M'Alister has been selected by Court Ward as their Lecture Secretary, and that Dock Ward, by an overwhelming majority, chose Miss Annie Loftus to be their Secretary. More power to the ladies.

The Labour Opposition Of Northern Ireland

Vol. 2—No.15   April, 1926   One Penny

Ali Baba And The Forty Thieves
Or, BRIGANDAGE UP-TO-DATE.
By HUGH GEMMELL.

THE ELEVENTH COMMANDMENT:—"THOU SHALT NOT BE FOUND OUT."

Thieves have succeeded in gaining an entry into the Belfast City Hall and making off with booty to the estimated value of £30,000. No arrests have been made. The stolen goods are of the most amazing variety, ranging from slates, tiles, bricks, stones, sand and gravel, but in one instance a sum of thousands of pounds was discovered to be missing, and this was ultimately traced to a Belfast firm of timber merchants bearing the sinister and significant name of Robb.

When clamant public indignation could no longer be ignored, a sworn inquiry was held, and the report of the inquiry not only confirmed the fears of honourable people, but revealed a deplorable depravity on the part of Mr. M'Cormick, Mr. Cutler and other public officials whose civic integrity had hitherto been beyond suspicion.

Mr. John M'Cormick, in his capacity as Town Solicitor, inserted special clauses in his own lease (and which were omitted from all other leases) securing that the buildings on his site should be of the largest and best houses the Corporation were allowed to build, with large gardens front and rear, and unusually wide roads, thereby enhancing the value of his **own** property.

Alderman Barron, Chairman of the Improvement Committee, negotiated for the purchase of 13½ acres of land on 2nd January, 1923, at a rent of £4 8s. per acre, and paid a fine of £600. Three days later he offered the same land to the Corporation at £12 10s. per acre, and the Corporation purchased at that figure in the autumn of 1924. The Commissioner states that the choice of site was largely influenced by the fact that Alderman Barron was the proposed vendor.

Marx was right when he said that money was welcome to a Capitalist, no matter how tainted was the source from which it emanated. Individual Capitalists may yet be found who are honourable men, but they are dying out, and as a **Class**, the Capitalists are prepared to do anything for money; from bombing babies to slaughtering strikers. Commissioner Megaw, K. C., has made definite charges in his report against definite people, who are mentioned by name. The charges are gross negligence; connivance at fraud; fraud itself; and utter incompetency on the part of many people entrusted with public moneys and with the direction of public affairs. Of Sir Crawford M'Cullagh, who was reputed to be a shrewd captain of industry, Mr. Megaw said, "he tried to justify the action of the Housing Committee by making a statement, recklessly and without regard to its truth, that Messrs. Robb's tender was 18% lower than the next lowest; a statement which an <u>intelligent</u> business man would on the slightest investigation have found to be untrue." The Big Business Bunch in Belfast have held the City to ransom for countless years, and it would be interesting to learn what graft, if any, has been associated with the members of the Corporation regarding our public street improvement and the erection of our public buildings. [A gap of a few words at this point in the original may be where names have been left out. Ed.] held the City to ransom for countless years.

When ordinary people commit theft, they are charged by the Police and consigned to gaol. In the present disclosures it looks as if the Police regarded it as a "family dispute" and will not "butt in" without instruction. The inquiry, though ordered by the Government, is not a "judicial" inquiry, and thus on the turn of a word criminals escape the consequences of their wrongdoing. The law of Moses and the Ten Commandments do not cover the crime, and the eleventh commandment has had to be tacked on: "Thou shalt not be found out." But who are the Lawmakers? Not Magistrates or Judges, but the people. The will of the people must and will prevail. Resignation of the culprits is not enough. They must go to gaol. The Council has 56 Capitalists and 4 Workers. Were it the reverse, Crumlin Road Gaol would long since have clanged on the evildoers.

Get rid of the Grafters! Let justice be done! Let the people rejoice!

Hits And Misses.
BY MARKSMAN.

ANTRIM.—Rural District Council have decided to raise the rents of labourer's cottages by threepence per week. Tenants have refused to sign the agreement to pay the increased rent. The Council are threatening legal proceedings and notices to quit have been issued.

*   *

BELFAST.—Six cow carcases and two carcases of mutton were destroyed in one day at our public abattoir because they were affected by tuberculosis and dropsy. What is happening in the Rural and Urban centres in Northern Ireland, particularly Ballymena, where slaughter houses are privately owned? "The health of the people is the supreme law," but is it, I ask.

*   *

BANBRIDGE.—Rural District Council have decided to raise the rent of the labourers' cottages by ninepence per week. The only Councillor who protested was Bob Getgood (Workers' Union) who moved that the matter be adjourned for six months, and failed to secure a seconder. Mr. Getgood stated that there was no justification for the proposed increase of rent. The Down County Council could grant an increase of £10 per week to an official, yet it was proposed to put up the cost of living on underpaid labourers and surfacemen whose wages had been materially reduced. He appealed to the Council to permit the labourers to live in their cottages at the existing rents. I wonder how many of these labourers will continue to vote for the Boss.

*   *

COLERAINE.—Chamber of Commerce have discussed Nationalisation of mines, electricity and broadcasting. Mr. Christie does not want nationalisation because he hates Socialists and Communists. Mr. Maclaughlin thinks that mines should be nationalised because coal is not the product of any individual. It is a natural product of the soil and should belong to the nation. My goodness, Mr. Mac, what do you mean talking like that and you the Chairman? The Chamber also passed a resolution drawing attention to the scandalously excessive charges of the Government official who recently held an arbitration inquiry in Coleraine in connection with labourers' cottages, which worked out at three guineas per hour for the twenty-three hours that he was engaged. Coleraine will be having a Soviet if they go on like this? I wonder what Sir James Craig thinks of it all.

BELFAST.—There are 357 vacant dwelling houses in Belfast. Yet hundreds of working class families are being denied shelter for their children. In many cases grown up boys and girls being forced to eat, sleep and bath themselves in one small room.

* *

DUBLIN.—The Capitalist Press informs us that the Dublin Union Commissioners are issuing thousands of food tickets to the unemployed and their dependents. That's the idea, keep them alive, but sap their independence.

* *

GALWAY.—Dwelling houses are being erected in Galway at a cost of £280 each.

* *

DUNDALK—Urban District Council propose to reduce all wages and salaries by five per cent. They also propose to dispense with public lighting during the summer months. This is the Free State for you. Some Freedom, eh!

* *

DUBLIN.—"The Irish Times" newspaper states that the nett price for best coal in Dublin is 47/- per ton as compared with 53/- in Belfast. What about the Belfast Municipal Coal Depots. Are they not long overdue?

* *

NEWRY.—Urban District Council have decided to pay relief workers for stated holidays. It was moved by the Labour members that the hour of meeting be changed from 11 a.m. to 7 p.m. The resolution was defeated by 10 votes to 6. There are only six labour representatives of course. See !

* *

NEWBRIDGE.—The Free State Government have made a grant of £12,000 to the Smithfield Wool Co., of Dublin, who are opening a factory at Newbridge. More bosses on the dole, eh !

* *

N. IRELAND.—The Belfast people are still being compelled to pay 3d. of an amusement tax as compared with 2d. paid by Britishers, whilst Free Staters escape scot free.

* *

COLERAINE.—Mr. D. H. Christie speaking at a meeting on 16/3/26, said, "If ever a country was saddled with a rotten Government, they in Northern Ireland were saddled with one." . . . "No wonder there were Socialists and Communists." Very strong language when one considers that Mr. Christie is Chairman of the Coleraine Urban District Council, and that Coleraine is a Unionist stronghold.

* *

The **Imperial Tobacco Co.**, report a net trading profit of about nine million pounds. What are we going to do about these **sheltered** shareholders?

The Christian Viewpoint.
THE CRIME OF POVERTY.

That "poverty is no crime" is of course true in the sense of the common use of the words, but in its social aspect the existence of poverty is a crime of the first magnitude judged only and entirely by Christian standards.

For poverty is criminal towards God by arresting the natural development of the faculties of body and mind, these being essential of the fulfilment of the divine purpose of man's being, and thereby plundering

"—From the immortal Mind
His bright and glorious crown."
and criminal towards man by robbing him of the opportunity of that full life which is his inherent right.

Aspiration after these things is the soul of Christianity and realisation its mission: "I am come that they might have life more abundantly" said the Founder.

And poverty blocks the way.

—J. M'A.

A Resolution.
Dear Comrade,

I have been instructed by the Committee to forward you copy of the following Resolution which was passed at a recent meeting of our branch:

"That the members of this Party demand that the Government of Northern Ireland shall reinstate all contributors to the Unemployment Fund who have been signed off the Register within the last twelve months."

THOS. M'DOWELL, Secretary.
SAM GEDDIS, President,
Shankill Labour Party

Reform or Revolution?

Evolution or revolution, confiscation or compensation. The Left Wing or the Right Wing?

Geology teaches us that in the aeons of time atoms of matter began to coalesce and gradually the earth evolved into its present conformation. Traces of revolt, more or less discernible, against this great work of natural forces can easily be noticed. Local volcanic eruptions, earthquakes, upheavals, etc., but still the growth or evolution of this world of ours goes steadily on and will. It is difficult to understand what purposes these serve, but somewhere someone will doubtless find out. One thing stands out clear and distinct, the natural law of evolution is undisturbed and pursues its course undeviatingly in spite of these sporadic outbreaks. The growth of humanity presents to us the same aspect: the individual on its self-defence; the community or tribe combining with others for protection against other tribes or communities, the evolution of tribes into nations and of nations into groups or empires seeking complete world domination.

It is a long time since the "Soul of Socialism" was born ('am I my brother's keeper'?) but gradually it is taking material shape and to-day despite janglings, or revolts, despite the bickering of individuals or the opposition of systems, the songs and prophecies of our poets are taking tangible shape and the brotherhood of man will be an accomplished fact.

Revolutionists, confiscationists, Left Wingists no doubt serve some useful purpose, someone will be able to depict it, but still evolution pursues its way undeterred by their outbursts till it reaches the altitude it has set for a goal and from that rises still higher. Mind is more powerful than matter. Socialism is bound to win; its soul is pure, its motto the "greatest good for all" is beyond and above all physical force.

Now for the query why we should compensate landowners, because it works out the same in the end and is the line of of least resistance. Confiscation says "take the land over at once even if force were required and have done with it." Compensation says, let the State buy the land, taking a period of years to pay off the purchase money and the result is the same. Violence has been averted, a gradual improvement has been effected and the law of evolution has been followed. The Left Wing will think this is slow work, but then it is a long time since the world was in infancy; doubtless it has a good while yet to go and if we too have "gone west" others will be 'left' to carry on and develop on lines far better than anything we have yet devised.

I am sure some readers will wonder why I have written in this strain. My attention has been drawn to some of the articles which have appeared recently. Evidently all is not well in the movement. Individual outbreaks, sectional revolts may make for good. My mind cannot comprehend how. If we want to destroy the evil system of Capitalism we need always to have a united front for the common enemy. If nationalisation of the land, of our banking system, or of any of our natural resources be our objective let us tackle the problem in earnest, not fritter away our time in the indulgence of petty personalities. Should we not be warned by the fate of the "Kilkenny Cats," the last two fought with each other till there was nothing left but a little portion of one tail.

Eastertide! a brief holiday of rest, peace and hope. Many minds will be engrossed by the beautiful thought of life springing to renewed vigour, through death. The cold desolate winter is at an end; spring is here. Little flowers are peeping forth in all kinds on unexpected places. The wild birds are calling to their mates, the air is filled with the music of their songs. Why should we not be carefree? The winter is past,. April showers we will have but the flowers of summer are sweet. **By SOWSEED.**

Belfast—The Profiteers' Paradise.

We Socialists have continually urged that the cost of living in Belfast is higher than it is across the water and Government records have been cited in support of this claim. The price paid by the Corporation for the very best English Coal, supplied to all its departments, is 29/3 per ton, but the price charged to the public by private enterprise is 54/- per ton. The difference of 25/- per ton is pocketed by the middleman, by the simple process of blocking the way between producer and consumer. Further, last May the price for English coal was 31s. 7d. per ton, so that the price has been reduced to the authorities during the last 12 months, but every housewife knows that the 10st. bag was increased by twopence during the same period, because of the threatened Miners' stoppage. Speaking frankly, we are paying double the price for coal that we need to pay, and if Municipal Coal Depots were established by the Northern Ireland Labour Party, the poorer people would not be left without a fire, and the more comfortably placed would be able to buy more coal. That would stimulate the mining industry, and the increased demand would be reflected in an equally increased demand for other necessaries of life.

The Socialist remedy for unemployment is complete social ownership of all the means of life, viz., land, industrial capital and finance capital. The Socialist position for alleviating unemployment under capitalism is higher wages, thereby giving increased consumption of goods, thereby increasing production.

The Capitalist remedy (sic) is lower wages and more production. It is an incredibly stupid "remedy," because when the workers are not given the means to buy back the greater portion of the wealth that they produce it causes a glut, and then the Boss sacks the worker and that cuts down consumption still further until the entire working class community is sunk in sheer apathetic misery: These are facts of the most elementary nature, and once a worker has grasped them he will be cured for ever of voting for the 'Boss' or for the perpetuation of Capitalism. Socialism is the scientific organisation of the resources of the community and its application to modern industry would immediately improve the status of every worker in Northern Ireland, but until the people send members of their own class to represent them on the public bodies, I am afraid that Belfast must still remain the Profiteers' Paradise.

HOTSPUR.

Belfast Housing Scandal.

Never has private interests been exposed so ruthlessly as in Mr. R. Megaw's report. It will be interesting to see what developments take place as a result.

Our men in the Council will have a golden opportunity to show up these people who are battening on the needs of the people. We would suggest that a resolution should be tabled asking the Council to dismiss Cutler, M'Cormick, Wardlow, M'Coll, and Mackie as these people have been proven to be incapable of their various posts.

Further, that Alderman Barron, Clifton Ward, Alderman M'Connell, Windsor Ward, Alderman Jones, Dock Ward, Alderman M'Cullagh, Cromac Ward, should be asked to resign their seats.

This report should be in the hands of every Socialist, and our M.P.'s should press for the reduction of the price to either 6d or 1/-.

The Cause Of Unemployment.

Several factors cause unemployment. Some of these factors we can control, and some we can't. One factor which forms a principal cause of unemployment is the evolution of machinery, and in this instance I want to point out the amount of labour that is being dispensed with in the following industries.

Road and Tramway work, Docks, Street-sweeping, Boot-making, Moulders, Bakers, Tailoring, Coal Miners, Clerks, Iron Dressers, Carpenters. In road and Tramway work, the introduction of the Pneumatic Crowbar displaces 60% of labour. Formerly, it required three men to operate: one who held the wedge, and two to drive the bar in to the ground. Now the bar is still held by one man, but the other two men are no longer required, as the force is supplied by a portable engine, which is capable of supplying the power to 4 Pneumatic Crowbars at the same time. In dock work, the employers have introduced the Electric Magnet for the purpose of unloading steel and iron ore. When the grain elevator was introduced to unload ships during a strike of dockers, it immediately displaced thousands of men, but the elevator itself has now been displaced by the suction pump. The elevator required some men to shovel the grain on to a travelling belt, whereas the pump is merely inserted in the hold, the power turned on, and the entire cargo of grain is sucked through a pipe and into storage without being touched by a human hand.

In street sweeping, the Motor Sweeper, is now in use in big cities. It is capable of travelling at 10 miles an hour, and watering, sweeping, and lifting the sweepings at the same time. I could not give you the percentage of labour that these motors eliminate, but you can imagine the amount of work they would do on a shift of 8 hours.

In the manufacturing of Boots, by Machinery, a pair of boots can be made every 1/2 hour. Whereas formerly, it took a man 2 or 3 days to make a pair. In Iron and Brass Moulding a Machine has also been introduced, and Lord Weir has recently erected a Factory in which these machines are installed. Moreover, female labour is to be used to operate the machine, and the effect of this is to oust the unskilled Worker.

The Pneumatic Chisel, which is now being used in the Iron, Steel and Brass Dressing, also does away with 50% of the labour required.

A great amount of labour has been dispensed with in the making of Bread by the introduction of Machinery for Dough Mixing, Weighing, and Wrapping.

Cigarettes, which formerly were made by hand at the rate of 1,000 per day, are now made by machinery at the rate of 5,000 per hour. In the Coal Mines, Machines are used for coal-cutting, and one machine can easily do the work of ten men. In the Tailoring trade, machines are being used that can cut out 40 Garments at a time, as against the old method of one at a time, and in the making up, the same increased production is manifest. And now we come to the clerks, who are also suffering from the advent of Adding Machines, Addressing Machines, and other "Labour-saving" devices. After considering all these facts it is obvious that the development of machinery has been one of the principal factors in displacing human labour in almost every industry. A second principal factor, or cause, is the loss of foreign markets, due to undercutting in the price of products by competitive nations. The principal factor is, again, the development of machinery, but this time in other countries. Various commodities which they formerly purchased from us they now manufacture for themselves. To support this I will quote you the official figures. Value of manufactured articles exported from Gt. Britain:

1920	1921	1922
£1,119,739	£588,889	£568,524
This shows a decrease of 50%.		

Another cause of unemployment is the payment of low wages, thus lowering the purchasing power of the workers, who are thereby unable to purchase goods that have been produced for the home markets. This has the effect of throwing out of work some of those who are employed in manufacturing these goods. For example, if the demand for boots and clothing falls off through lack of the purchasing power of the community, the workers in these particular industries become unemployed.

Man, by his wonderful energy and genius has created machinery that can perform wonders of wealth production, but man has been robbed of the fruits of his genius by the employing class seizing control of the machinery and using it to enslave its workers.

Machinery should be the servant of Man, and not his master. They are socially produced, they should be socially owned and controlled. If that were done, they would not only lighten labour, but their wonderful powers of wealth production would enrich a world impoverished by the greed of the capitalist class. Social ownership would absolutely solve the unemployment problem, and the final solution of that problem is the establishment of Socialism.

Let us all work hard to get it and let us all work together.

Alex Stewart.
Born, 1854, at Glasgow.
Died, 26th March, 1926, at Belfast.

With the passing of Alex. Stewart, the Socialist Movement has lost a fighter for freedom that could be ill spared at any time, but is the more missed because of the strenuous days that lie ahead. He was a propagandist to his finger tips, and wherever he moved he carried an atmosphere of active revolt and a dynamic sense of action. Present at all meetings, out in all weathers, at 71 years old he was an inspiration to those who are already tired at 20. Although he worked all his life, he left no material wealth of consequence, but he enriched the Movement with his devotion and loyalty, and we can best honour his memory by following the example he set. At the funeral, a large gathering of Comrades paid their final tribute ere his remains were taken to Marlin for interment. **H.G.**

Parliamentary Notes.

Parliament reopened on Tuesday 9th March, with the usual blaze of magnificence, which was rather damped by the very unroyal weather on that day. Apparently, even Jupiter Pluvius was expressing discontent with our Northern Administration. Much speculation has been indulged in by the local press as to the attitude of the Labour Party on the opening day, but we were glad to see that the three Labour Members occupied the front bench, and that in the procession to the Senate, Mr. S. Kyle acted as Leader of the Opposition. The Address from the Throne was debated with greater gusto than has ever yet been shown in the Northern House.

The Official Amendment, demanding work or maintenance was introduced by Mr. Wm. M'Mullen, Labour Member for West Belfast, who was in good form, and he pointed out that instead of Unemployment getting less it was getting worse. He reminded the House that since Sir J. Craig promised to solve this question, the number of Unemployed had risen from 37,000 to 61,000.

Mr. Beattie, Labour Member for East Belfast, gave a number of illustrations of hardship arising out of the more rigid application of the Unemployed Insurance Regulations. Mr. Kyle supported the Amendment, and claimed that it was the duty of the State to provide work, or failing that, maintenance. He said that the amendment would mean a fundamental change in Society as we know it to-day, a change from production for profit, to production for use. He pointed out that the workers produced all wealth, and that it had been demonstrated that one man with machinery could produce in one year, enough woollen goods to clothe 300 people. Enough cotton goods to clothe 250 people in a year, and that 5 men with machinery on the land, could produce enough food for 1,000. He said that in Karl Marx's Analysis of the Capitalist System it was pointed out that Capitalism was breaking up, and that that was true, was evidenced by the fact that the Government are supplying State credits to private enterprise as private enterprise has failed to house, clothe and feed the workers.

At this stage the Speaker said the speeches on this Amendment should be confined to Unemployment.

Mr. Kyle pointed out that he was showing the implications of the Amendment.

The other Labour Amendment was on the question of Rent Restriction, and was introduced by Mr. Kyle who gave a number of instances of extortionate rents being charged by Landlords. These charges are all too common, and the clause permitting One House Owners to get their houses by giving six month's notice is being abused. A very interesting sidelight on the intelligence of the Independents was shown in the debate on the Employment of Ex-Service men, when the proposer of the resolution was paired and so could not vote for his own motion.

Sir James Craig has stated in the House, or at least it has been stated for him, that Proportional Representation is to be abolished before the next General Election. The significance of this decision is obvious; the Government want to get rid of the Labour men in the House; perhaps they will succeed —and then, perhaps they won't!

How The I.L.P. Drowned The Shamrock.

St. Patrick's night in the I.L.P. Hall must forever stand as a night of memory, and after Councillor Midgley had introduced the Choir in a neat little speech, we all settled down to listen to the fun and frolic. The Choir sang their very many items with sustained brilliance, but in "Barry Brallaghan's Courtship" they surpassed themselves with sheer wholehearted joyousness. No wonder the crowded audience asked for more. The Choirmaster, Colin C. Caldwell, not only conducted the Choir and the Orchestra, but he had arranged an attractive series of solo items which were rendered by Molly M'Larnon, Bob Johnstone, Mrs. Smith, Jack Moonan, Dorothy Lynn, Stuart M'Laughlin, Mrs. Crawford, Archie M'Comb, Lily Davison, and Sam Moneypenny.

Pipe Major Magee was there from West Belfast and he set us lilting, and our feet tapping with his lively Irish Airs. Everybody declared that our Irish Night was a great success, and when Harry thanked the Choir, the Orchestra, the Choirmaster and the Soloists, and peeped round the piano to pay a tribute to the accompanist Mrs. Davison—the applause that was released was more than ample reward for all the dull discipline of practice nights. And all of us sang "The Red Flag" with a greater gusto.

Then followed the Social; and from 10-30 until 3 in the morning we forgot the work-a-day world and gave ourselves over to merrymaking and the pleasures of the dance.

Why could Robb not rob the Corporation?

Because M'Cue kept "Dick."

The Ministry of Labour And Belfast Registry Offices.

BY R. E. BEL.

I wonder how many kind hearted ladies and gentlemen are aware of the amount of bare-faced robbery that is carried on by certain Registry Offices in Belfast. The scandal is so rampant that something will have to be done to end it. Our Ministry of Labour has opened a registry office at Arthur Street, where girls with the very best references can be secured, and it is important to note that **No fees are charged to employer or to employee.** An agitation has been going on for some time to try and compel the Ministry to advertise the fact that no fees are charged at the Arthur Street Registry Office, but a very highly placed member of the Government says, "No! don't advertise the fact or we may do harm to the people who have been in the business for years." Who are these people and how do they charge? Well, they charge a fee of 4/- to the employer in each case, and they charge the unemployed worker anything from 2/6 to £5 for each job secured. The method adopted usually is—a Register fee of from 2/6 to 5/- and remember that a servant may be registered at four different offices, which means four fees of 4/- each. At the end of a month there may be no sign of a situation and the unemployed worker is then persuaded to pay the price of an advertisement in the local press. After the Ad. is paid for, it may appear and it may not, and if you are a betting person, I suggest you back the "may not."

Eventually a situation may be secured, and the poor victim is compelled to pay to the Registry Office shark, her or his first week's wages in addition to the Register fee and the advertisement fee. In order to bear out what I have said I would like to cite a few cases at random.

(1). Lady Housekeeper, unemployed. Fee of 5/- paid and at the end of four weeks an advertising fee of 2/6. All the local newspapers were carefully scrutinised but the Ad. never appeared. Two weeks elapsed and the applicant was successful in obtaining a temporary situation with a former employer. An Agent from the Registry Office called at the house where applicant was employed and demanded a further fee of £2 5s. "Applicant" as I have called her, refused to pay, and agent left, murmuring all kinds of threats and called back a second time when a lively scene took place. A trade union official came on the scene later, and threatened the Registry Office proprietors with legal proceedings unless the persecution of the poor victim would cease. I am glad to say that the threat proved effective.

(2). Male Waiter, paid a fee of £1 and secured a job in the Free State. At end of Summer season returned to Belfast and again registered, paying a fee of 4/6 and signed an agreement promising to pay his first week's salary in the event of a job of any kind being found for him.

(3). Male Waiter, paid registry fee and secured situation in an Urban Centre. Total fee paid 24/-.

(4). Domestic Servant—paid a fee of 5/- at one office and 3/6 at a second office. She has been told that a situation may turn up soon.

(5). A Chef—paid a fee of 4/- and agreed to pay first week's salary. Secured a job at £4 10s., but it only lasted for one week. Is being pressed to pay up as per written pledge.

(6). Domestic Servant, paid fee and secured situation in Belfast, and paid a further sum of 13/- and received a receipt from Registry Office. "For Vacancy procured, with thanks," "Received 13/-."

Signed "Gullem and Cheetem."

In conclusion, I would appeal to the Ministry to advertise the fact that they are in a position to place Domestics and others whose references have been fully certified and "**No Fees Charged.**"

Northern Farmers And Trade Unionism.

George Simpson of North Belfast I.L.P. made a gallant attempt to form a new branch of "The Workers' Union" at Garvagh, near Coleraine. The meeting was held in the Temperance Hall on Saturday 27th March.

Farmers, farmers' sons, and pettifogging employers of labour turned up in force and gave George a rough passage. After the meeting he was brutally assaulted by a gang of farmers' sons, and had to secure medical attention. However, nothing daunted, George is going back again, as farm labourers are working for 12/- per week and many of them have five or six small children to keep on this princely wage. Some employers in Garvagh are paying able-bodied men 15/- per week. It is only right to say that the local paper gives a good deal of space to the incident, and in the "Northern Constitution" for the week ending April 3rd, at least three correspondents condemn the farmers' sons for their cowardly action.

* *

Sir James Craig is a Home Ruler ! ! Sir James is not satisfied with a pig's foot or a slice of bacon. No, he wants the whole Hog!

Speaking in the Old Town Hall on 30/3/26, Sir James said "If Southern Ireland said to-morrow, 'We want to go back to the old conditions under the Imperial Parliament,' he would refuse emphatically on their behalf to follow." Why, Sir James is stronger in the Home Rule faith than ever Parnell or Gladstone was.

* *

Mr. Dan Christie, a well-known public man in Coleraine, still criticises our Northern Government. Speaking at a very important meeting a few days ago, he said—"There is as much intelligence, in Co. Derry as in Belfast, where you have this clique, who have put their aunts and uncles, their sisters and brothers into jobs. There are Ministers drawing £2,000 and over it, who never made the half of it in their whole lives."

* *

Coleraine Rural Council had a meeting on 3/4/26, when Mr. J. Morrow, J.P., condemned the Rt. Hon. H. M. Pollock for making misleading statements in the Northern Parliament. He said—"It was a shame that Ministers should make such statements without knowing the facts, and it was a disgrace that a man working 23 hours should be paid £72 9s. It was no wonder there were Socialists in the country!!

* *

Holywood Unionists had a meeting the other evening in the Orange Hall. Major R. E. M'Clean, M.A., said—"Dangers are ahead of us in the shape of Socialism, Communism and other evils. We have only to look at the case of Russia, and of Italy, to get sufficient cause for thinking about the greatness of this danger." We agree, my dear Major; Italy *is* a menace to the peace of the world, and Mussolini should be imprisoned or detained in a madhouse. I am glad that I can agree with the Major on the Italian danger.

Correspondence.

We print the following letters sent out and received by the Shankill Labour Party, because of the light they shed on problems of current interest to the workers of Northern Ireland. The Divisions should persistently press their demands to the Government, both local and national, and we will give them as much publicity as our somewhat limited space will permit. A bigger kick means a bigger movement, a bigger paper and a more active Opposition.

To Secretary Northern Ireland Labour Party.

Dear Comrade,

I have been instructed by my Committee to forward you Copy of the following resolution which was passed at a recent meeting of the above Party: Asking for a united front to demand the Poor Law Guardians to adopt a **money relief** to able bodied unemployed persons in keeping with other Poor Law Guardians in Great Britain.

Yours fraternally,   T. M'Dowell, Secretary. S. Geddis, President.

(This resolution has been adopted by the Labour Party, Northern Ireland, and forwarded to the proper quarter. It is up to the workers to see that it is enforced. Ed. L.O.)

Ministry of Home Affairs (N.I.)
To Secretary, Shankill Labour Party.
Sir,

—With reference to your letter of the 11th inst., addressed to the Prime Minister, containing copy of a resolution passed at a meeting of the Shankill Labour Party on the subject of the Rent and Mortgage Interest (Restrictions) Act, I am to point out that under the provisions of the Act referred to only vacant houses with a valuation over £8 are being decontrolled. The policy of the Government is to effect gradually the decontrol of houses and I am to state that the proposals contained in the resolution referred to would be contrary to such a policy.

I am, Sir, Your obedient Servant,
Geo. A. Hanna, Assistant Secretary.

Ministry of Labour (N.I.),
8/3/1926.
Dear Sir,

Mr. Andrews desires me to acknowledge the receipt of your letter of the 4th inst., forwarding copy of a resolution passed at a recent meeting of your Branch. He wishes me to point out that it would not be possible to adopt the suggestion contained in the resolution in view of the Government's policy of keeping on parallel lines with Great Britain in matters relating to unemployment Insurance—a policy which, it is felt, is in the best interests of the working people of Northern Ireland.

Yours faithfully, W. N. M'William,
Private Secretary.

Ministry of Labour (N.I.),
16/3/1926.
Sir,

I am directed by the Minister of Labour to reply to your letter of the 4th March which has been forwarded to him by the Prime Minister.

It is the statutory duty of the Ministry of Labour to administer the Unemployment Insurance Acts as passed by Parliament. Certain conditions, as in Great Britain, have been laid down in these Acts which must be satisfied by all applicants for Unemployment Benefit and the Department cannot continue to make payment to individuals who do not comply with these conditions.

In these circumstances, the Department cannot re-admit to Unemployment benefit disqualified persons until they again qualify within the provisions of the Acts.

I am, Sir, Your obedient Servant,
R.R. Bowman.

Book Review.

"The Devil's Business."—By A. Fenner Brockway. One Shilling Net.—From the Literature Secretary.

This little book is a play described by the author as 'a comedy in one act.' Four principals are needed; one super, and a crowd 'off.' The stage setting and directions are simple, and the story in brief, is this:

There is a war on, and the Prime Minister, the War Minister and the First Lord of the Admiralty are gathered to discuss the matter and to await news of an impending naval battle in which, *of course*, their ships will be supreme. The news comes. They have suffered a smashing defeat. Dazed with disaster they discuss details. A staccato knock, and enter the 'female,' young, vivacious, unconventional and brilliantly witty, but with a head for business like a Burroughs Adding Machine. She is the representative of the International Armaments Trust and it was one of their hellish weapons—Aero-bombs—that smashed the navy. It transpires that the Minister for War is a large shareholder in the Trust and the First Lord caustically congratulates him on *his* victory. After some ordinary 'business,' the young lady offers an anti-aero invention to obtain revenge and to prevent further defeats. They abuse her. She is anti-patriotic and a murderess. Through her, their ships are sunk and thousands of homes bereaved. She is unmoved. Her trust has no country—they dominate the world. Besides, is not the War Minister a large Shareholder? They hesitate; they discuss; they bargain. She asks one hundred million pounds, and—gets it!! They have tea, cigarettes, and a B. and S., when she quietly tells them she has another little Trust Invention that will render futile the one they have just bought. They blow their noses, make speeches, burn their fingers with cigarettes, threaten the Police and "to be shot at dawn." She laughs at them. If they do not want it, there is no harm done. The enemy will be glad of it, and indeed, are being approached now. Hopelessly incompetent to run a country, the Cabinet yields and the Treasury is ransacked for another hundred million pounds. A startled knock! With drawn, haggard faces they await the unknown terror. The door opens and the harsh cries of a multitude in anger pervade the chamber. They have heard the news of the naval defeat. Resign, Resign, Resign! The insistent clamour growns in volume. The "Patriotic" War Minister will handle the curs. He will order out the soldiers. No, no; not that! Let the Prime Minister speak to them. He will soothe them, and explain. A silver tongue is better than a silver bullet. He hands them out the sob stuff and the band plays the National Anthem. The crowd cheers, but a stone is thrown and cuts the Prime Minister's head He faints. A rattle of musketry, a sharp command, and the agonised cries of a mob "dispersing" The War Minister has secured an important victory. Cheers, groans, hisses and ambulance. That will teach them a lesson. The Prime Minister recovers. The representative of the Armaments Trust suggests gently that the contract has not yet been signed. The Premier rises; anger and horror mingle in his passionate outburst. The War Machine is too strong for him. Suddenly he stops, staggers, collapses. He has seen the Angel shape and the end is near. In gasping phrases he gives order for the Foreign Secretary to negotiate peace. Then in crescendo accents he describes the great vision. He hears the tramp of thousands of feet. The people are singing,

"There shall be no more wars, nor Kingdoms won,
But in thy sight whose eyes are as the sun,
All names shall be one name, all nations one."

A breathless hush and his lips are stilled foreever. With pallid cheeks, shining eyes, and hands steady with a great purpose, the young lady steps to the table and tears up the contracts of the infernal machines.
The Devil's business is finished.

HUGH GEMMELL.

S. O. S.
(Speed On Socialism)
The Labour And Socialist Movement Is Calling.
The Capitalist Press Of Northern Ireland Is Hostile To Us.
We Must Have A Press Of Our Own.
We Made A Start With The "Labour Opposition" Of Northern Ireland.
BUT
If Our Little Paper Is To Live And Develop,
You Must Come To Our Assistance.
You Must HELP Us!
GIVE US 2/-, HERE and NOW, and we will post you a copy of each issue to be printed during the next twelve months.
We must have 2,000 new readers at once.
Please do your little bit for Socialism.
Signed on behalf of the Press Committee.
HUGH GEMMELL, EDITOR

Socialism is simply Common Sense.

Socialism is the Only Hope of the World.

The Labour Opposition Of Northern Ireland

Vol. 2—No. 16   May, 1926   One Penny

LABOUR AND CO-OPERATION.
BY MARGARET M'COUBREY.

Eighty-two years ago the Pioneers of the modern Co-operative Movement opened their now world-famed Store at Toad Lane, Rochdale. It seemed a paltry and insignificant affair, but the principle of which it was the visible manifestation holds great potentialities for human betterment. Out of small beginnings has grown not only British Co-operation but a great International Movement.

The Annual Congress of the Co-operative Union meets in Belfast at Whitsuntide. Delegates will assemble here from every corner of the British Isles, hundreds of them our comrades in the Labour Movement, men and women convinced that whilst on the march towards the Co-operative Commonwealth their place is in the ranks of a Movement which stands for the overthrow of the present competitive and capitalistic system of society and the establishment of a system of collective ownership and control.

There are socialists who think themselves above the consideration of what might be termed the bread and butter aspect of life. Marxian theory is to them more important than Pure Milk! There are also so-called socialists who support the multiple shop or any other shop offering a cut price, regardless of the conditions of labour or the destination of the profits of the concern. Out of the depths of an abyssmal ignorance both types, upon occasion, grumble, grouse, and sneer at the Co-operative Movement. But the majority of socialists recognise that the Movement is a powerful organisation composed of working class people; that in the very nature of things its policy must lean towards industrial collectivism rather than individualism; and that in a transition period here is the machinery for the organisation of production and distribution. Across the water, members of the Labour and Socialist parties are strong supporters of Co-operation, and in some quarters wield considerable influence on Co-operative policy.

In view of the coming Congress a few facts and figures may be of interest. At the end of 1924 (the latest year for which we have the official statistics) there were 1,445 Co-operative Societies in Great Britain affiliated to the Co-operative Union. The aggregate membership of these societies was 4,752,636. The majority of members represent families. The British movement, therefore, represents at least one-third of the population.

"Where is the Capital to come from" whines the anti-socialist working-man when we talk of the workers owning and controlling the means of production. At the end of 1924 the members of Co-operative Societies owned £91,926,203 Share Capital. These members are working men and women. Millionaires do not shop at the Stores. No Government has ever made a grant to the distributive Co-operative Movement; no capitalist ever made a contribution to its funds. We want neither donation nor subsidy. It has been said that the possession of a few pounds Share Capital tends to make the workers think and act as if they were capitalists. We do not believe that this danger exists, but may we remind critics that Co-operative policy; when the people are ready to advance policy can be altered. In some continental societies capital is collectively owned in a more real sense than in our own country.

The co-operative sales of distributive societies for 1924 totalled £281,950,901. Of that amount there was returned to the members as dividend on purchases £21,396,596.

At the end of 1924, 207,211 workers were in Co-operative employment, 111,820 in the distributive end, and 95,391 in productive enterprises. The working classes have it in their power to increase these figures. As trade grows, greater will be the number of men and women co-operatively employed. Thus industrial power, like financial power, will gradually pass from the hands of those who now possess it, and through Co-operation the people, organised as consumers and producers, may achieve the control of industry.

If the people will, a peaceful revolution can be brought about through Co-operation. When the Labour Movement comes to a fuller realisation of the potentialities of the Co-operative Movement, and when Co-operative members see the folly of supporting Co-operation in the economic field, and at the same time on the political field supporting the sworn enemies of Co-operation, we shall keep step better and move forward rather more rapidly than we are doing to-day. At the heart of both Labour and Co-operative Movements is the hope that -

"One day, without a trumpet's call
This news will o'er the world be blown.
The heritage comes back to all,
The myriad monarchs take their own."

Hits And Misses.
BY MARKSMAN.

Newtownards Rural District Council are in trouble because they have decided to raise the rent of labourers' cottages. It was reported at the last meeting that 131 tenants in the Portaferry area have stopped paying rent and that the trouble is spreading to other areas. Mr. Alex. Adams of Millisle, and Miss Woodside of Arkdeen are fighting the tenants' battle on the Council and the Rev. Scott of Ardkeen is fighting outside for the tenants.

* *

Ballymena Rural District Council have decided to build 175 labourers' cottages at a cost of £60,033. At an inquiry held recently it was stated that houses in the Rural District were tumbling down by the score, and that many existing labourers' houses were unfit for habitation. Craftsmen and labourers continue to build mansions for the rich and themselves continue to live in hovels.

* *

Monaghan Urban Council have been told by Dr. Ward, Medical Officer of Health that they must have a proper drainage system as the death-rate is higher than in any town of a similar size in Ireland. The Council have reported that they cannot afford a drainage scheme but are prepared to carry out minor improvements. Dr. F. Ward retorts that evidently the Council don't want an Officer of Health. I admire the Doctor because he is a real Medical Officer of Health.

* *

Cork Harbour Board propose to reduce salaries of officials by 20 per cent., salaries of office staffs 10 per cent. and all skilled and unskilled workers to be put on short time—four full working days weekly to be worked. Evidently Protection and trying to make the foreigner pay is not bringing prosperity to the Irish Free State.

* *

Tipperary Commission on Destitute Poor heard a witness named Mr. J. Kelly, who recommends that all those who refuse to work should be flogged. God help the idle rich people if Mr. Kelly had his way with them.

* *

Lord Justice Best, formerly Dick Best, M.P., is also a physical force man. At Belfast Commission Dick recommends all parents to give their boys a weekly spanking. Evidently Dick thinks we are still living in the Middle Ages.

* *

R.I.P. stands for Rent, Interest and Profit. I have been examining the Census returns for Ireland (1911). I find that out of a total of 1,250,531 persons enumerated in the six counties, almost 300,000 persons were returned as of no occupation, and all over 19 years of age. In other words these people were living on Rent, Interest and Profit, and not giving any useful service in return. Leaving out of account the 500,000 persons under 20 years of age, 215,810 were engaged in industry; 147,371 in agriculture; 25,881 in professions; 30,715 in domestic duties; 32,263 in commerce.

I anticipate the 1926 returns will reveal an increasingly large number of people who toil not but yet are able to enjoy the good things of life. Yes! The number of idle rich is increasing day by day.

* *

Belfast Corporation can stand thieving, lying and hypocrisy, but they cannot stand Sunday music or Sunday games. They also love the Royal Family. I notice that the Prince of Wales on a recent Sunday was playing golf on the links at Sandwich. I also notice that he has decided to run some of his many horses under National Hunt Rules. I am also in a position to inform the sanctimonious members of the Belfast Corporation that his racing colours are red with blue sleeves and black cap.

* *

Dunlop's Rubber Co., Ltd., report that the profits for 1925 amount to £3,200,000 or an increase of 85 per cent. over the previous year. Dividends will be paid at the rate of 15 per cent., although the profits on money invested amounts to 35 per cent. Sir Eric Geddes, who is Chairman receives a time rate of £15,000 per annum or £288 per week. All broken time and holidays paid for. "To him that hath, more shall be given."

* *

Mr. Crawford M.P., says poor people in Antrim can be kept for £53 15s. per head. Marvellous! Our Ministry of Labour asks insured persons to keep their children for £5 4s. per head per annum.

Thousands of insured persons are being denied benefit and are being allowed to starve.

* *

Sir Dawson Bates says—"The maintenance of prisoners per annum worked out at an average of £102 per head." You will notice Sir Dawson said maintenance. Is it a fact that maintenance and establishment charges work out at £149 5s. per head, or almost £3 per week, per prisoner?

* *

Coalisland is a prosperous (?) mining village in County Tyrone. The wealth from Sir Sam Kelly's mine has not materialised at time of writing. Last week 40 wage earners at the pits were paid off to swell the ranks of the unemployed. The Roan Spinning Co., at Coalisland is still closed down, and the spinners and other workers are travelling miles each day trying to get a day's work at anything. Old people who have been employed in the mill for 50 years have been denied their benefit by the Headquarters of the Ministry of Labour. The local representatives on the Rota Committees are recommending that benefit be paid, but the Secretary of the Ministry says "No," and this is happening in dozens and dozens of cases.

I called at one home and found the household consisted of two young women and one middle-aged woman, all highly-skilled textile operatives. These three people had been denied their benefit and a generous (?) local authority allows them the large total of 5/- per week to live upon, and three adults are supposed to live on 1/8 each for a week of seven days.

Open Air Campaign.

STEPS	Sunday	..	3 p.m.
STEPS	Sunday	..	7 p.m.
LIBRARY STREET	Wednesday	.	8 p.m.
PEEL STREET	Wednesday	..	8 p.m.
PERCY STREET	Thursday	..	8 p.m.
MOUNTVIEW STREET	Thursday	..	8 p.m.
CARLISLE CIRCUS	Friday	..	8 p.m.

Slumdom Philosophy.
BY SLUMDOM JACK.

As I visualise the worker from the angle of this old rat-trap, I can readily realise what a tremendously important fellow the worker is, but when you attempt to drive that message home to him, he merely grins and asks you, apparently in all sincerety, if you imagine you can, in that way, take him a wee dander. It seems to me that the worker was born in the wrong street, and after the educational system has done with him and the nice pulpit chaps have succeeded in getting into his napper a quantity of dope sufficient to last a life-time, all the powers of heaven, hell, and earth are totally inadequate to open his eyes to the true state of his relationship, and he goes to the grave a mere **thing,** after existing for a number of years as a wealth-producing land-crab. Of course, during the whole of his blind alley existence, it was perpetually dinned into his ears that if he were a good boy here, and paid strict attention to his religious duties and looked up to his "betters," he would go straight into Abraham's bosom, when all wealth-producing vitality was well squeezed out of his machine-like composition.

Of course, I am all awake to the fact that I'm not credited with being in possession of much intellect, but I can claim to have sufficient horse gumption clearly to recognise the utter folly of a worker getting down on his bended-marrow bones, and shutting his eyes tightly, and offering up an emotional string of verbosity for the daily bread he has succeeded in creating by his Labour power. It does strike me that if the worker could only learn the wisdom of keeping his peepers open when he is saying the Lord's Prayer, he wouldn't have to say it so often. When he opens his eyes, he finds that the loaf, which was the result of his own industry, and for which he prayed so earnestly, has disappeared before the magic-wand of the Capitalist oracle workers. This miracle so upsets his mental equilibrium, that it drives him right into the realms of pure imagination, where you will find him scratching his poor befogged napper in utter amazement, and getting it off his chest like this: "I am but a stranger here, heaven is my home."

From the boss-point of view, when the worker reaches this lunatic stage he is rightly considered to "be landed." The one thing that has always struck me as being rather peculiar, is that when the worker prays for his daily bread, he studiously refrains from "mooching" a bit of "kitchen," but seems to be entirely satisfied with dry "rooty," for doing which he is characterised a virtuous creature, which is just about equal to saying that before getting into his shake-down at nights he must needs plant himself down at the doss side and offer up a prayer, as long as York Street, for the temporal and eternal salvation of the rogues who have been chiefly responsible for creating, and keeping in existence, the politico-economic machinery that breeds slums, and consequently all their humanity-killing and diabolical concomitants. To me, it is quite obvious that so long as we allow ourselves to be fooled into believing that this lunatic mental condition, which is nothing other than a pure dope condition, is allowed to stand between the worker and his best interest, economic salvation will remain a mere will-o'-th'-wisp affair.

When followers of the lowly Carpenter of Nazareth teach the people that poverty serves a useful purpose, it is hard to get the thousands who have been denied the right to work, to realise that nothing outside efficient working-class organisation will ever succeed in effecting their economic freedom in this world. The professional class constitute an active instrument in the hands of some of our rulers, by means of which the worker has been led up the wrong street, **and kept there**. Think for a moment of the down-and-out who has been taught to believe that outdoor relief is calculated to demoralise his character, and so effectual has that type of mental dope proved, that there are practically thousands of men and women in this politico-theologically ridden city prepared to starve rather than seek assistance at the hands of the Guardians. We Socialists, however, are fully alive to the fact that, when the Prince of Wales stretches out his paw for his cheque, he doesn't think it is likely to degrade him though, of course, it is just derived from the same source as outdoor relief . . . . . AMEN.

Union of Postal Workers' Film.

I was privileged to attend a Film Lecture on the U.P.W. by Mr. Houlihan, and I was very much impressed by the propaganda possibilities of this film and the admirable lecture by Mr. Houlihan. The film showed in no uncertain fashion the advantages of the broad basis of organization rather than the narrow and restricted benefits possible under the old style sectional or craft basis of organization. The pictures that impressed me most were the graphs and diagrams showing the privileges gained by members of the union, and the pictures of the Head Office Staff at work, proved the advantages to be gained by a Union such as the U.P.W., as such an efficient staff and head office could not be obtained by a small union.

The day of the small craft or vocational Trade Union is done and the day of the One Big Union is fast approaching. Speed the day. Congratulations to the U.P.W. on their enterprise.

SAM KYLE.

"The Opposition" is steadily growing in Power, Circulation and Influence. What we need now is a Weekly, and every new reader and every fresh subscriber is a definite step towards that goal.

The Red Peril.
BY MURTAGH MORGAN.

We in Belfast are a singular people. So perfect has been our development that periodically we proceed to exterminate each other. During the "peaceful" periods in our lives we still harbour sentiments of hatred.

The local Press has always been a powerful agent in the manufacturing of a specific type of mentality; a mentality that outside our city has almost become, in an inverse fashion, as famous as our linen. However, certain changes have occurred of late; not the least remarkable perhaps being the temporary discarding of the religious "bogey," and the directing of all the energies of a russophobia infected Press towards creating a "public opinion" compatible with the system of capitalism. Thus it is we have that exceedingly peculiar individual known as the "loyal -worker" in possession of absolutely fantastic ideas relative to the near approach of the "Socialist Menace" and "Red Peril," and the increasing circulation of "Moscow Gold."

Now, for the especial benefit of those highly intelligent members of the working class inebriated with the "Tele" philosophy we will tell of a "Socialist Menace;" not the special 1926 product of a turbid Press, but a little local side light of the last century.

Towards the middle of the last century a movement was on foot in the North to have the old Ulster custom of Tenant-right sanctioned by law. In other words the farmers, who were suffering severely at the hands of a tyrannical landlord-class, wished to have a legal right to their own improvements. There was established for this purpose what was known as the Tenant League. Now, any movement which sought to better the conditions of the farmers would naturally be antagonistically received by the landlords, who had no desire to part with any of their plunder. From the first the League was met by all the forces which, by virtue of the monopolistic position, the landlords had at their command. It was asserted that at that time the Orange Society, then completely controlled by the landlords, was used effectively in election times to defeat candidates who were favourable to Tenant-right. Many of the Ulster farmers then as now were Presbyterians; and we find that many of the ministers of that religion, notably the younger, were ardent advocates and champions of the farmers' cause. These Ministers were accused of preaching Socialism because they had the courage to oppose a brutal landlordism. At a meeting of the Synod of Belfast in 1850, the Rev. J. Rogers, a Comber man and ardent Leaguer, moved that a petition be presented to Parliament in favour of Tenant-right. Here is an illuminating extract from the proceedings:-

Mr. Rogers—"With regard to the Socialist doctrines alleged to have been taught by Tenant-right advocates, I shall just say that for the last two hundred years Socialism has been all on the other side. The entire outlay of the tenant farmers has gone periodically into the pockets of the landlords. **A small minority have swallowed up the property of nine-tenths of the province.**"

Dr. Cooke—"Now, here it is; we have Socialism preached here in the Synod."

Mr. Rogers—"I state a fact. It would seem to be forgotten by some members that the poor man has property which should be as fully secured as that of the rich." Despite the opposition of the trenchant Dr. Cooke, whose statue I have seen hanging around somewhere, the petition was carried by a large majority.

The above little incident will serve to illustrate the fact that although various measures and reforms are **not** Socialism, any and everything which tends to decrease profits is to the ruling-class a formidable and evil "Socialist-Menace". Tenant-right was not Socialism; yet because he took upon himself its advocacy, the Rev. Rogers became the recipient of all the vile abuse that a reactionary landlord-class and its ignorant partisans could hurl at him. Those workers, who, through an assiduous assimilation of certain dope gain a knowledge of Socialism akin to Sam Weller's knowledge of London, which was "extensive and peculiar" should occasionally attempt to think for themselves. The benefits derived will certainly compensate the pain incurred in the effort.

Our position at the moment is certainly not satisfactory. Looking around we find everywhere scurrilous attacks oupon Socialism in general and the "Reds" in particular. From time immemorial our local papers have reiterated in their own obsequious and reprehensible fashion the aspirations of the cross-channel capitalist gutter-press. The tragedy is that there are people who honestly believe these vituperative outbursts. Let all such wage-slaves realise that in Society to-day there are only two classes—the capitalist-class and the working-class —and that inside or outside of Parliament the Socialist Party alone is engaged in fighting that capitalist-class. Capitalism seeks to divide the workers; to render them impotent and disorganized, and thus sink them deeper in the mire of mean submissiveness. Socialism seeks to unify, consolidate and educate the working-class, and thus render them capable of moving forward to the abolition of the existing order, and the erection in its place of a system of society based upon co-ordinated effort and mutual good-will. That is the historic function of our class. We have toiled long and the process has been slow. First from Slavedom into Serfdom. Second, from Serfdom into Wagedom. The Third and decisive step has yet to be taken from Wagedom into Freedom. To quote the late James Connolly:

"Then send it aloft on the breeze boys !
That watchword, the grandest we've known,
That Labour must rise from its knees, boys !
And claim the broad earth as its own."
GET TO IT !

What May-Day Is To Ireland.

BY HUGH GEMMELL.

(Reprinted with acknowledgements, from the "Sunday Worker" Labour's only Sunday Newspaper).

On the 1st day of May, all over the Globe, the workers of all countries send fraternal greetings to each other. It is the great call of Democracy demanding its release from the bondage of wage-slavery. From Red, Black, White and Yellow, the great urge to freedom goes forth, and in the fight for international freedom and unity, Ireland has played a conspicuous part.

On May the 5th, 1818, the world's foremost internationalist, Karl Marx, was born, and on May 12th, 1916, his staunch disciple, James Connolly, of beloved memory, laid down his life in tragic consummation of a life's devotion to the principle of human freedom.

Ireland does well to remember the month of May, for it was during that month, over many hundred years that her people were stripped of possessions and liberties, and an effort made to debase them to uncouth savagery.

It was on the 9th of May, 1604, after a year of plotting and chicanery, that Chichester reached out his blood-stained hands for the coveted prize of Lough Neagh and the River Bann, adding a fresh chapter to his theft of the Common Clan Lands in Ulster, and paving the way for the Plantation that ruptured our Land from Malin Head to the Cove of Cork. On the 18th May, 1606, the notorious spy, James Hamilton, better known as

"THE HUNGRY HAMILTON."

obtained possession by fraudulent means of the lands of Westmeath and Longford, and laid the foundations of the *noble* house that to-day gives a Viceroy to Ulster, and draws a "dole" of £160 per week for the privilege.

In May, 1608, Cahir O'Doherty's turbulent spirit flamed into the tempest of rebellion, while in May, 1613, the Planter's Parliament met to place the seal of legality upon theft and public corruption.

The sinister shadow of Chichester again fell athwart the page of Irish history in May 1611, and this time it was the Clan territories in Wexford that passed into the avaricious grasp of the freebooters. The plan was completed in May 1613, and thousands of innocent families were uprooted from the soil and evicted from their homes.

In May, 1628, one of the "graces" (No. 29) asked "that the inhabitants of Connaught, Thomond and Clare forthwith have their surrenders enrolled in the most beneficial manner possible, and that the passing of patents be carried through on terms favourable to the tenants." The surrenders were made, but the regrants never matured, and the peasantry of the west learned to appraise the worth of a King's pledge. It can no longer be denied that the repeated thefts provided the economic base from which the flames of the great rebellion rose in 1641.

On May, 29th, 1650, Cromwell sailed from Ireland to conceive, give birth to and nurse in England, the notorious edict of

"TO HELL OR CONNAUGHT."

It was on the 1st May, 1654, that all the Irish were to remove beyond the Shannon on pain of instant death, and the great trek of a nation began.

It is estimated that 100,000 Irishmen were butchered to please the "Republican Parliament" of England, and punish the gaiety of a foolish king.

The supreme folly of the wholesale banishment was soon apparent to the new land owners. They could not till the soil nor reap the harvest, and the hated Irish were permitted to trickle back to reap the harvest for others. This is the birth of the wage-earning class in Ireland, and as May the 1st marked our downfall in 1654, so now the 1st of May, 1926 heralds our rise towards human freedom. Let us be strong in our determination, staunch to our great cause, loyal to our class; and when the moment of victory crowns our age long efforts with final triumph, let us be restrained and dignified in our freedom.

Marksman Misses But Scores A "Bull's" Eye.

Ballymena Poor Law Guardians. A meeting was held on 13/3/26, when the Master reported that one of the Union's pigs took sick during the week and had to be killed, being sold to a firm in town. Mr. Henry, P.L.G., said—"It was a serious matter to sanction a sick pig to be killed and sold in town for human consumption."

* *

Ballymena Rural District Council held a meeting on the 6/2/26, when Meat Consumption was discussed. Mr. Reid, R.D.C. said—"There is some meat offered for sale in this town that would not be fit for a dog (laughter). I would not eat it from this to the Day of Judgment."

* *

A friend takes me to task for saying in our last issue—"What is happening in the Rural and Urban centres in Northern Ireland, particularly Ballymena, where slaughter houses are privately owned." I admit I was misled, and stated in error there were private slaughter houses in Ballymena Urban District. I hasten to correct my error. I learn that all meat sold in the Urban District of Ballymena must bear the stamp of the Abbatoir. I also learn that in Ballymena Rural District there are practically no restrictions on the sale of meat, and the slaughter houses are all privately owned. Mr. Kyle, M.P., put a question to the Home Secretary on the matter on 25/3/26, and Sir Dawson Bates replied that the question of uniformity of inspection of meat is at present engaging the attention of the Local Government Commission.

MARKSMAN.

Book Review.
The Ulster Year Book—One Shilling Net.

This is the book we have been waiting for since 1920. It is the Domesday Book of Northern Ireland, wherein are gathered all the resources of production and distribution of the six counties. There are maps, charts and diagrams, and pages of statistics that will delight the student of Economic Home Affairs. It is the text book of our everyday industrial life. We know now who our masters are, and the resources in material wealth whereby they oppress the poor.

Our 60,000 unemployed Workers will find comfort in the assurance that the Capital of their masters has increased while the mills, factories, and shipyards lie idle. Our victims who are scalped, maimed or broken in our factory hells will no longer be mixed with the cross channel lists, while our table of diseases forms a formidable percentage that climbs with steady persistence. The Capitalists were always great bookkeepers, and the first effort of the Belfast Bosses betrays no trace of a novice hand.

Every worker should read this book, and, having learned the wealth he produces, demand the full fruits of his industry. We are learning slowly in Ulster to do our own work ourselves and every day provides fresh evidence of our drift from English domination. But where do the workers stand?

H. G.

The **Dungannon** Rural District Council have been discussing the advisability of carrying out necessary work as relief work, but the matter stands adjourned until a later meeting. A meeting of unemployed workers has been held in the Market House, Coalisland, and a deputation appointed to wait on local Clergymen of all denominations, to persuade them to approach the local farmers and ask them to make a gift of the potatoes which will not sell, and which will only rot in the fields. As everyone knows there has been a bountiful harvest of potatoes with the result that farmers cannot get a decent price for them, and tons of good potatoes are being allowed to rot in the fields in each of the six counties, while our unemployed workers in town and country are being denied access to this most valuable food. In Belfast I understand, business people and public representatives are wining and dining at big dinners and luncheons practically every day of the week at a cost of from 20/- to 40/- per head. I think the time has arrived to call a halt to this gross extravagance. People mouthing sympathy with the unemployed and at the same time acting like gluttons.

Notes And News.

As a result of the exposure in the LABOUR OPPOSITION of the privately owned Registry Offices in Belfast, many of the abuses have been remedied. One Registry Office has been closed.

Senator Dorman has been the means of printing, and distributing free, 31,000 leaflets on "What is Socialism," and "The Record of Queensland's Labour Government."

Dick M'Connell won his spurs last Wednesday at Library Street with one of the best constructed and most appealing lectures ever delivered at that historic spot.

Mr. Kyle, Labour M.P. for North Belfast, received a very unsatisfactory answer to this question which he put to the Home Secretary.

"To ask the Minister of Home Affairs whether he is aware that a brutal assault, necessitating medical attention, was made recently on a young ex-Serviceman who was holding a trade union meeting in Garvagh; whether the police are entitled to decide who is to be permitted to hold such meetings; whether he has received any report from the police on the subject; and will he take steps to prevent a recurrence of such incidents in future."

Co-operation Calling!

Belfast Trade Unionists & Labourites

Your income may be small, but the Store will show you how to *spend it wisely* and at the same time *Save while you Spend, Assure yourself Without Premiums, Create your own Capital,* and use it to *Control your own Business* through Co-operation.

28 Grocery Branches 9 Pastry Branches Bread and Milk Deliveries Daily

One Shilling Makes You A Member of the

Belfast Co-operative Society, Ltd., 20/44 York Street, Belfast.

Join The Store To-Day!

The Co-operative Congress.

The undernoted meetings are open to the public.

SATURDAY, 22nd MAY.
Propaganda Meeting and Concert in the Assembly Hall at 7-30 p.m. Speaker: MR A. V. ALEXANDER, M.P.

SUNDAY, 23rd MAY.
P.S.A. in the Assembly Hall at 3-30 p.m. Address by the REV. H. J. ROSSINGTON.

SUNDAY, 23rd MAY.
Co-operative Party Demonstration, Empire Theatre, 7-30 p.m. Doors open at 7 p.m.

MONDAY, 24th MAY.
Guild Rally—Assembly Hall, 7-30 p.m. Speakers: MRS. ELEANOR BARTON, (England); MRS. MURDOCH, (Scotland); MR. T. W. MERCER (Men's Guild).

TUESDAY, 25th MAY.
Propaganda Meeting and Concert in the Assembly Hall at 7-30 p.m. Address by DR. LIVINGSTONE, Vice Chancellor, Queen's University, on "**Some Educational Lessons from Denmark.**"

EXHIBITIONS IN THE ULSTER HALL AND Y.M.C.A. will be opened on Saturday, 22nd May, at 3 p.m. and will be open daily until Saturday, 29th May. Musical programmes afternoon and evening.

TO ALL WHOM IT MAY CONCERN.
EAST BELFAST LABOUR PARTY HALL.

(Corner of Mountpottinger Road and Short Strand).

Now available for Lettings to Trade Unions and others.

Seating Accommodation 150 to 200. Terms Moderate.

Apply to Secretary, Mr Frank M'Auley, 11 Vulcan St., City.

Alexander Stewart.
AN APPRECIATION.

With feelings of painful surprise I learned of the passing of Aleck Stewart as I dipped into the columns of the **Labour Opposition**at the recent Protest Meeting in the Ulster Hall. Can it really be, one asks oneself, that we shall never again hear that voice so vigorous, so characteristic, so challenging; and because of those outstanding qualities, so familiar, so much an accepted, integral part of current life in the local Labour Movement. It seems well nigh incredible; yet such is the tragedy of our common, human experience. Continually, as the years go by, we must keep making these sorrowful readjustments, and still, in spite of grief, "carry on".

It was not my privilege to be an intimate acquaintance of Aleck's and I can only write of him as a comparative outsider—indeed as one for whom, it is to be feared, Aleck could not readily find a place in his practical "scheme of things." For he was too deeply committed to the cause he had at heart to palter either "with the enemy in the gate," or with others of whom he could not be certain at a glance; and with a kind of Cromwellian "thoroughness" and austerity he would be inclined to bid them all begone, to share the common fate. His was the type of the old Crusader—bold, aggressive, downright, taking no heed of blows received, and but little notice of minor skirmishes and incidental defeats along the route mapped out; but ever pressing forward with his eye upon the goal.

Such was our good Comrade Aleck Stewart, as I was enabled from time to time to take his moral measure. And indeed it is particularly because of these outward things that separate that I feel impelled to say a word of appreciation. When a friend passes to the Great Unknown, "beyond these glimpses of the moon," it becomes possible to be frank without running the risk of being fulsome; and thus not infrequently death provides an opportunity of explanation concerning things that have been somewhat baffling and mysterious, and to that extent at least, "making our sorry scheme of things complete." No one who knew Aleck Stewart, even at some little distance, and observed his manner of life could be in any doubt as to his mission in the world—as to the work to which he had set his hand. It was to champion the cause of the downtrodden and the oppressed; to wring justice out of a luxurious and self-regarding generation; to set free the victim of the stupidly selfish exploiter; to blast with scorn the strong-hold of the oppressor; to create a new world for the honest wealth-producers. And who shall say it was not a great ideal in the heart of this working man?

Aleck Stewart was a type of the hard-hitting, pioneer Socialists; a type which perhaps only the hard-bitten ranks of the sons of labour can produce. But this is not all in his case. He was a Scotchman; and there was about him the characteristically Scottish saving grace of magnanimity: the subtle, yet not uncertain implication that ultimately forgiveness and reconciliation were not beyond the bounds of possibility; that there was still "a place left for repentance." This is a very high achievement and one only possible to the greatest of men and of races. It is to be feared that we Irishmen all too seldom reach to it—we are typically so tragic in our expressions of bitterness and rebellion; so frequently do we give the fatal impression that there will be nothing ultimately but perdition for "the enemy."

Such, briefly stated, was what one gathered concerning the character of this honest working man. Not "dour" so much as downright and sincere; not hard so much as earnest in his cause; not an irresponsible buccaneer but a Crusader in a holy war. In these respects his life will continue to be an inspiration to many who knew him; and he, although passed hence, will continue to speak for many years to come. Peace be with his spirit !

THOMAS BROWN.

Order Form.

Correspondence.

Lecke, Ballymoney.

To The Editor Of The Labour Opposition.

Dear Comrade,

Please forward four dozen copies of the OPPOSITION by return of post. The OPPOSITION and "Glasgow Forward" are doing good work here. I have every reason to believe that a Labour Candidate would at least save his £150 deposit in this constituency. Please try and get agents to sell the OPPOSITION in the following towns. Ballycastle, Armoy, Dervock, and Stranocum. You will get some annual subscribers there if the paper can be brought to their notice.....   Yours in the cause, —A. C.

We are asked to express the sympathy of the entire movement to Comrade Alex. Adams, whose sister was killed under such tragic circumstances.

Labour Party (Official).—The allegation that a Labour P.L.G. did not attend the Relief Committee Meetings is without foundation. The member is on three Committees of the Institute, and has the highest possible attendance on each.

The Labour Opposition Of Northern Ireland

Vol. 2—No. 17   June, 1926   One Penny

Socialism for Ulster;   Now!!
BY HUGH GEMMELL.

The birth and growth of the Labour Party of Northern Ireland is a political event of the greatest significance. It marks the final passing of cross channel domination in our political affairs and is a sharp reminder that Ulster Labourists must put their own house in order before turning their eyes either to Dublin or London. In this we are but following the example of the Ulster Tories who have consolidated their position in Northern Ireland and no longer trouble about the Imperial House. The secession is all in favour of the Workers of Ulster, who can now trace their economic misery and political injustice directly to their source. We now know our masters.

The Labour Party claims that what is produced by labour ought to belong to labour, and their Constitution declares that its purpose is "To secure for the producers by hand or by brain the **full fruits** of their industry, and the most equitable distribution thereof that may be possible, upon the basis of **the common ownership of the means of production** and the best obtainable system of popular administration and control of each industry or service."

CAN ULSTER SUPPORT HERSELF?

The six county area has a population of 1¼ million and they occupy a territory of approximately 3½ million acres. All wealth is produced by the corporation of two agents, Land and Labour Power. Land is the Mother of Wealth (Mother Earth), Labour Power is the Father (Father Industry) and

Wealth, i.e., Food, Clothing and Shelter, is the child of the marriage.

Within our Province we have arable and pasture land that is easily the equal of any in the world, and with comparative ease we can produce grain to make our bread and other basic foods, and we can produce in abundance winter roots for feeding our live stock. Our pastures are world famous for their succulent grasses and from their bounty our people could get enough dairy produce and flesh meat to preserve our child life and sustain our adults. Yet people die in our midst from sheer starvation. Why? What is wrong? The answer is simple. The people are divorced from the land and denied access to the storehouse of nature. No man made the land, yet the soil of Ulster is "owned" by five or six great landowners who draw literally tons of thousands of pounds each year from the blood and sweat of our peasantry, and call it rent. We Socialists say that rent is robbery, that the land should be free to all our people, even as our roads are free, and that the social produce from the land should be socially owned and controlled by all our people. If the Londonderrys and the Abercorns desire **individual** ownership let them individually work the soil. Literally they would die in a month. Private ownership of land is as dead as the ancient highwayman, and the corpse stinks, but these modern Dick Turpins still stand on the highway between producer and consumer and levy toll on man's industry. They call it Rent, and Rent is robbery. The land must be socialised.

CAN WE CONTROL INDUSTRY?

The entire wealth of Ulster, both agricultural and industrial, is produced by approximately 300,000 workers. 60,000 wealth producers cannot find a buyer for their skill. 40,000 highly skilled men and women, dying slowly in Belfast, are not allowed to build ships, make machinery, erect houses or weave cloth. Why? Do we not need these things? We obviously do. Why then are our shipyards idle, our linen mills stagnant and bankrupt, and our housing schemes flung into the waste basket. The answer is the same as before, the workers are divorced from the tools of wealth, the factories and workshops. Great Industrial Magnates, sometimes alone, but more often banded together into Companies, Trusts or Combines, stand between the producers of clothing and shelter and the consumers of these goods, and say that unless the workers give them the greater portion of their product, they will shut them out altogether from their shipyards and factories. They call it profit, and the Labour Party says that profit is plunder and that the means of wealth production should be as free as the Rivers, Roads and Seas. No individual made these things. They are a social product and what is socially produced ought to be socially owned and controlled. Every unit of wealth that is produced, from the needle to the anchor, contains the embodied labour-power of the entire working class, and the skill, experience and co-operation of every trade is dovetailed into its production.

If the Clarkes, Craigs, Andrews and other Industrial Magnates deny this and assert that production is **individual**, let them **individually** build a ship, distill whisky, or spin linen thread. In one day they would discover their futility. These are social processes, yet individuals, again like the highwayman, stand between producer and consumer and take the fruits of industry. Robbers and Pirates used to call themselves Captain Kidd, Captain Drake or Captain Moonlight, now they call themselves Captains of Industry. They call it Profit and Profit is plunder.

Our great industries must be socialised.

Socialism is not a thief, it is a policeman preventing the robbery of the workers.

CAN WE LIVE WITHOUT MONEY?

"Ah," say our doubters, "where is the money to come from? You cannot do without money." It is a fallacy, a bluff, a "hidden horde" mysteriously created by the Highwayman to frighten his victim into yielding up the spoil without resistance.

The amount of money in circulation in Ulster is less than one tenth of the wealth we produce and its legitimate function is to act as a connecting link between producer and consumer. Modern industry is a complex affair and the road between producer and consumer is often very long and very tortuous. The Robbers know this, and again like the Highwayman they stand in the road and exact toll from the workers.

They call themselves Bankers and Financiers and when asked to point the way between producer and consumer they produce a mysterious money token and say it will act as a safe pass for the worker. They ask payment for the service and call it Interest and the Labour Party says that Interest is Usury.

Phantom millions and hidden "Hordes" hover always between producer and consumer until the worker is wearied and bewildered by the Money Lords' trickery.

Socialism would abolish the robbery and make a straight, secure road for all.

SOCIALISM IN OUR TIME.

Our task in Ulster is to abolish private ownership and establish socialism. To-day there is a contradiction in Ulster because what is socially produced is privately owned. Socialism would abolish the contradiction. Northern Ireland is practically self-supporting, and, if properly organised, could give immediate economic security to every person within its confines. Industry would revive, invention would be encouraged, unemployment would be unknown, personal possessions, as distinct from social wealth, would be greatly increased, and our women and children would no longer be faced with the misery that enthrals them to-day. We must all come into the great fight for the liberation of mankind, and we must all support those who are victimised in the class struggle. Let us all get together into one big movement for the abolition of Rent, Interest, Profit, and when victory crowns our effort with triumph, let us inscribe on the tombstone of Capitalism: "Here lies the enemy of Man,". . . R.I.P.

The Social Mirror.

Strange Place, Belfast!

Look at those twinkling little legs darting along Royal Avenue; look at the happy expression on the face of the owner of the aforesaid "shanks." With a bundle of "His Masters' Voices" tucked under his arm, and a husky voice reciting the latest news—there you have the Belfast typical newsboy complete. No, not exactly complete, as his clothes have not been mentioned; yet even they are not complete. But why quarrel about the absence of a patch or two, as no one ever heard of a well-dressed vendor of "Tele's"

And the life! How those little beggars enjoy it. Think of the exultant delight of darting along, through the dusty, dirty passages (commonly called slums), on a "Summer's Eve,"—as Shakespeare would put it—blinded with sweat, and racing as hard as a piece of broken glass in the foot will allow. Think of the beautiful thoughts which the handful of coppers conjure. And the thoughts of the mother who had striven to give her boy a chance. But what are her ramblings anyhow? Doesn't she belong to the working class? She surely does not expect Editors to stand at a "pitch" on a frosty day, suffering the pangs which are the inevitable inheritance of some workers.

But then, a Belfast Newsboy is not like an ordinary person—nauseous tea and hard crusts constitute quite a satisfactory menu, don't you know?

However, everyone doesn't enjoy an illuminated sign in their honour; and any hunger or worry the "boys" may feel is speedily alleviated when they see the electric sign portraying their cherished profession in Royal Avenue. You don't think so? That's because you are not a "tele" boy, and don't possess that poetic outlook, born of frugal meals and ancient dwellings.

The Police Committee of the Belfast Corporation, having heard of this state of affluence existing amongst the "messengers of tripe"....I mean truth...is considering the question of regular "pitches" and the means of stopping this "abominable practice." One can almost hear an apoplectic Alderman or Councillor, in tones resembling the "ould flute," urging that something must be done to take these hawkers of Editorials out of the rut and set them on the run. Apart from the Municipal justification for this action, I would suppose that, eventually, they would become lazy and indolent, by habitual lounging, unless some restriction were immediately brought into operation.

It is quite a natural thing, in this city of certificates and guns, to have your paper handed to you at the door. There you can read how the Socialists are never able to outvote the Government of Northern Ireland; or how general strikers are the inevitable outcome of allowing the Reds too much rope. But to return to the subject or object of this literary inspiration—the Newsboy. The Education Committee, I believe, have some clause or other, to the effect that terrible consequences to the culprit shall ensue, should he be found guilty of selling those sheets of expositions, accusations and omissions, if the aforesaid criminal be under the age of 14 years. Their education must not be neglected. Agreed. But what happens after they are "eddicated?" Why, they can sell their literary burdens, of course. They are then better able to read, pronounce and shout the startling headlines. And their future? Well, one might become a Lord Mayor or a Prime Minister, or a few may seek the hospitality of the Workhouse. But then, what does it matter? They are born for the life, man; actually predestined to measure their happiness by 4d. on every dozen. Strange Place, Belfast!....

"RAMBLER."

Hits And Misses.
BY MARKSMAN.

Newry Petty Sessions, 5/5/26, Henry Acheson, Nicholson's Court, Newry, was sentenced to one month's imprisonment for the larceny of two old railway sleepers valued at 6d. each. Acheson was a fool, he should have stolen a whole railway and he would have escaped going to jail, because, as "Old Moore's Almanac," says, "You can steal the commons from the 'sheep,' but you cannot steal the sheep from the commons."

* *

Newry.—A contractor name J. J. Rodgers, was **discharged** at Newry Petty Sessions. Informations were refused in a charge against him, alleging the larceny of a quantity of seed oats and grass seed from the Newry Workhouse, where he had a contract for sowing seeds on the farm. Are the Socialists right when they say there is one law for the rich and another for the poor?

* *

Dungannon U.D.C. invited tenders for erecting a lattice work front on the fowl shelter at the market place. Contract prices were too high, and it was decided to carry out the work by direct labour.

* *

Ballynahinch Hiring Fair was held on 6/5/26. Strong men suitable for all classes of farm work were hired for 26 weeks, the average price being £20 per man, for the whole period. Women were to be had in plenty, from £5 to £13 for the half-year. Strong boys fetched from £7 to £16. The price of strong men has fallen by 30/- since last hiring fair.

* *

In England the half-yearly hiring of human beings has almost ended. Thanks to the Labour Government re-introducing the Legal Minimum Wage, wages of farm labourers in England and Wales have been increased on an average by 4/6 per week.

* *

East Anglian Daily News reports that a farmer named Nelson Williams was summoned for not paying the Legal Minimum Wage. He was ordered to pay arrears of wages amounting to £24 18s. 9d., and was fined in £6 6s. 6d., and costs. This is where parallel legislation would be welcome . . . and beneficial.

* *

"Irish Independent," 6/5/26. "One thing the British Industrial dispute can teach us is that setting up a general tariff wall round present-day Ireland would not in itself remedy our economic ills. Industries which rely on foreign markets ought not to seek protection at home."

Ship-lords and Linen-lords please note.

* *

"Belfast Telegraph," 7/5/26. "As a result of the coal strike there is a glut of salmon in Galway, and poor people who have never before enjoyed the luxury of the kingly fish may now purchase it at 1/- per lb." The usual price averages 3/- per lb., and a man on the "burroo" with 18/-, or a farm labourer working for 15/- per week, has to content himself with a 1/4 lb. of liver or a black pudding. It is only when there is a general strike that he can afford one quarter of a pound of the kingly fish at 3d.

P.S.—There was no coal strike. The coal owners locked out the miners. If you want the truth, buy the Labour papers.

* *

Sir Dawson Bates says the present estimate for the R.U.C. represents a saving of £35,000. Sir W. Coates says Belfast is being asked to pay an additional £33,000 for the services of the R.U.C. Figures cannot lie, but Sir Dawson and other liars can figure. If Bates and Coates are both right, then Belfast people are paying £33,000 extra in local rates while the people of the six counties (including Belfast) are saving £35,000 in taxes. Robbing Peter to pay Paul is the employers' idea of government. The Socialist method is to stop the robbery of the people.

*   *

Scabs were employed at Dundalk to unload the S.S. Iveagh, and many British people have been employed as tools of the capitalists to scab on their fellow-countrymen during the General Strike. A pickpocket, a cut-throat, a burglar or an assassin is a decent citizen compared with the contemptible creature who scabs on his fellows during a strike or lock-out..

The dotted lines is the remainder of what I wrote, but the type melted with the heat.

Thanks To Labour.
How Farm Workers Wages Have Been Increased.

How the wages of farm workers have been increased as a result of the Legal Minimum Wage which the Labour Government established during its term of office is shown by the following examples of increases that have been put into operation in the various counties:—

	per week. s. d.		per week. s. d.
Berks	3 2	Herts	5 0
Beds and Hunts	3 6	Kent	5 6
Cambs	5 0	Kesteven and	
Cheshire	3 0	Lindsey	4 6
Dorset	3 0	Middlesex	5 2½
Isle of Ely	5 0	Norfolk	4 0
Essex	2 11	Oxon	5 0
Gloucestershire	5 0	Rutland	5 6
Hants	5 0	Somerset	3 6
Herefordshire	4 0	Worcestershire	4 0

It should be remembered that the previous Agricultural Wages Boards were abolished by the Liberal-Tory Coalition, and that neither of these parties displayed a helpful attitude when the Labour Party attempted to restore some measure of legal protection for the farm worker.

VOTE LABOUR NEXT TIME.

The Reflections Of A Mug.
BY SLUMDOM JACK.

It doesn't require a mountain-like heap of logic to enable a bloke clearly to figure it out that the capitalist system is badly in need of a radical over-hauling. We can certainly appreciate those blind bats who are born into this world in the midst of luxury, when they venture to adduce arguments in substantiation of their claim that this is considerably the best possible system in which to live, but when we hear the bloke who is nothing other than a denizen of the cesspool, endeavour to argue in terms of appreciation and justification of a system of society that has obviously been responsible for changing the direction of the laws of nature and turning him from a human being into a land crab and gutter snipe, it does, you will agree, require a considerable measure of that immaterial wealth called moral rectitude to prevent the itch that invariably creeps into your wrist working a fistic miracle.

When I was approached and requested to write an article for this issue of the **Opposition**, I readily enough consented, my intention then being to furnish the readers of this little Socialist paper with the fruits of my study of the evolution of the bug; and to draw a more or less philosophic analogy between the bug and the humbug, but domestic events have induced me to change my mind, and, indeed, at the moment my chief regret is that I cannot change my shirt with anything approaching the facility with which I find it possible to change my mind, such indeed is one of the economic tragedies which perpetually obtain in the down-and-out-world. Let it suffice here to say that my investigations in the scratchy land of bugdom have succeeded in revealing to my mind the fact that in its rather melancholy pilgimage down through the ages the bug has been most indefatigable in its endeavour to stick as closely to the heels of submerged humanity as possible, and that its labours have been richly rewarded. I am, I can assure you, in the position to know. The bug's chief consolation rests in the fact that it was evolved minus the soul, hence in its struggle to live it is not disturbed in the least by other worldly influences; and can thus bite, suck, and generally torment to it's heart's content, without wasting much time moralising as to where its conduct is likely to land it when one day it is called upon to undergo the inevitable "crack."

THE HUMBUG.

A detailed biographical account of the humbug necessarily opens up wide fields of inquiry, covering such interesting subjects as anthropology, enthnology, sociology, and of course a thorough study of the bogey we are in the habit of calling our ethical system. The humbug is a typical product of a system of society that rests on an absolutely false basis, and the one outstanding and chiefly distinguishing characteristic of his miserable existence is that he is endowed with sufficient physical strength to wield an effective anti-socialist tomahawk. We have seen that the bug was evolved minus a soul, not so, however, the humbug; for this miserable creature, having come through many phases of evolution, now finds himself high and dry on the rugged rocks of economic insecurity, and in addition to this he is also endowed with a semi-soul, and his chief concern in life seems to be that of securing for this half spiritual thing, eternal bliss. Bless the name!

That the humbug is a most effective instrument in the hands of our idea bankrupt ruling class, no man with an iota of reasoning power will venture to deny. And one of the most difficult things to understand in this world today is how this humbug wealth-producer has been built up so as to act constantly in a manner diametrically [opposed] to his own best interests and incidentally those of class-conscious workers. I am, as most of the reader of the **Opposition** know, a Socialist propagandist of the bottom-dog order, and I am endowed with a reasonable measure of the thing called optimism, but I frankly confess that I entertain no hope of ever converting the humbug, especially of that brand who serenely refuses to raise his voice against the factors which go to make social degradation in all its horrible moods and tenses, but will come to the street corner, Bible in hand, and sing to people who are threatened with eviction, like this:- "There is a happy land, far, far away," and I feel quite sure that this land would be all the happier if he were as equally far away as the mythical land referred to in the emotion stirring and non-stomach-filling song.

Despite the existence of the multitudes of societies claiming to be reforming agencies, slums exist in Belfast in abundance, and the ghost of poverty is stalking through this city working incalculable havoc among a long-suffering people; and in face of the huge volume of poverty prevailing, the churches are about as active as tombstones.

The time is certainly ripe for an absolute avalanche of intensive social-ist propaganda. So let the intellectuals come out of their shells and get stuck into work.

Since the *Co-operative Bakery* was established in Belfast, 22 years ago, the huge sume of
£180,000
has been returned to the consumers *In The North Of Ireland* as *Dividend* on
Bread Alone. Did You Participate?
United Co-oprative Baking Society Ltd., Ravenhill Avenue, Belfast.

THE BATTLE OF GARVAGH, 1926.
Being the History of the Exploits of that gallant soldier of the Red Army:— COMRADE GEORGE SIMPSON.

"Labor Vincit Omnia."
Chapter 1.

T'was on a pleasant Saturday evening in the Spring of the year, in fact, 'twas in the month of April, 1926, that our story had its birth.

E'er the Town Hall clock in the busy market town of Coleraine had struck the hour of seven, a solitary cyclist might have been seen, wending his way swiftly along the road that leads to the boglands Town of Garvagh, famed throughout the civilised world, even to the Free State, for its wee fir tree.

Leaving the swift flowing Bann on his left, our hero, the aforementioned cyclist, struck through the leaf screen, and was soon lost to view behind the heights of Somerset, and in due course, by following his nose, and relying on his two-wheeled steed, he reached his objective.

And now, dear readers, a word as to our hero: behold a red-haired, freckly-faced young man of middle height, a typical son of that glorious and mighty Province on which the sun would not dare to set; that Province, which is the keystone of the mightiest Empire the world has ever seen, the British Empire, before which the Roman, the Assyrian, and the Babylonian Empires, have to bow down in speechless worship. A Province, the creator of the Empire, its Flag, its Army and Navy. The fountain of its Law and Honour, the creator of

its Colonies and Dominions, in short, a little bit of Heaven that had got misplaced, and slipping in its efforts to get back into its place, had fallen into the Atlantic Ocean, and become the germ which grew into the noble and never to be forgotten handiwork of the Almighty, the British Empire.

This, then, was the land which had given our hero birth, the land of praties, pigs, and peelers, of Prods, Papishes and Presbyterians.

In his veins flowed the blood of countless fighting ancestors, the stern defenders of the Maiden City, the glorious victors of the Boyne, and of the Scottish Covenanters, who risking their all, fought to the death for civil and religious liberty; this was the stuff our hero was made of.

But enough, let us return to our subject.

When our cyclist had arrived at his destination, he quickly dismounted, and walking smartly into the Temperance Hall, encountered a few recruits of the Red Army.

Jumping smartly to attention, they saluted him, and the band, in their smart uniforms of corduroy, played the first verse and chorus of the "Red Flag."

Barely had the last note died away, when the sentry on guard, running in with blanched face, yelled out, "Look out, ye boy ye, here come them damned fermers."

Immediately all was confusion, but in a few moments every man had recovered his composure, his hat and his head.

"To your posts," cried our hero, and "prepare to repel the invaders."

No sooner said than done, but on came the foe, shouting and gesticulating, every man armed to the teeth, with ashplants, naggin bottles, and rotten praties.

The defenders, though poorly armed, put up a gallant defence, but were overborne by force of numbers.

Fiercely the battle raged, skulls got broken and rebroken, still the defenders fought bravely, until one of the attackers, with a well aimed shot, blinded the leader with a rotten spud.

"All is lost!" cried one defender, "No, no, it isn't, ye damned fool," replied the gallant George, "its in me eyes."

Swiftly the garrison retreated, carrying their badly wounded leader, leaving the victors in possession, and by devious ways, reached their homes.

Thus ended the Battle of Garvagh, 1926, and though the Red Army lost, they were not disgraced, for they fought against greater forces, armed to the teeth, and yet they managed to carry away some of the enemy's ammunition in their leader's eyes.

Round the boglanders turf fires, the fame and heroism of the gallant George Simpson will be told and retold in years to come, and all the childer will emulate him.

THE END.

Editor's Note.—Thinking this was a serial, we allowed the Author to begin his story with Chapter 1., but potatoes are not a "cereal" and . . . help! . . . the damned things are in my eyes too, and I cannot see to finish.

From The Northern Whig Of 1826.
Thursday, May 4.

Disturbances at Blackburn.—"It is with heartfelt sorrow that we have read in the English papers accounts of a very serious disturbance having taken place at Blackburn on the 24th ult. A dense mass of population are in a state of actual starvation. The weavers, who compose the great majority of the rioters, consider the power-looms as the cause of their present distress, by preventing a demand for manual labour, in consequence of which the population are thrown out of employment and subjected to all the horrors of idleness and want. This belief has induced them to wreak their vengeance on the power-looms. At Blackburn several manufactories have been destroyed by the mob, and damages are estimated at not less than £10,000. The military was called out, the Riot Act read; but the mob instead of dispersing returned the fire of the soldiers, and several lives were lost."

The Socialist remedy for this is to socialise all new inventions, thereby giving the people the benefit of their ability and industry. What is socially produced should be socially owned and controlled.

Labour's Fighting Forces.

Court Ward Labour Party is, undoubtedly, the most virile and advanced of all our locals. Their Friday Fixture at Carlisle Circus has become a weekly demonstration, and here the young men of the Party get their opportunity to declare their faith in Socialism. But the spoken word is not enough, and several of their members push the Party papers with a purpose and persistency that plumps the propaganda right into the workers' brain box. Their Literature Secretary is a real live-wire and he and his assistants disposed of 41 doz. of the May "**Opposition.**"

It is a great pleasure to see Tommy Geehan returned from his trip to Canada, and . . . he is already in the fight for freedom.

Clifton Ward Labour Party is putting in some fine work, and their big meeting on Thursday at Clifton Park Avenue is an inspiration to tired toilers.

The Branch possesses some good earnest fighters, but the work needs to be spread out a little more evenly, and some comrades could quite easily take the chair and sell literature in order to lighten the burden for others. A little more help all round and two meetings could quite easily be run each week in the Ward. The humble helper is just as important as the splendid speaker. At one of their meetings, 5 doz. **Oppositions** were sold in 10 minutes.

Dock Ward Labour Party broke new ground by holding a Connolly Memorial Anniversary on the 12th May, and Councillor William M'Mullen, M.P., gave an interesting lecture on the life and teaching of that stern fighter who literally gave his life in the cause of Socialism.

From 10-30 until 2 a.m. a really enjoyable social was held and the fun was so great that the clock stopped at 10 minutes to 2, when we were in the middle of the "Rinkie Mor." May we suggest that the next "Anniversary" should be enriched by Connolly's songs and poems, "The Watchword of Labour;" "The Rebel Song;" "The Call of Erin;" "We want the Earth;" etc., and that his masterpiece of working class history "The Legacy" should be staged with the full dramatic effects and appropriate setting. It isn't right to pander to cross-channel prejudices while our own worker playwrights and song makers are neglected.

East Belfast Labour Party has launched its summer campaign and every Monday night witnesses a huge crowd at Templemore Avenue. Newtownards Road is a changed place, and many who used to scoff and jeer now embrace the policy of the Labour Party as the only hope of the workers. The problem of the East Branch is the large area it caters for, and some effort ought to be made to get a Ward Party for Victoria and another for Pottinger. This would divide and extend the work and yield results on the spot. There is more talent lying latent in East Belfast than would man half the meetings held each week in Belfast. This is no time for dawdling. It is a time for ACTION!

Shankill Ward Labour Party is the oldest divisional Labour Party in Belfast, being a continuation of the old Woodvale Labour Party. Some alleged left-wingers seceded from Woodvale leaving a few live trade unionists and

Labour men to carry on as best they could; later it was decided to re-organise the old Woodvale Labour Party, and to change the name to that of Shankill Labour Party. After re-organisation our first trouble was in securing new premises. We secured a meeting place at the back of a "Pub" on Shankill Road, but our landlord, Mr. Bung, was threatened by some of his customers and by the alleged Loyalty League. We got notice to quit and later secured an old stable at No. 2 Luke Street, which we renovated and made habitable. We are still open for new members who are heartily welcomed. Debates, Lectures and games are carried on at 2 Luke Street.

Our first attempt at electioneering was to throw down the gauntlet to Alderman John Graham, which meant that we were up against all the power and influence of West Belfast Unionism. We were satisfied with the result as we succeeded in polling 2,800 votes. Many of our young members were in the thick of the fight for the first time and acquitted themselves like veterans. At the present time Shankill Labour Party are holding very successful open-air meetings at Percy Street and Ligoniel and our message of Socialism is attentively listened to by people who twelve months ago would have made a lot of noise (to say the least of it), if any of us had advocated Socialism in its mildest form. In conclusion I want to say that there is need for propaganda in Shankill Division and we appeal to left and right wingers one and all, to roll up their sleeves and work for "Socialism in our time." (S. G.)

South Belfast Labour Party is our last born, and like all fledglings, lingers long in the nest before trying its "wings" for a flight. Yet why delay? Why not "hop" out and begin "chirping" to the 9,000 "birds" who voted for Socialism last Parliamentary Election? Seasoned campaigners are among the membership, the ground has been broken, zeal and youth are ready for the great adventure, and all that is wanted is for someone to say "go." Who will take the initiative? Surely Comrade Gordon is not shut up in a political Khartoum awaiting the coming of a relief expedition. Rally the rank and file and fight your way to freedom. Success is sure to come.

Women's Section Labour Party sent a deputation to the Belfast City Council to tell them what they thought about their working class houses, and to suggest several practical reforms. They came, they saw, but damn the conquer!—for the Belfast Bosses don't have to live in the houses that the workers build for themselves. Women's work is never done, and recent political developments in Belfast make it imperative that our Womens Section should intensify their propaganda and secure recruits for our Party. A central pitch, well chosen, sustained entirely by their own efforts and their own speakers, would increase both the numbers and the prestige of the Section and allow the work to be gradually extended to the Wards. Hard work, perhaps, but you have proven yourselves capable of propaganda power, and a definite plan of campaign, doggedly persisted in, will reap its reward in a very few months.

West Belfast Labour Party came through the streets last week with silent tread and muffled drums to honour the memory of James Connolly, whose leadership is so sadly needed and missed today. At Smithfield Square a meeting was held and Sam Haslett and William M'Mullen, M.P., paid tribute to one whose class loyalty was unsmirched by any compromise , any truck with publicans or politicians who slavered sympathy for our Party while plundering the pockets of the Poor. We hope to see the West conducting a big summer campaign, with an alert rank and file watchful of the Party's principles.

The I.L.P. meeting at the steps on Sunday night has become a tremendous affair, and the enthusiasm for Socialism is wonderful. Many notable cross-channel speakers have delivered their message there, and recently, Neil M'Lean M.P., Thomas Scollan, Helen Crawfurd, and Tom Henderson, M.P., (Glasgow) have been among the speakers. The midweek rally on Wednesday at Library Street is another big meeting, and hundreds of passers-by come over to find out what the crowd is about and remain to listen to our message. The strain on our speakers is a heavy one but they give gladly for the great cause of Socialism. We have only touched the fringe of the work that is waiting, and there is room for Chairmen, speakers, and literature sellers. Why not come in and help? No nobler cause ever asked for recruits.

ARMAGH ABU !

A monster Labour Demonstration was held in the Shambles Market, Armagh, on Saturday, 22nd May, organised by the Armagh District Committee of the Workers' Union, the following towns sending contingents to take part in the parade of the principal streets of the historic city: Coalisland, Cookstown, Dungannon, Keady, Belfast, Monaghan, Richhill and Portadown. The weather was ideal for the occasion and the parade of trades unionists and labour men, with bands and banners, created great enthusiasm. The Flax-dressers' branch sent a beautiful silk banner which showed an Irish girl seated at the spinning wheel, and the reverse side showed a modern flax dressing workshop. The Belfast Shipyard Branch also lent a beautiful silk banner. Mr. T. O'Gorman, U.D.C. presided, and said that the meeting had been arranged in order to focus attention on the unemployment problem; and also to point out the necessity of all workers to be organised in their trade unions. Mr. R. M'Clung proposed that—'This mass meeting of citizens call upon the Government of Northern Ireland to immediately initiate national schemes of employment to relieve the unemployed, as the problem is so far reaching and wide-spread that it has got beyond the scope and power of the local authorities to deal with, and suggest that until the percentage of unemployment is the same in Northern Ireland as in Great Britain, our Imperial contribution be retained to provide the capital charges of national relief schemes in relief of unemployment." This was seconded by Mr. M. Kearney, R.D.C., and ably supported by the following speakers; Mr. Sam. Kyle, M.P., Senator Dorman, Mr. James Duff, P.L.G., Mr. John M'Mullan, and Mr. James Callaghan. The following points were made by the different speakers:-

"The wealthy classes of Gt. Britain and Ireland have six thousand million pounds invested in industrial concerns in foreign countries, and are living well on interest and profit while the working people, who are the true patriots, can starve or go to the workhouse."

"1842 claims for U.I. Benefit are downed each month in Northern Ireland."

"Northern Ireland has one motor vehicle for each 48 people."

"The Employers of Armagh are still

licking their sores because their representatives suffered defeat at the recent elections at the hands of 8 labour representatives."

"The old gang in Armagh Urban Council refused to hear a deputation of unemployed workers, and left the Council room in disgust."

"It costs £2,000 to educate a rich man's son and put him through Trinity College, Dublin."

"There are 6,073 building trade workers unemployed in Northern Ireland, yet there is an urgent need for homes for heroes."

"Gas in Dungannon costs 7/11 per 1,000 cubic feet. Armagh charges 6/3 and Belfast people get it for 2/11 less 20% discount."

"There are 46 different railway companies in Ireland.'"There are 258,000 insured persons in Northern Ireland and over 60,000 of them are unemployed.

"Malone Reformatory will maintain a youthful offender for 43/7 while a Co. Council surfaceman gets a wage of 27/6 to maintain himself and a wife with three or four youthful offenders."

When Sir Austen's Father Preached Bolshevism.

"For my part, neither sneers nor abuse nor opposition shall induce me to accept as the will of the Almighty and the unalterable dispensation of His providence a state of things under which millions will be condemned to sordid, hopeless, and monotonous life without pleasure in the present and without prospect for the future."—The late Mr. Joseph Chamberlain, father of the Tory Foreign Secretary and the Tory Minister of Health.

THE CHRISTIAN VIEWPOINT.—Social Salvation.

Where was God in the Titanic disaster? The question and its answer were used as an illustration by a member of an American delegation of ministers addressing a Belfast congregation. His answer being that God was in the self-sacrifice of the men passengers of both countries, who relinquished the boats to the women and children. The purpose of reference here is to point out a far reaching implication of this view, namely, that if God was seen in the saving of those women and children, then contrawise, acquiescence to present day conditions of social and industrial life with consequences vastly more tragic is downright atheism. This thought gives tremendous emphasis to the words of another member of the same delegation who said that the social claims of religion had not been stressed one tenth enough.

Small wonder the churches are emptying.—J. M'A.

"PROVERBS"

1. Feed the hungry who are fatherless, feed them with bread and meat, and don't pelt prayers at man or child, when his belly is empty, for man cannot live by platitudes alone.

2. Don't take from the lean to give to the fat, for that is the way of the world and the devil, and a good many pious persons as well.

3. Don't waste silver on statues to a man's memory and let his widow and bairns want bread.

4. If you know a man praising God with a loud voice, and putting the bailiff on his neighbour the next minute, honour him not, a dead dog by the way-side is sweeter than he.

Epilogue.

Towards the end, though still with its characteristic spirit and vigour, the **Labour Opposition** succumbed to the desperate confusion within which it was forced to operate. Left as it was to its own devices by the official structure of the British Labour Party (to which it was connected only through the ILP), and the subject of half-hearted anti-partitionist manoeuvres on the part of the Irish Labour Party, it began to turn in on itself, beginning to reflect within itself the confusion that surrounded it..

Henry Dubb appears in the columns of the **Labour Opposition** as the example-to-be-converted of a confused and gullible worker (in which guise, it seems, he first appeared in the propaganda of the American IWW, the Wobblies). In 1926 Henry Dubb was coming into his own.

The first sign that the movement's lack of direction was becoming a problem for its propagandists appeared when Tommy Geehan, a Catholic textile worker and Secretary of the Court Ward Labour Party, returned home from a brief sojourn in Canada, where he had been seeking work. Almost immediately, he wrote the article which appears in the March issue of the **Labour Opposition** under the *nom de guerre*, Plebeian. Though this is phrased in the language of the far-left entryism of the period, Geehan's political history, the political history of Court Ward and the shadow-boxing quality which characterises all the NILP's public debates on the matter, all suggest to me that behind the revolutionary phrases lay a decided anti-partitionism. Gemmell and *Sowseed* replied with a reformist argument which clearly implies a pragmatic attitude to the fact of Unionist control of the devolved administration of Northern Ireland, an acceptance of the mundane detail of the problem in which they were imprisoned (the British and Irish Labour Parties, between them, having decreed solitary confinement, and thrown away the key).

The subsequent political history of Hugh Gemmell and Tommy Geehan seems to me to confirm this account of their dispute in the pages of the **Labour Opposition**. In 1927, Geehan was closely associated with Roddy Connolly's, Communist in all but name, *Workers' Party of Ireland*. He left the NILP in 1929, and joined the Belfast Workers' Group, the Belfast section of the, Communist, *Revolutionary Workers' Groups*. In 1932, he was prominent in the RWG's confrontationalist activity in the Belfast Outdoor Relief agitation.

Hugh Gemmell stayed with the NILP. In 1931, he contested the Chairmanship of the party against Bob Getwood and Sam Kyle, and won. When Harry Midgley was expelled from the NILP in 1942, Gemmell's wife chaired a stormy meeting of the North Belfast Labour Party which passed a resolution supporting him. They both (along with most, if not all, of the North Belfast Branch) followed Midgley into his *Commonwealth Labour Party*.

Insofar as the dispute of March and April 1926 can be said to have been resolved (at that point the **Labour Opposition** had only two months to go), its resolution was along the lines of Gemmell's reformism and his pragmatic attitude to the existence of the Unionist Government. Neither sentiment, nor any degree of sympathy were involved in this, simply a recognition that it had, crudely and brutally, established its credentials and would not, rhetoric about the absurdity and expense of the constitutional experiment to one side, be lightly overthrown.

By 1926, the Unionist Government had proved itself to be politically viable and militarily secure. Its success in consolidating devolved structures which Britain had designed as, and expected to be, a short-term expedient was inimical to the sound development of local Labour politics.

Harry Midgley described the NILP's dilemma well in a speech, as its Chairman, to the Annual Conference in August 1933. Labour, he explained, was concerned to engage the local government on bread and butter social issues, but:

> '...the northern Government pays a Scale of Benefits which were, in the first place, authorised by the Imperial Parliament, and for which workers and Employers contribute about two-thirds of the total cost, the Government contributing the remaining one-third, which is collected in taxation from the people who pay the two-thirds. The Government of Northern Ireland has merely duplicated the legislation passed in the Imperial Parliament, and has never been called upon to display any legislative originality in the matter. But the Ulster people ought to know this: that the Ulster Unionist representatives in the Imperial Parliament have always voted for any reductions which were carried out in Unemployment Benefits; and, indeed, always opposed legislation for the benefit of the working class. When beneficial social legislation has been carried in the Imperial Parliament despite the opposition of the Ulster members, Ulster politicians then make the claim that they initiated the legislation, because it is copied in Ulster."

The social and economic issues upon which Northern Ireland Labour wished to agitate, the social and economic policies it wanted to influence, the essential raw material of any Socialist politics—all this was centred on, considered in, and decided at, Westminster. For that it needed the active moral, organisational and financial support of the British Labour Party.

The continuing refusal of the British Labour Party to consider issues of principle, or considerations of mutual obligation and history, in relation to Northern Ireland was made clear by its General Secretary, Arthur Henderson, in his report to the NEC on 20th June, 1927. In response to a request from the NILP that the political levy collected from Northern Ireland trade unionists be paid over to it, the Executive decided to lose it in bureaucratic procedures:

> "That further inquiry be made as to whether political fees are being paid by National trade unions in respect of their membership in the North and South of Ireland, and if so, to what extent: and that the further consideration of the application from the North of Ireland Labour Party be deferred until this information has been secured and until the revision of the constitution and rules of the party is undertaken when the present Trade Union Bill becomes an Act ."

Henderson commented that:

> "The National Executive has taken the line, since the establishment of separate Governments in Ireland, that the operations of the British Labour Party were confined to England, Scotland and Wales,"

At that time Northern Ireland was still functioning as an organic part of the British Labour Party through the ILP. But the ILP was not, as it demonstrated when it disaffiliated in 1932, an effective electoral machine. It could not help secure the return of Labour MP's from Northern Ireland to Westminster, which above all else is what was required.

On the other side of Catch-22, The Irish Labour Party could, had it been prepared to distance itself sufficiently from the general nationalist movement to argue a consistently democratic anti-partitionist case, have provided the Northern movement with the broader context it required within which to stretch out and develop itself. But the Irish Labour Party very quickly showed that it was devoid of any independent spirit.

At its Annual Conference in 1926, the Northern Ireland Labour Party passed a resolution from North Branch ILP (where else?):

> "That the Labour Party (Northern Ireland) proceed immediately with a plan to link up the LPNI with the Irish Labour Party, while retaining a separate identity."

Due to the previously mentioned difficulty about affiliating the ILP branches, the proposal did not proceed beyond the discussion stage. When the ITUC and the Irish Labour Party separated in 1930 the proposal became a practical possibility and took the form of a Joint Council consisting of three representatives of each executive, meeting twice a year, in Dublin and Belfast alternately.

The Joint Council accordingly met and produced a report which was debated at the 1931 NILP Conference. Victor Halley of Belfast Central ILP moved the reference back of the paragraph of the report which dealt with agriculture. This stated that:

"......the council did not desire to interfere with the present system of peasant ownership of land, but favoured co-operative marketing with, if necessary, the use of compulsory powers to ensure its success."

According to the News Letter account of the debate:

"Mr. Halley contended that it was anti-socialist not to interfere with peasant ownership." (BNL 7/4/31)

Halley and his seconder, J. Glen, argued that Labour Party policy was nationalisation (a policy which was anathema to the Southern bourgeoisie, and hence to the Southern Labour Party which tail-ended it), proving that the spirit of the Rev. J. Bruce Wallace and *Sowseed* was still alive at that time. The reference back was defeated but the recommendations of the Joint Council were never adopted as party policy. The Joint Council itself may have continued to meet but it produced no further reports.

Senator Thomas Johnston, the fraternal delegate from the Irish Labour Party, delivered an address at that 1931 Conference which gave Northern Ireland Labour a flavour of the low regard in which it was held by an Irish Labour Party which was at that time, briefly, full of itself, entranced by the prospect of holding the balance of power in the Dail. He said:

"The Labour Movement has always insisted that it was a political crime to divide the country but, speaking without authority, but with fairly clear views, I do not think the anxiety for union comes from our side of the Border.

"We are not very anxious at this stage for political reunion because we feel, and I think I speak the views of the majority of the people—that it would be something in the nature of a liability rather than an asset, and, frankly, if the choice was forced on one, I would rather have steady employment, and maintain high wages, if that were accompanied by our present standard of social ameliorative services, than have your higher ameliorative services, plentiful unemployment and low wages." (Northern Whig, 7/4/31)

The true character of the Irish Labour Party was made clear within a year when, having achieved the balance of power in 1932, it put De Valera into government, unconditionally, because it could think of no conditions about which it felt strongly enough. The Irish Labour Party was not independent, it was not socialist, and it did not have the backbone to argue consistently for the social and economic reforms that could have given Northern Ireland Labour something to work on to make a practical case against partition. Since Senator Johnston spoke, the Irish Labour Party has only intervened in Northern Ireland when it felt it necessary to disrupt a situation that was stabilising to the disadvantage of nationalism.

Tommy Geehan's plebeian intervention in the **Labour Opposition** of March 1926 crystallised Catch-22, confronting Hugh Gemmell with the terms of a dilemma that it was not within the power or ability of anyone caught within its ambit, living in Northern Ireland, to resolve. For the first time the propagandist surrendered to the confusion, and confused himself. In May, Gemmell was arguing for the literal reconquest of Ireland. In June, he was calling down a plague on both their houses, London and Dublin both, and advocating an effectively independent Ulster. And such was the end of the **Labour Opposition.**

These introductory and concluding remarks have not been intended as, and certainly do not constitute, a definitive history of the Northern Ireland Labour Movement or, within that, of the NILP. I hope to have presented sufficient of the raw materials of such a history to encourage its production in the not too distant future.

No history, at least no history which takes itself seriously, can affect to be disengaged. This contribution to the history we require most certainly is engaged, with the project lately embarked upon by the South Belfast Constituency Labour Party, in association with Athol Books, to provide the factual basis of those arguments by which the British Labour Party will be persuaded, cajoled or simply bludgeoned into at last organising in Northern Ireland.

In anticipation of that, it is addressed in the first instance to that favourite target of the **Labour Opposition,** the ubiquitous Henry Dubb. For the vindication of Slumdom Jack, **Wake up, Henry Dubb, Wake up.**

NOTES.

1. **The Workers' Union:** Its ads and information concerning its activities in the pages of the **Labour Opposition** indicate the importance of the Workers' Union in the life of the Northern Ireland Labour Movement.

Largely forgotten now, the Workers' Union was a major force in its day.

It was founded in 1898 by the Syndicalist pioneer, Tom Mann, and aimed at:

"The organisation of all sections of the community on an Industrial and Political Basis for the purpose of raising the standard of social life of the workers, and the ultimate realization of an Industrial Commonwealth."

In 1900, it played a part in the formation of the Labour Representation Committee.

Having started with a few hundred members it had almost half a million in 1920. Throughout the period covered by the **Labour Opposition** that membership was declining drastically.

In 1929, the Workers' Union was absorbed into the Transport and General Workers' Union.

2. **Pre-Decimal Currency:** Hard as it is for some of us to accept, a whole generation has grown up which knew not the old money. As that generation might find the financial calculations of *Marksman*, et. al., somewhat esoteric, I have been asked to point out that before 1971, the Lsd system of pounds, shillings and pence worked like this:

There were twelve pence to a shilling, and twenty shillings to a pound. There were, therefore, 240 pennies in a pound. A penny today is equivalent to 2.4 old pennies.

What was then a shilling is now 5p. Two shillings and sixpence then (written 2/6) would today be described as 12½p. Four shillings then (written 4/-) is equivalent to 20p in current notation. Eleven shillings and three pence (11/3) should be rounded down from the fraction as 57p in today's money.

The 100,000 pennies which Court Ward Labour Party was attempting to raise was £416 13s. 4d., which was a very substantial sum of money in those bygone days.

A guinea was twenty-one shillings, £1.05p.

Nuf sed?

3. **P.L.G.** These letters after a person's name indicate Poor Law Guardian. Elections to the Poor Law Boards staffed by these Guardians were held regularly, on the local government franchise, but were all-too-frequently uncontested.

It should perhaps be pointed out that Hugh Gemmell and his team on the **Labour Opposition** were not disinterested observers describing the operation of the Poor Law in a dispassionate spirit of scientific enquiry. They were propagandists, working up an agitation for change, and their spirit was that of the old song which ends:

"I hope to God, when my life is through,
My life is through, my life is through,
Where I go there won't be any bloody buroo,
Like the bloody buroo in Belfast."

The only full and accurate (and thoroughly readable) account of the development and operation of the Poor Law in Ireland is by Angela Clifford and is available from Athol Books (**Poor Law In Ireland**).

BIBLIOGRAPHICAL NOTE.

The project on which the then South Belfast Labour Association embarked some nine months ago was described in its reprint of W.H. McCullough's 1945 article on Ireland as:

"...to familiarise the workers of South Belfast with the secret history of Labour politics in Northern Ireland."

And it is literally that, a matter of uncovering a secret.

There is one reasonable explanation of this state of affairs: during the Blitz the NILP's premises in Belfast, and all its unpublished records, were destroyed.

The explanation for my reluctance to provide a comprehensive list of the few books which have been written on the subject is less reasonable. It is simply that I see no point in listing works which are no longer available in the Belfast reference libraries. As the young lady on the desk at the Linenhall Library euphemistically put it, when asked for numbers 1-12 of the **Labour Opposition** (which are listed in the catalogue), they have *"gone missing"*.

I feel I have to limit myself to saying that **The Politics Of Frustration** by

Graham Walker, which deals with the career of Harry Midgley, is available in the Central Library and the Henry Collection at Queen's. Austen Morgan's **Labour And Partition** is available in the Henry Collection. John Harbinson's Msc. thesis on the history of the NILP to 1949, is available in the Linenhall Library.

Of those, there is nothing of interest to be found in Walker and Morgan which is not to be found in Harbinson's thesis. Harbinson has the inestimable virtue of being free of the irritating affectations of petty academic careerism. It is the only one worth taking the trouble to consult.

Alan Carr's pamphlet, **The Belfast Labour Movement**, which deals with the period 1885-1893, is available from Athol Books.

The development of Labour politics in Northern Ireland to 1932 is dealt with by Angela Clifford in a series of articles in The Irish Communist, 1979-80.

Her pamphlet on the Poor Law deals comprehensively with the Belfast Outdoor Relief Agitation of 1932, and includes a great deal of documentary material which throws light on the concerns of Irish Socialists and Trade Unionists in the first half of the twentieth century.

Two articles of an unfinished series of articles by the late Tom Bates in The Communist Review No.'s 3 and 4 (May and June 1974) deal with relations between the Labour Parties of Northern Ireland, Great Britain and the Free State, 1902-13.

Index.

The Origin Of Irish Catholic-Nationalism. Selections from Walter Cox's "Irish Magazine": 1807-1815, Introduced and Edited by Brendan Clifford, Athol Books, ISBN 0 85034 53 5
Irish Education: The Case For Secular Reform by David Alvey
Preface by Michael D. Higgins, TD. Experiences of the system, the facts and figures, historical appendices. Church & State Books and Athol Books, 1991, ISBN 0 85034 047 0
Faith And Fatherland by Fr. Pat Buckley
The Irish News, The Catholic Hierarchy And The Management Of Dissidents
Belfast Historical &Educational Society, 1991, ISBN 1 872078 02 8
Scripture Politics by Rev. William Steel Dickson, *The Most Influential United Irishman Of The North. Introduced and edited by Brendan Clifford.* Athol Books, 1991, ISBN 0 85034 044 6
Billy Bluff And The Squire (A Satire On Irish Aristocracy) by Rev. James Porter, *who was hanged in the course of the United Irish Rebellion of 1798.* Introduced and edited by Brendan Clifford. Athol Books, 1991, ISBN 0 85034 045 4
The Causes Of The Rebellion In Ireland by Rev. Thomas Ledlie Birch, *who was exiled after being courtmartialed during the rebellion of 1798.* Introduced and edited by Brendan Clifford. Athol Books, 1991, ISBN 085034 046 2
The O'Neill Years by David Gordon
Unionist Politics 1963-1969. Athol Books, 1989, ISBN 085034 039 X
From Civil Rights To National War by Pat Walsh
Northern Ireland Catholic Politics 1964-74. Athol Books, 1989, ISBN 085034 040 3
The Constitutional History Of Eire/Ireland by Angela Clifford
Post-1921 Constitutional developments, set in their political context. Athol Books, 1987, ISBN 085034 032 2
A Story Of The Armada by Captrain Francisco De Cuellar, Joe Keenan and others. *Additional material by Madawc Williams, Pope Sixtus the Fifth and Admiral Monson.* Athol Books (for Bel. Hist. & Educ. Soc.), 1988, ISBN 085034 037 3
Poor Law In Ireland by Angela Clifford. *Historical review starting in 1838, detailed account of 1932 Outdoor Relief Dispute, refutation of Paddy Devlin's book on subject.* Athol Books, 1983, ISBN 085034 033 0 (a 163-page, A4 pamphlet)
An Argument On Behalf Of The Catholics Of Northern Ireland by Joe Keenan. *A political biography.* Athol Books pamphlet, 1987
The Road To Nowhere by Brendan Clifford. *A Review Of The Party System In The British Constitution, With Relation To The Anglo-Irish Agreement.* Athol Books pamphlet, January 1987
The Unionist Family. *How Protestant communalism replaced politics in the political vacuum caused by devolution and party-of-state boycott of Northern Ireland.* Athol Books pamphlet, 1987
Queen's by Brendan Clifford. *A comment on a University and a reply to its Politics Professor* Athol Books pamphlet, 1987
Federalism, Northern Ireland, And The 1920 Government Of Ireland Act by Eamon Dyas. IRG pamphlet, June 1988
The Mater Hospital (Belfast) By Angela Clifford. *Includes a review of the NHS, Past, Present and Future.* Athol Books pamphlet, 1990
Legal Systems, North And South by Angela Clifford. *Comparison of law systems* Athol Books pamphlet, 1990
Connolly Cut-Outs by Brendan Clifford. *Review of some caricatures.* Athol Books pamphlet, 1984
The Belfast Labour Movement, 1885-93 by Alan Carr. Athol Books pamphlet, 1974
All the publications are available, by mail order only, from:
Athol Books,
10 Athol Street, Belfast, BT12 4GX
SEND FOR A FULL CATALOGUE